# Quarrels with Himself: Essays on James K. Baxter as Prose Writer

# Quarrels with Himself: Essays on James K. Baxter as Prose Writer

Edited by Peter Whiteford and Geoffrey Miles

Victoria University Press

TE WHARE WĀNANGA O TE ŪPOKO O TE IKA A MĀUI
VICTORIA
UNIVERSITY OF WELLINGTON

VICTORIA UNIVERSITY PRESS
Victoria University of Wellington
PO Box 600 Wellington
vup.victoria.ac.nz



First published 2017

ISBN 9781776561711



A catalogue record for this book is available from the National Library of New Zealand.

Printed by Ligare, Auckland

## Contents

# *Foreword*

## John Weir

To a considerable extent, I regarded *James K. Baxter: Complete Prose* as a resource book that would make it easier for scholars to research the prose literature of an iconic New Zealander and thus help others to better understand his life and pattern of thought. This collection of essays, edited by Peter Whiteford and Geoff Miles, begins that process wonderfully well.

The *Complete Prose* did not have an easy birth. It was first seeded in 1959 when I sent Baxter some poems I had written and asked whether he thought there was any point in my continuing to write. In his reply he encouraged me to be bolder in the matter of content and to avoid the 'poetic phrase'. He added: '. . . I know very little of the making of verse, except the extreme difficulty of doing it well; and I am sure we face identical problems when we sit down to write. Intellect on its own is not enough – the best poems are always written from the rack'.

He also situated the writing of poetry in the context of a vocation: 'Can it just be a "hobby"? I think not – I suggest that you should regard it as a secondary, very difficult vocation. A man, whether priest or layman, may have one or more than one secondary vocation. For example, my own primary vocation is of course marriage: after that, poetry and membership of that interesting organisation Alcoholics Anonymous probably run a close second: and after that, who knows?'

I did my best to adopt his suggestions and continued making poems. But I did not write to him again until almost eighteen months later when I sent him a poem, 'Letter from

Waimarama', which I hoped to dedicate to him. The opening words of his reply were generous and welcoming: 'Your poem has been a delight to me at a time when there was no other source of delight: like water from the dry ground.' He went on to remark that 'The silences and the famines are I think always the times that bear most fruit in the end. Your voluntary silence in not corresponding with me may have given you far more than you could have gained by writing to me.' Now he invited me to begin a correspondence.

Between 1959 and his death in 1972 I received eighty-four letters from him. They often included poems or prose pieces which he had written recently, so I began making a list of these mainly unpublished items. From 1959 onwards, also unsystematically, I had begun collecting whatever published items in prose or verse I came across. Then in 1967, in preparation for my MA thesis, I began systematising this information into a formal bibliography. In the following year the thesis was presented to the University of Canterbury under the title 'Man without a Mask'. The bibliography was further refined for my 1974 doctoral thesis, 'Five New Zealand Poets'.

On 25 October 1972 Frank McKay drove me from Wellington to Baxter's tangi and requiem mass at Jerusalem. During the trip we discussed our friend's literary legacy and I mentioned that I would like to edit his collected poems and collected prose. My preference was governed by the fact that I had already done a great deal of the essential bibliographical research. I also suggested that Frank undertake the research for a biography. (*The Life of James K. Baxter* was published by Oxford University Press in 1990.)

In the early 1970s, when I was teaching New Zealand literature in the English Department at the University of Canterbury, I was aware that there were few relevant bibliographies. So I was gratified when Barbara Lyon, a member of the library staff, offered to help me compile a bibliography of significant New Zealand poets. So we became co-authors in 1979 when the results of our research were published as *New Zealand Poetry: A Select Bibliography 1920–1972*. Because of my focus on Baxter it was decided that his bibliography should be published separately. Consequently *A Preliminary Bibliography of Works By and Works About James K. Baxter* appeared in the same year, again published by the University of Canterbury.

Ever since then this little book has proved invaluable to me. It enabled me to compile various collections of Baxter's poetry in the lead-up to his *Collected Poems*, which was published by Oxford University Press in 1979, and it provided me with the information I needed to collect copies of his published prose. Most of this was uncollected; so the very large typescript I sent to Oxford University Press at some stage during the 1980s was entitled 'The Prose Writings of James K. Baxter'. It included the text of many unpublished talks and articles that I had unearthed up and down this country.

Realising that Oxford seemed reluctant to publish such an extensive manuscript, Jacquie Baxter eventually suggested to me that Price Milburn or Victoria University Press might be more welcoming. I chose the second but found once again that the size of the manuscript posed a difficulty. A further complication occurred later when Jacquie declined permission to publish any of her husband's prose apart from selected book reviews from the *Listener*. I countered that such a proposal was entirely inadequate and would do an injustice to his achievement, but she did not budge – presumably because she did not want to permit the circulation of his remarks on personal and family matters.

After she died in 2009, her son John became literary executor for both his parents. In this role he welcomed the publication of his father's prose. Fergus Barrowman had always been interested in the project, but up to this time had been deterred by the costs involved. Eventually, seeing a light at the end of the financial tunnel, he suggested that I do even more research and turn the manuscript into James K. Baxter's complete prose. In late 2015 it was published by Victoria University Press.

Subsequently I have felt gratified that Peter Whiteford and Geoff Miles conceived the notion of inviting a group of scholars and writers to breathe life into Baxter research by writing articles about the topics that most concerned him. It seems to me that his views on what it means to be human are at least as relevant in the twenty-first century as when he first put them down many years ago.

On 29 June 1926 a child was born in Dunedin. The name he was given was James Keir Baxter. By the age of seven, realising that he was on a journey, he felt compelled to write notes in prose and verse about his place in the world. From that time on he never abandoned the craft of writing. Now his poetry and prose have become the footprints he left upon the earth.

He did not find life easy. In a letter he sent to me in 1969 he remarked, 'I lay down in exhaustion yesterday and shut my eyes. And I saw a most beautiful landscape – rolling green steppes, rocks, cliffs, waves breaking – the empty paradise of the earth without man – and I know that paradise was not for me – my paradise is the tight close dark furnace of the human heart – to be there, where the seed of the Kingdom is sown in pain and darkness.'

His journey seemed to have ended when he died on 22 October 1972. But in 'The Instruments' (*CP* 4. 76–77) he had already anticipated that moment and decided that the journey did not end then:

> . . . one must still go
> Another journey to another place
> Where without kisses, without the clasping of fingers,
> The snake-haired women will appear
> Naked, clothed in our own deformity,
> And take us singly through the gate in the rock
> To the paddock of the slavegirl Blandina,
> To where the soul is broken or else becomes
> A bird, born out of blood, another creature.

The voice that resonates from Baxter's poetry and prose is a voice for the living. It tells how one person found a way in the world, often with difficulty, frequently walking in the dark. This collection of essays helps to explain that journey.

# *Bibliographical Note*

Unless otherwise noted, quotations from Baxter's prose works are taken from the Weir *Complete Prose*, and references by volume and page number are to this collection:

Baxter, James K. *Complete Prose*. Ed. John Weir. Four volumes. Wellington: Victoria University Press, 2015.

The following works by and about Baxter are listed here rather than in the 'Works Cited' for the individual chapters:


Baxter, James K. *The Bone Chanter: Unpublished Poems 1945–1972*. Ed. and intro. J. E. Weir. Wellington: Victoria University Press, 1976.

———. *Collected Plays*. Ed. Howard McNaughton. Auckland: Oxford University Press, 1982. Cited as *CPlays*.

———. *Collected Poems*. Ed. J. E. Weir. Auckland: Oxford University Press, 1980. Cited as *CPoems*.

———. *Jerusalem Sonnets*. Wellington: Price Milburn, 1975.

———. *The Man on the Horse*. Dunedin: University of Otago Press, 1967.

———. *Poems to a Glass Woman 1944–1945*. Ed. and intro. J. E. Weir. Wellington: Victoria University Press, 2012.

———. *James K. Baxter: Selected Poems*. Ed. and intro. Paul Millar. Auckland: Auckland University Press, 2010. Cited as *Selected*.

———. *A Selection of Poetry*. Wellington: Poetry Magazine, 1964.

———, Louis Johnson and Anton Vogt. *Poems Unpleasant*. Christchurch: The Caxton Press, 1952.

McKay, Frank. *The Life of James K. Baxter*. Auckland: Oxford University Press, 1990.

——— (Ed.). *James K. Baxter as Critic: A Selection from his Literary Criticism*. Wellington: Heinemann Educational Books, 1978. Cited as *Baxter as Critic.*

Miles, Geoffrey, John Davidson and Paul Millar. *The Snake-Haired Muse: James K. Baxter and Classical Myth.* Wellington: Victoria University Press, 2011.

Millar, Paul, ed. and intro. *Spark to a Waiting Fuse: James K. Baxter's Correspondence with Noel Ginn, 1942–46.* Wellington: Victoria University Press, 2001. Cited as *Spark.*

Newton, John. *The Double Rainbow: James K. Baxter, Ngāti Hau and the Jerusalem Commune.* Wellington: Victoria University Press, 2009.

Oliver, W. H. *James K. Baxter: A Portrait.* Wellington: Port Nicholson Press, 1983.

O'Sullivan, Vincent. *James K. Baxter.* Wellington: Oxford University Press, 1976.

Weir, J. E. *The Poetry of James K. Baxter.* Wellington: Oxford University Press, 1970.

Māori words are macronised except in quotations from Baxter and others who did not use the convention. Following Baxter's practice, 'pākehā' is not capitalised.

# *Introduction*

## Geoffrey Miles

At the age of nineteen James K. Baxter wrote a private memorandum, 'Thoughts Concerning a Career'. He declared, 'I do not wish to lose my religion. In nature, in the mere sight of the natural world, in looking over wide distances, I find a self-delighting peace. This is the primary source of my poetry, and all that I know of a God I know from natural things' (*Complete Prose* 1. 10). Poetry, nature and religion, inextricably intertwined, are at the centre of the young Baxter's self-definition, and were to remain so, however much his 'religion' might develop past this early Romantic pantheism. A couple of paragraphs further on, however, he declared a supplementary ambition: 'I know now that later in life I will write prose and good prose. This will not be aesthetic prose, but rather realist. That is I will describe the life of people, ignorant so-called, but men and women nevertheless' (1. 11). The young Baxter's vision of his future prose writing suggests Tolstoyan fiction or Orwellian reportage. That was not in fact the main direction in which his prose-writing career would take him; the prediction that he would 'write prose and good prose', however, was as accurate as his self-dedication to poetry.

The full range and depth of Baxter's prose writing only became visible with the publication in 2015 of John Weir's monumental four-volume edition of his *Complete Prose*. Its first three volumes, containing the Baxter texts (the fourth being devoted to notes and background materials), weigh in at over 2000 pages and contain 710 separate items. Along with the previously published prose writings which were already an established part of Baxter's oeuvre – including the lecture-essays in *The Fire and the Anvil* (1955) and *The Man on the Horse* (1967), the popular Catholic homilies of *The Flowering Cross* (1969), and the posthumously published autobiographical novel *Horse* (1985) – Weir has assembled a mass of unpublished or ephemerally published material: short stories and prose sketches, essays, autobiographical pieces, talks and lectures, newspaper interviews, book reviews, letters to the editor, journals, private meditations and prayers. The writings range from personal and informal jottings to highly crafted literary essays or political polemics. The subjects also range widely, especially early on; in the first volume in particular, Baxter's many book reviews demonstrate his omnivorous interests and his gift for seizing the points of interest to him in the most diverse and improbable materials. In the second and especially the third volume, his focus gradually narrows and becomes more fiercely concentrated on his central spiritual and socio-political preoccupations, his determination to diagnose and cure what he saw as the spiritual sickness of modern New Zealand society. His core concerns remain consistent throughout the *Complete Prose*, and Weir offers a succinct summary of his main 'five topics: himself, the nature of literature and art, spirituality and religion, social injustice, and, a thread of this, the plight of Māori' (4. 124).

Baxter never swerved from the central assumption made in 'Thoughts Concerning a Career', that he was first and foremost a poet: that was the core of his identity and inextricably tied up with his relationships with the world and God. Prose writing came far behind as a secondary vocation, carrying little of poetry's mana. His sister-in-law Lenore Baxter made a shrewd point when she told his biographer Frank McKay that Baxter's essential mode of expression was poetry: 'Other people talked and thought in prose and had to switch to "poetic mode" when they began to write; with [Jim] it was the other way round' (quoted in Miles et al. 18). In reading through the *Complete Prose* it is notable that, whereas Baxter returns repeatedly to questions about the nature of poetry and the role of the poet, he hardly ever explicitly addresses questions about prose writing, and then only in a rather casual and dismissive fashion. In a 1966 newspaper interview he developed (perhaps with a certain conscious irony as a recovering alcoholic) an analogy between modes of writing and types of alcohol:

> My best verse is like a liqueur. A good poem may affect three hundred people at the most, but the effect will be considerable. Short stories are more like wine. They are taken in more quantity by more people. An article would be like beer. It's shallower. It might affect three thousand but the butter is spread thinner.

The key point is the concentration and potency of the form. Poetry ('good' poetry) is the pure essence of literary art, prose fiction a somewhat watered-down textual experience; but the comparison of non-fictional prose to beer (in the age of the 'six o'clock swill', before the advent of craft beers and boutique breweries) suggests cheap, mass-produced stuff, a weak brew. Nevertheless beer is popular, and prose writing offers a useful way to get one's point of view across to a mass audience.

Critics who have discussed Baxter's prose writing have tended to agree with his own low valuation of it. C. K. Stead, in a 1973 review of *Jerusalem Sonnets* and other volumes of Baxter's late work, contrasted the 'wisdom' and poetic concentration of his best poetry with his 'prose where, for all his colour and horse sense, he is often rambling and partial.' In tune with Baxter's remark on the mass popularity of beer, Stead rather snidely suggested that 'it was the prose Baxter who had followers.' Such followers would admire 'Elegy for Boyle Crescent' (3. 536–42), a late prose piece about spiritually enlightened junkies and brutal 'fuzz', which Stead sees as 'a shabby exercise in rhetoric, a giving in to the sentimental self that rises most readily when we believe we have a just cause.' In his best poetry, on the other hand, 'the prose Baxter yields precedence to the deep implacable will of the artist to discover the real and the true' (Stead 220–21). Gregory O'Brien cites this passage in his essay in this volume, and adds, 'Another way of putting this: the poet gains access, through his art, to the subconscious, whereas the Prose Baxter is speaking his conscious mind, usually immoderately. . . . [T]he prose tends to march a few steps behind experience, its mind already made up.'

Countering the low valuation of Baxter's prose by both the writer himself and his critics, this introduction would venture to make a case that Baxter is not only one of New Zealand's great poets but also a prose writer of some distinction. Such a judgement is not necessarily based on Baxter's fiction – his 'wine', in the 1966 metaphor. In 'Thoughts Concerning a Career' the young Baxter seems to have envisaged becoming a realist novelist or short-story writer, chronicling the lives of the common people. But he did not have the central gift of a writer of fiction, the ability to enter imaginatively into the internal lives of people different from himself; as Sharon Matthews demonstrates, Baxter's short stories are essentially autobiographical, portraying lightly fictionalised versions of himself, and, while fascinating for what they reveal about the writer, never spring to life as creations in their own right. *Horse*, perhaps, is a partial exception to this judgement. Although Timothy Harold Glass is transparently a version of Baxter's younger self – and John Grummet, as Janet Wilson notes, a parodic version of his current self – the blend of sympathetic identification and self-mockery with which Baxter regards them, and the novel's anarchic mixture of gritty realism, lyricism and bawdy slapstick, give it a vitality comparable to the fiction of his acknowledged model, Dylan Thomas.

Baxter's best prose writing arguably comes out of traditions closer to poetry and fantasy than to realist fiction. The young Baxter experimented with 'prose poems', such as 'The Dead House' (1. 26–27). In a 1944 letter to Noel Ginn he surprisingly declared that 'Prose is greater than poetry:

infinite horizons'; poets in middle age and old age naturally turn from poetry to prose, since 'Poetry is of the child, prose-poetry is of the adult' (*Spark* 345–46). This early enthusiasm for prose poetry did not last, and the 'prose poems' now have a somewhat faded air of *fin-de-siècle* aestheticism. A more lasting form of 'poetic' prose writing was his fondness for symbolic fables: wryly satiric Aesopic fables like 'Apple Mash' (1. 198–202) or 'The Story of Butch' (1. 272–74), or (more seriously) parables like the tale of the man in the iron tank in *Jerusalem Daybook* (3. 295–96) – extended images which might equally easily have become the seed of poems.

Baxter's finest prose writing combines crispness of argument with an imaginative use of metaphor and symbolism. An interviewer in *Critic* in 1966 noted that Baxter 'talks all the time and shifts the subject frequently – usually through metaphor' (2. 9–10). The interviewer's perhaps slightly bemused comment underlines the fact that Baxter's habitual mode of thought is poetic and metaphorical. His prose, like Metaphysical poetry, tends to work through and pivot around images, often witty or unexpected ones. And the 'whiplash turns' of thought and image (as Hugh Roberts calls them below) frequently go along with disconcerting shifts in tone and register, between the academic and the colloquial, the vatic and the bathetic.

A nice example is the opening paragraph of *Aspects of Poetry in New Zealand*:

> The archetype that best expresses the situation of New Zealand poets is, to my mind, not Orpheus, the man whose music made the stones dance, but Phaeton, who stole the sungod's chariot and did not drive it well, or Icarus, whose father unwisely made him wings, and the wings fell apart when he ventured too near the sky. These images signify the minor talent determined to be major; and I do not find the ambition in any way unsuitable or singular. Major talents are not born into the world fully fledged. They develop by struggle, strain and the endurance of frequent unsuccess. The Muse after all is a tall girl. Sometimes

> all that a growing poet can do is put a bucket over her head and swing on the handle. (2. 325)

Baxter's point, that contemporary New Zealand poetry aims high but (understandably) often fails to achieve its ambitions, is reflected not only in the mythological allusions in the first sentence – Phaeton and Icarus as archetypes of vaulting ambition plunging to earth – but also in the paragraph's beautifully calculated bathos, as it descends from those grandiloquent names to the deflatingly comic image of the Muse with a bucket on her head.

For a more detailed example we might look at a less well-known text, 'Portrait of the Artist as a New Zealander' (1. 405–06). This apparently slight journalistic piece, written for the *Otago Daily Times* in 1960, similarly works through unexpected images and mercurial shifts in tone. Starting with a solemn declaration that 'It can be dangerous for a writer to pass judgment on the state of literature in his own country,' Baxter goes on to characterise that state as 'shapeless as an unmade bed'. In the next paragraph he describes a photograph he has recently seen of a 'vegetable caterpillar', infected by a parasitic fungus which had gradually transformed it into something resembling wood. 'It seemed to me an instructive natural parable. The vegetable caterpillar is myself or any New Zealand writer, slowly becoming a public figure, consumed by the spores of kudos, developing the reviewer's shamble, the critic's stoop, and accepting finally a permanent job at a university' (one of Baxter's characteristic side-swipes at academia, discussed in John Davidson's chapter). This grotesquely comic-horrific image of artistic death is set provocatively alongside Allen Tate's lofty statement of the artist's role: 'a man of letters must recreate for his age the image of man.' How often (Baxter implies) do our writers live up to that ideal?

He goes on to personal reflections on the publication of a volume of his poems, the production of his play *The Wide Open Cage*, and the general question of 'honours'. Expressing surprise at the play's warm reception, he writes,

> I have a genuine horror of success. Neither God nor the Muses visit a man who has bandaged his wounds and settled down to fulfil the expectations of his relatives, his audiences, his bosses and his religious advisers. When someone likes what I have written, it seems to me probable that they have misunderstood it.

Baxter's confession of his 'horror of success' is a provocative paradox which nevertheless expresses an uncomfortable truth – he had a genuine terror that worldly success and respectability would destroy his poetic gift. The image of 'God and the Muses' abandoning the wounded-but-bandaged writer is simultaneously dramatic and self-mocking, while the last sentence is a rather sour joke not very far from Stead's gibe about Baxter's followers only admiring him for his worst work. The joke leads into a serious statement in the final paragraph about the importance of humour: 'In a quite primitive sense, it is the job of a writer to entertain. He may or may not instruct, as he chooses' (a reworking of Horace's classic dictum about the writer's duty to combine *utile et dulce*, the instructive and the pleasant). And the piece concludes by circling neatly back to the image of the vegetable caterpillar: 'Vitality rather than politeness seems to me the most essential virtue of a work of literature. The living caterpillar is always less polite than his vegetable brother.' 'Portrait of the Artist as a New Zealander' is a casual piece which Baxter probably dashed off in an hour, but it sums up much of his view of himself as a writer and his role in society, and exemplifies the imagination, wit and precise control of tone of which he was capable in his prose writing.

Baxter's best-known prose works are the 1967 lecture-essays assembled in *The Man on the Horse*. Lawrence Jones's chapter is a close reading of one of these texts, 'Conversation with an Ancestor', which traces not only the twists and turns and backtrackings of its argument, but also its radical mutations of form and register, as it shifts through personal reminiscence, artistic ecphrasis, poetry (both comic and serious), a chunk of the then unpublished novel *Horse*, philosophical argument about bourgeois and Bohemian values, a passage from an African funeral chant, and the 'conversation' which gives the text its name, an imagined dialogue with a Scottish Highland ancestor whose blunt questions Baxter turns off with subtly metaphorical responses. This is not a conventional academic lecture (though it assumes that voice at times); it is neither an academic essay nor a personal essay in the tradition of Bacon or Montaigne or Hazlitt – it is entirely its own thing, a hybrid form of Baxter's own creation. It could be argued that Baxter has, consciously or not, recreated the classical genre known as Menippean satire: a rambling form which mingles prose and verse, wit and seriousness, the personal and the public. Almost as much as Baxter's poetry, these essays can be seen as a distinctive contribution to New Zealand literature. The same could be said of the very different blend and interweaving of poetry and prose in late books like *Jerusalem Daybook*.

Most readers who come to Baxter's *Complete Prose*, however, are more interested in his content than in his form and style, and that is where the emphasis falls in almost all the essays in this volume (hence the introduction's attempt to redress the balance a little). Weir's judgement that on the whole 'his prose is more important for *what* he said rather than *how* he said it' (4. 123) expresses not only the general view but almost certainly Baxter's own priorities: his prose was an instrument to communicate as clearly and forcefully as possible with his readers about the issues he cared most passionately about. The criticisms by Stead and O'Brien, quoted earlier, focus on Baxter's use of prose as a blunt instrument of persuasion rather than an exploratory scalpel. They hark back ultimately to Yeats's famous distinction: 'We make out of the quarrel with others, rhetoric, but of the quarrel with ourselves, poetry' (Yeats 8).

Undoubtedly such critics have a point. Baxter's warmest admirers would have to admit that in polemical mode he can be drearily sermonistic, gratingly hyperbolical, or crudely reductive in his division of the world between sheep and goats. But the criticism should not be taken too far. Yeats contrasted the rhetoricians 'who get a confident voice from remembering the crowd they have won or may win' with himself and other poets who 'sing amid our uncertainty' (8). Baxter, despite a usually confident voice, was very often singing amid his uncertainty, in prose as well as in poetry. He famously wrote (in a quotation featured on the slipcase of the *Complete Prose*) that 'In contradiction . . . I was born' ('Home Thoughts', *CPoems* 256). One of the most consistent themes of the essays in this collection is how much more complicated Baxter is than his popular stereotype, and how often in his prose writings he is wrestling with his own contradictions, anxieties and competing impulses, so that – as the title of this volume suggests – the *Complete Prose* as much as the *Collected Poems* could be read as a series of 'quarrels with himself'.

*

*Quarrels with Himself* is designed as an accompaniment and a tribute to the monumental achievement of Weir's *Complete Prose*. In putting the volume together we have tried to cover as broad a range as possible of Baxter's concerns and of contemporary approaches to Baxter. As an organising principle we have adopted Weir's list, cited earlier, of Baxter's key topics: 'himself', 'literature and art', 'spirituality and religion' and 'social injustice' – though the topics inevitably shade into one another in the volume just as they do in Baxter's writing. (The fifth topic on Weir's list, that of Māori, presents a special problem that we will return to.)

The collection thus begins with Baxter's writing about himself, and Janet Wilson's 'No Middle Ground: Baxter's Writing of the Self' strikes a keynote for the volume in its opening sentence: 'In a very real sense all of Baxter's writing . . . is autobiographical.' But, as Wilson demonstrates in close readings of a series of autobiographical texts, Baxter's 'life writing' is not straightforward but a complex and fraught endeavour, as he attempts to reduce the messy chaos of his lived existence to 'textual images of wholeness and self-agency'. He is continually pulled between the desire or need to write about his own life and a reluctance to pin himself down in a coherent factual account. His conflict issues in repeated textual images of violence, wounding, and the death of the subject, perhaps prefiguring the kenotic impulse of his last years in which he tries to abolish 'the man James K. Baxter'.

If Baxter's autobiographical writing is a kind of fiction, his fiction is equally a kind of autobiography. Sharon Matthews's '"Women are all mothers to him": Displacing Fear in James K. Baxter's Short Stories' offers a close and sympathetic psychoanalytic reading of the dysfunctional male–female relationships in Baxter's stories from 1949 to 1960. She demonstrates how these stories enable 'the playing out of long-held inner dramas at a displaced symbolic remove', as the virgins and temptresses of the stories reflect Baxter's own psychic wrestling with the figure of the 'monstrous mother'.

Paul Millar's chapter, taking its title from a rueful comment in a 1962 letter from Baxter to his mother – 'There may be something wrong with my mind' – likewise explores the psychological roots of his prose fiction and traces the route which led to the writing of *Horse*. Millar points out that almost all of Baxter's fiction was written in two major spurts, one in late adolescence, one around the time of his return to Dunedin, and both directly inspired by his reading of Dylan Thomas. The root of Baxter's fiction, Millar suggests, is his attempt to deal with the 'monstrous postlapsarian metamorphosis' of adolescence, in which the innocent wholeness of childhood gives way to a divided adult self. His stories are attempts to 'master the incubus', to negotiate a relationship between the respectable public persona and the repressed, demonic private self which found its most vivid embodiment in Horse – the 'schizophrenic twin' who resides in 'the cellblock in the basement of my mind'.

Lawrence Jones offers a more close-grained study of Baxter's self-writing in his reading of 'Conversation with an Ancestor' as Baxter's 'prose exploration of his personal poetic situation'. In what must surely be the most meticulous close analysis ever applied to a piece of Baxterian prose, Jones shows how 'Conversation' combines 'the techniques of the creative writer [and] of the conceptual analyst' as Baxter works through his conflicting views on the writer's role in society, the tension between bourgeois and Bohemian values, and his own particular 'personal unease' at his position as holder of the Burns Fellowship at the University of Otago.

That uneasy relationship with the world of the university is further explored in John Davidson's 'Baxter, Academia and Academic Writing'. Davidson demonstrates that, in spite of Baxter's frequently expressed scorn for academics and intellectuals (as 'a lifelong fugitive from all forms of Higher Learning'), his relationship with academia was more ambivalent and conflicted than it might appear, and that essays like 'The Man on the Horse' have an excellent claim to be considered as 'serious academic writing'.

Davidson has taken us into the topic of Baxter and literature, and Nicholas Wright's 'The Incarnational Formalist' takes a deeper look at Baxter as literary critic and theorist. Challenging the orthodox view of Baxter as a writer much more interested in content than form, Wright provocatively characterises him as a 'formalist', and demonstrates that his critical assumptions and principles are closely linked to those of the New Critics of the early and mid-twentieth century. Wright sees formalism as a fundamentally mystical (or mystified) critical doctrine which ultimately refines both poetry and criticism out of existence in favour of a contemplation of ineffable truth – a movement which Wright links to the kenotic self-renouncing mysticism of Baxter's final years. This is a dense and subtle essay, which arguably overemphasises the elitist strain in Baxter's thought at the expense of his earthy, populist, ballad-writing, pamphleteering, intellectual-baiting side;

but it makes a powerful case which any future discussion of Baxter's writing will have to engage with.

If Wright challenges the stereotype of Baxter the anti-formalist, Hugh Roberts's 'Invisible Boulder: Baxter among the Nationalists' challenges the stereotype of Baxter the anti-nationalist. Baxter persistently set himself up in opposition to Allen Curnow's 'nationalist' school of New Zealand poetry; but his representations of Curnow's positions are (as Roberts demonstrates) 'crudely reductive caricatures', and actually their views on poetry and nationhood are quite similar. Roberts argues that the split is ultimately a theological one: both poets see New Zealanders as exiles from paradise, but in Curnow's view the exile is a historical condition which time will repair, while in Baxter's tragic Christian perspective it is a permanent and irreparable consequence of the Fall. His contradictory view of Curnow's nationalism was, Roberts argues, 'a paradox that Baxter could not resolve without erasing the very grounds from which his writing, prose and poetry, sprang'.

Kirstine Moffat's essay on 'James K. Baxter and Puritanism' similarly explores the territory between national identity and theology, and once again sets out to complicate a stereotype of Baxter – in this case, that of the bitter critic of New Zealand's repressive and life-denying Puritan ethos. Teasing out the implications of Baxter's description of Puritanism as an 'austere anti-aesthetic angel', Moffat finds overtones of reluctant admiration alongside the hostility, and a strong Puritan strain in Baxter's own character and in the role he stakes out as radical social critic. Baxter's quest is 'to transcend both the Puritan and anti-Puritan selves that lurked within to refashion himself as a prophet of freedom, mercy and justice.'

Moving fully into the territory of religion, Paul Morris offers some reflections on 'Baxter and God'. Commenting on the perhaps misleading impression given by the 'monumental' *Complete Works* of a 'cogent and coherent' theology and a life built on a consistent journey towards

Catholic orthodoxy, Morris instead calls for a less structured reading of Baxter's 'scattered and unsystematic theological ruminations' as he searched for a understanding of God – a spiritual quest that, Morris suggests, remains an example and challenge to contemporary New Zealand.

Doreen D'Cruz's 'Kenosis: The Difficult Spirituality of James K. Baxter' offers a close analysis of the key theological idea that preoccupied Baxter in his last years, that of kenosis or self-emptying: a process which demanded 'the dying of the self, a loss of the self's ordinary coordinates for negotiating existence, an unmooring from its habits and habitats'. D'Cruz carefully traces the three stages of this process. Of course, as Baxter would have ruefully acknowledged, to write about the emptying of the self is still, inevitably, to write about the self, which bring us back to Janet Wilson's initial proposition that all Baxter's writing is self-writing.

Peter Whiteford's 'Becoming the Sore Thumb of the Tribe: The Development of James K. Baxter's Social Voice' takes us to the final topic (implicitly present in much that has gone before), Baxter's concern with social injustice. Whiteford observes that, while the poet's role as social critic is an important theme in his writing from the beginning, actual social criticism is surprisingly sporadic in the earlier prose. It is only in the Burns Fellowship years and after that Baxter takes on the role of radical social critic which we now see as so central to his persona, and part of that new role, Whiteford suggests, is the development of a new 'voice' in his prose, whose 'immediacy and urgency' can carry conviction. Whiteford traces the implications of the changing metaphors Baxter uses for the writer as social critic: the 'cell of good living', the 'sore thumb of the tribe', the 'bad smell' – the last image ironically implying the writer's inevitable implication in the corruption he diagnoses.

The last essay in the volume is Gregory O'Brien's 'A Green Baxter', chosen for that final position both because its patchwork form (mingling verbal and visual materials) is a creative response to Baxter's own experiments with the essay genre, and also because it offers a distinctively twenty-first-century take on Baxter's legacy. In a series of short sections, snapshots of its subject from various angles, O'Brien explores the idea of Baxter as environmentalist and ecologist – terms that, as he acknowledges, would have been strange to the poet. In the Romantic tradition that Baxter inherited, he suggests, nature tends to be seen as 'landscape' rather than 'environment', a background and reflection to what is going on in the poet's soul; but the late Jerusalem writings develop a grungy anti-pastoral sensibility and a sense of the inextricable involvement of human beings in nature which look forward to contemporary Green concerns. In this area as in others, O'Brien suggests, Baxter's writing remains 'a call to new ways of thinking and living'.

As a kind of coda to the volume, and in particular to the discussions of Baxter as social commentator and critic, we have included a 'new' piece by Baxter himself. It is an unpublished 1971 essay titled 'The Rich and the Poor', rediscovered by Richard Hill after the publication of the *Complete Prose*, and he has generously allowed us to include a transcript here. As Peter Whiteford observes in his headnote to the piece, it is almost certainly not the last scrap of Baxter's prolific prose writing which will turn up to qualify the '*Complete*' title.

There is, of course, one obvious gap in *Quarrels with Himself*: the final topic on Weir's list, 'the plight of Māori', is nowhere formally addressed. We were keen to have at least one essay dealing with Baxter and the Māori world, and if possible a Māori voice to deal with the issue; but in the event we were unable to find a contributor, Māori or pākehā, able to take it on. Of course any edited collection is limited by the available time and energy of its possible contributors; this is not the only absence we regret from the volume, though it is the most important. Nevertheless, we suspect that the difficulty in finding someone to write on this topic is connected with the difficulty of the topic itself. Baxter's relationship with the Māori world – as a pākehā who moved into te ao Māori, adopted a Māori identity, and set himself up as a spokesman for Māori causes, a few years before the Māori political and cultural renaissance really hit its stride in the late 1970s – is now, in the second decade of the twenty-first century, a somewhat uncomfortable one. It may be a decade or two before a hypothetical future survey of Baxter will be able to put the figure of 'Hemi' into historical perspective. In this area as in others, Baxter in the twenty-first century remains a problematic figure – still 'the sore thumb of the tribe', and likely to remain so.

## *Works Cited*

Stead, C. K. 'Towards Jerusalem.' In: *In the Glass Cage: Essays on New Zealand Literature*. Auckland: Auckland University Press, 1981. 215–226.

Yeats, W. B. '*Per Amica Silentia Lunae*.' In: *Later Essays*. Ed. William H. O'Donnell. Collected Works of W. B. Yeats, vol. 5. New York: Charles Scribner's Sons, 1994. 1–33.

# *No Middle Ground: Baxter's Writing of the Self*

Janet Wilson

In a very real sense all of Baxter's writing – verse, prose and drama – is autobiographical, for, as has been noted, the impulse to record his life experience in all kinds of writing, and particularly in verse form, was with him from the time he started composing poetry (*Complete Prose* 2. 217–19; McKay 26). Keeping a prose record in note or diary form alongside the drafts of poems was a habit that he acquired in childhood, and the working and reworking of subjective impressions drawing upon observation, memory, dream and fantasy was part of his education as a poet. This intuitive reach for words to articulate his life experiences suggests he recognised that prose could give voice to his inner world in ways that differed from those of poetry or drama.

Prose narrative as a medium reflects the realities of life in a mundane way, as well as dramatically, and Baxter's early narrative fragments show him in everyday situations and settings grappling with sensations of fear, anxiety, guilt, registering pain and wounding, and using impressionistic modes – dreams, images and reflection – from which to construct textual images of wholeness and self-agency. This indicates that writing was an essential coordinate of the drama of his life. As Vincent O'Sullivan comments, 'he saw himself as *naturally* at the centre of forces which made any movement of his own feelings or thought of more than passing significance' (5), and he aimed to recreate these reactions both in verse and prose. Baxter himself read the need to tell stories, or the will-to-narrative, as creating meaning out of the chaos or disorder of life, which is how experience manifested itself to him, by mythologising it: 'What happens is either meaningless to me or else it is mythology' (2. 217; see also McKay 203). In the terms of Paul Ricoeur (28–29), his narrative understanding was anchored in his actual experience of human acting and suffering, and he formulated this understanding as the crux of his poetic identity: that is, suffering was essential for writing poems, and to turn away from human suffering was to be involved in self-betrayal. This was dramatised as a dialogue between his two sides: the one that writes, and the one that does the suffering and reminds the writing self, 'you can't do without me' (2. 137).

That narrativisation was an irreducible element of his self-understanding appears in the way Baxter entered wholeheartedly into mythological constructions of himself, and in his determination to create and live out his own biographical legend. The many versions of his early life suggest that his creative acts came from these involuntary drives to tell and record. Ricoeur claims that there is a '*pre-narrative quality of human experience*', namely that 'life [is] a story in its nascent state, and . . . an *activity and a passion in search of a narrative*' (29; italics in original), and this passion can be traced in the discovery of narratives. But Baxter went further in narrativisation in the application of narratives or mythologies for self-projection, locating himself at the centre of his work so as to act out new identities and roles of his poetic self. This unusually complex relationship between identity, life and art meant that his narrative self-inscriptions, whether in verse or prose, not only projected a public identity but helped sustain his life. For just as life produced narratives, Baxter's compulsive self-mythologising meant that narrative was a source of his life, as his textual inscriptions helped him move from one stage to the next.

Baxter's ongoing drama of life was defined by crises or high points marked as 'conversions' to new life structures

– marriage, Alcoholics Anonymous, Anglicanism, Roman Catholicism – often gaining visibility because of his public status as a poet and speaker. His self-mythologising as poet and prophet, his anti-authoritarianism and his crusading ambition to reform culminated in the desire to live a life that blended Franciscan poverty with aroha, inspired by the 'missionary' call to Jerusalem. Here a new configuring of life and art was made possible by a retreat from the social spheres of domesticity and institutionalisation through his self-transformation from the poet James into the prophet Hemi (Newton, *Rainbow* 1–3). This messianic destiny was delivered in a vision in 1968 – in another narrative form, a message from his unconscious in sleep that he believed to have come from God.[1] Baxter developed his social vision into the reality of founding of communes, first at Boyle Crescent in Auckland and then at Hiruhārama (*Rainbow* 23). With the inflation of his public life into a rapidly growing legend, feeling about Baxter became more adulatory, causing what John Newton calls the 'Baxter effect': the problem of disentangling the mediating presence of the public persona from the poems themselves ('Baxter Effect' 4, 6).

This essay examines selected 'autobiographical'[2] prose writings by Baxter, which belong to two different stages of his life and serve different purposes, to show how self-writing practices function in relation to his poetry and to discuss the role they play in his life trajectory, to the point where he seemingly exhausts the attempt to construct an account of his life in prose. It will begin with his earliest writing, which can be defined as 'life narrative', that is 'acts of self-presentation' or 'autobiographical acts' (Smith and

1 The account was written in a letter to his friend Noel Hilliard (*Rainbow* 23).

2 Baxter made no attempt to write autobiography (*autos* 'self', *bio* 'life' and *graphe* 'writing') in the accepted sense, and this generic term is used here only to refer generally to writing about himself and his life, and the self-reflection and comment that often infiltrates his lectures, reviews and so on. Terms like 'life-writing' or 'self-narrative' are more appropriate for describing these prose texts (Smith and Watson 1, 4).

Watson 4-5) in which he constructs and projects an image of selfhood, usually as a basis for his self-fashioning in verse. It will then turn to the autobiographical writing of the late 1950s and 1960s after Baxter had become an established literary voice and respected poet, in particular the collection titled 'Notes on the Education of a New Zealand Poet'[3] and then the posthumously published, semi-autobiographical novel *Horse,* which includes a reworking and adaptation of sections 3–5 of 'Notes on the Education of a New Zealand Poet'. Although vastly different in tone and genre, both these works can be categorised as 'life writing' because Baxter's own life is their subject, and they are a combination of the 'biographical, novelistic, historical, or explicitly self-referential and therefore autobiographical' (Smith and Watson 4).[4]

In consciously mythologising his life, Baxter was often motivated by feelings of violence and violation, and indeed the imagery of pain, wounds, scars, battles and wars recurs in all his accounts of his life. This might be formulated in terms of the 'originary violence of language' where the inscription of difference, the very act of naming, of turning something into a linguistic sign, what Derrida calls the violence of the letter, splits the subject by introducing a gap between the thing and its representation (Derrida 112, cited by Slaughter 26). For Baxter such a split might have been explained in biblical, mythological terms of man's fate due to Adam's Fall. But he also perceived his own deep psychological discord, and in all his writing represents these internal divisions as symbiotically linked, sometimes warring selves, whose conflict is necessary for creation to occur.

3 This consists of previously published lectures and articles including his 'Beginnings' account in *Landfall* (1965), and three sketches published in the late 1940s and the 1950s.

4 Smith and Watson introduce these terms as more inclusive of the heterogeneity of self-referential practices (4), and to encompass the expanded meanings of 'autobiography' (or 'self life writing', which they shorten to life writing) and 'memoir', which they consider to be types of life writing. See also Schwalm 7.

Moments of such recognition are recorded in prose when he perceives himself as another external self, articulated in his work in the language of uncanny doubles (twins, mirrors, doppelgängers, ghosts, illusions).[5] There was also what he perceived as injustice and discrimination, such as the persecution of his socialist pacifist family members for their anti-war ideology during the Second World War, his feelings of a gap between himself and others due to a sense of being different, and the plight of social outcasts.

A perception of the inherent violence in life led Baxter to claim that his poetry was partly inspired by 'a sense of grief – even at times a sense of grievance' with life which is in part 'a quarrel with the status quo' (2. 217). Given the interlinking of the poems with notes and sketches in the notebooks, it is likely that his life writing was catalysed by similar sensations. He describes himself as experiencing 'the sense of having been pounded all over with a club by invisible adversaries which has been with me as long as I can remember' (2. 217). The drama of a violent and bruising encounter with society also appears in later life through sexual misadventure, being scarred by the 'wars of Venus' or social dysfunction, the 'sickness of the heart' caused by social malady (McKay 197, 199, citing 'Pig Island Letter' 2). It is fictionalised in *Horse*, in his hero's antisocial behaviour, drunkenness and non-conformity, his vulnerability in sexual affairs, and his social and political moralising. The sense of being damaged and wounded by life, therefore, or of being a social irritant, or of perpetrating violence, gave Baxter the writer powerful roles within his inherited moral structure which he learned to project in both verse and prose.

The violence that triangulates the relationship between narrative and life often takes the form of law and is subject to its commands (Slaughter 17), for 'Narrative in general,' according to historian Hayden White, 'has to do with the top-

5 Folkenflik points out that autobiography is like the mirror stage (Lacan's symbolic) in that it allows one to reflect on the self by presenting imagery of the exterior self for contemplation, as in a mirror (234).

ics of law, legality, legitimacy, or, more generally, *authority*' (17, italics in original).[6] In all Baxter's work, efforts to legitimate his voice in different roles that often mask his psychological conflicts and 'quarrel with the status quo' hint at a thematics of violence as well as a violence of representation. Attempts at making meaning from this pre-narrative perception are also negotiated though his strong moral awareness, concern for justice, and dedication to social reform. These were central to his poetic creed. In 1951, in his speech to the New Zealand Writers' Conference, he pronounced the view that the artist should aim for the moral reform of society, and assumed the role of prophet with the declaration 'that poetry should contain moral truth and that every poet should be a prophet', a visionary perception of his future political activism. Justice has a defining role in this vision, for it 'demands . . . something more difficult' of the artist than living in romantic isolation or departing into the wilderness. Baxter famously declared that the artist should 'remain as a cell of good living in a corrupt society and in this situation by writing and example attempt to change it' (1. 75).[7]

Self-writing, therefore, enabled Baxter to deal with guilt as the fallen son of Adam, to rebel against the status quo, to unleash the unruly forces of chaos and disorder that lurked in the unconscious, and to construct his identity in diverse mythological or archetypal forms. It helped him to define new freedoms for writing poetry, as appears, for example, in the relationship between the more demotic narrative style of *Horse* and the vernacular idiom that distinguishes the poems of *Pig Island Letters* (1966) which followed *Horse*, and the loss

6 Cited by Slaughter, 19–20. Slaughter refers mainly to testimonial memoir and the prose of counterinsurgency, but this may be said of all kinds of life writing. He argues that the originary, generative role that violence plays in narrative is generally underestimated.

7 Baxter's argument that the artist should be politically committed to the social good anticipates Salman Rushdie's stance of 1984 that writers should act 'outside the whale', in critiquing George Orwell's assertion, made in an essay of 1940, that they should remain 'inside the whale'. Rushdie (1991) denounced Orwell's political quietism whereby the writer was 'allowing himself to be swallowed, remaining passive, *accepting*' (95).

of distinction between verse and prose in *Jerusalem Sonnets* and *Autumn Testament* (Oliver 146). Hayden White points out that meaning in narrative may come from an 'impulse to moralize reality, that is, to identify it with the social system that is the source of any morality that we can imagine' (18). Baxter's life trajectory in prose ended precisely because his opposition to the social system's morality, to which he had committed himself with his marriage, made continuation seemingly impossible; he abandoned the attempt to write his life in the search for a deeper meaning which he found in turning to Māori language and culture, as the fusion of Māori aroha and Catholic spirituality in *Jerusalem Sonnets* and *Autumn Testament* testifies.

### *Early narrative fragments: 'Before Sunrise' and 'The White Gull'*

An apprehension of the violence inherent in rural life, where death – whether arbitrary or deliberate – is often made casual, emerges from Baxter's earliest prose fragments. Written in the early 1940s when he was between sixteen and twenty years of age, the three versions of the sequence titled 'Before Sunrise' record his subjective processes of understanding victimhood and vulnerability, guilt and expiation, pain and wounding and his own death. These essential blocks of his moral and theological framework, forged from his childhood in the township of Brighton and its rural hinterland, would recur throughout his work. They all display the animism that Baxter valued: the narrator's identification with creatures and birds – e.g. 'I am the animal unsad and blood-aware' (1. 1, 5) – and they draw upon images from nature and the Otago landscape, reflecting this use in his early poetry for the expression of mood and subjectivity.

The sketches begin with his awakening from sleep and dream in early morning, and leaving the family tent in the camping ground for a walk and ocean plunge. The short first version, subtitled 'A description', only hints at the swim by referring to the waves as either 'death or longing' (1. 1, 5).

In versions two and three the narrator's immersion in the sea is followed by his reflection on the killing of a rabbit, his return to the camping ground and an exchange with his father. Version three is the most developed, with a more resolved tone and mood: swimming underwater, the narrator finds mussels on the sea floor and brings them up, grazing his ankle, and in the recollection that follows he converts his earlier guilt at killing the rabbit into a sense of accomplishment.

The manipulation of narrative technique suggests that Baxter was already developing an understanding of events as if defining two separate lives: according to Stephen Spender,

> one of these lives is himself as others see him – his social or historic personality – the sum of his achievements, his appearances, his personal relationships. . . . But there is also himself known only to himself, himself seen from the inside of his own existence. (116)

He uses the third person predominantly (as if writing biographically), and reserves the first-person, autobiographical narrative voice for representing inner thought, memory and subjective comment, moving between outward projection and interiorisation. Version two registers his pain and anguish at the animal's suffering – 'It shrieks, it is agony, the sound cuts my eyes' – but switches back to the third person in associating rain with 'purification', possibly of sin (1. 6).

Responsibility for the death of an innocent creature is something that Baxter the artist cannot leave unmarked without a dramatic projection of self-immolation, and in versions two and three the narrator imagines, commensurate with this act of destruction, his own solitary death by drowning. In version two he thinks, 'If I had been drowned . . . they would not have known: pity of his parents, not self pity' (1. 6), and this thought is followed by a change of heart over killing the rabbit: 'Why worry over a rabbit?' (1. 7). In version three speculation on his death is now represented in italics: '*If I had drowned,* he thought, *no one would have known*' (1. 38). This sentiment precedes his reflections about killing the rabbit, dramatising himself as catching it by the hind legs and delivering the 'rabbit punch' (1. 38). Version three also differs from the other two in that the first-person voice appears only once – in considering his own death; all else is recounted as if the narrator is looking at himself from the outside – a public image. 'He saw his drowned body floating . . .' (1. 38). This version is also stylistically closest to narrative proper, in contrast to discourse, through 'the use of the third person and of such forms as the preterit and the pluperfect' (White 7, citing Genette 11). In place of the anxiety and troubled conscience of the narrator of version two is dispassionate observation: 'The eyes were sad with the terrible remoteness of all dead things' (1. 38).

Version three presents a new self-image marked by a triumphant confidence: 'He had walked proudly through the plantation with the rabbit hanging heavily' (1. 38). In his poem about the same incident, 'The Killing of a Rabbit', dated c. 1943/44, the self-doubts of version two of 'Before Sunrise' are hinted at but put to rest in the final line: 'shall I be blamed? / I walk back unashamed' (*CPoems* 20). In another prose sequence about shooting a bird, 'The White Gull', written about this time, he unhesitatingly embraces the new identity: 'More than the desire to kill, it was the myth of the hunter that gripped him' (1. 35).

The three versions of this episode offer insight into Baxter's processes of revision and rewriting, as he reworks his memories and preoccupations with guilt and death. He uses observation to relate one experience to another 'until the subjective is objectified' (Spender 117). Incorporating the fantasy of his own death enabled him to come to terms with his role as huntsman and killer through what James Olney calls the 'processual memory model' (19–20); that is, with each revision a slightly new self is created until he arrives at an image of self-empowerment. These apprenticeship pieces show Baxter as less interested in narrative credibility than in developing a mythic dimension that can be related to Christian theology, and in striking the right pose, as 'The White Gull' confirms: 'His luck was out today. He would not be able to pose as the experienced hunter' (1. 36).

The rich imagery of these early pieces provides a seminal Christian metaphysics which reappears in Baxter's subsequent writing and especially in his poetry about the South Island. Not only does Baxter transform the phenomena of water, wounding and death that constitute this initiation rite into sacramental images familiar in religious symbolism, but the graze on his ankle in version three evokes an image of the wound that he later would associate with the writing of poetry.[8] His narrator's descent into the sea – the source of the wound, analogous to the movement through the unconsciousness and the activating of creative energies in writing poetry, and at a more archetypal level of the descent into hell – has affinities with the poetry and lyrical drama of the Martinican francophone poet and critic, Aimé Césaire. For Césaire, the 'secret wound' of the sea is associated with the trauma of the Middle Passage, the Atlantic slave crossing, and the descent into the sea is also a quest to give birth to poetry (Allen).

In reconciling his feelings to present an image of wholeness and psychic unity, the narrator 'authorises' his presence: for the reader, the text converges with the world, the life with the narrative. Version three confirms that writing about himself in prose narrative enabled Baxter to gain textual self-agency: self-exculpation from the stain of sin in killing the rabbit requires the ritual enactment of his own metaphorical death, including the witnessing of his corpse through the eyes of his parents; and this enables him to celebrate the dead rabbit in the poem 'The Killing of a Rabbit' in semi-religious terms for its 'miraculous life of the soul' (*CPoems* 20).

8 For example the comments of George Barker that his 'poetry flows like a jet of blood from a wound' (1. 319). The wound is also associated with the later, important concept of the gap which required 'an act of trust in . . . something, someone quite unknown whose image is the wound and the darkness itself' (Baxter, letter to Maurice Shadbolt, 22 September 1963, cited in McKay 196).

## *Life Writing: 'Notes on the Education of a New Zealand Poet'*

If the early prose fragments show Baxter authorising his text with positive self-inscriptions and developing his poetic persona through the mythopeic imagination, the later self-writing shows the impact on that reflective and creative imagination of his role as public commentator, poet and critic. By the late 1950s, now famed as 'the leading poet of his generation' (McKay 114) and 'our profoundest critic' (McKay 132), Baxter embarked on a major autobiographical project, catalysed by commissioned pieces such as his 'Beginnings' piece for *Landfall*, and the lectures given in the mid 1960s when he was Robert Burns Fellow at the University of Otago. Speaking and writing about himself flowed from Baxter's reputation as a major poet and critic and his compulsive urge to reach a wider audience in communicating his understanding of his early life. Yet such self-referential writing failed to gain narrative momentum and remained sporadic, reflective and anecdotal, and was often interspersed with other discourses, such as lectures, comment and reviews. John Weir comments that for Baxter poetry became a substitute for autobiography (*Poetry* 40–41; cited by McKay 203), that verse rather than prose had the role of shaping the meaning of his life. It is also true that Baxter's public orientation as an oppositional, anti-authoritarian voice, and his internal conflict between being both a poet and a domestic family man made for a confusing and contradictory narrative, unconducive to a full-blown biography. He does not incorporate into accounts of his life any reference to his marriage, family life, alcoholism, Alcoholics Anonymous, conversion to Catholicism or his various occupations, although these topics are mentioned in his poetry, public addresses and comment, such as the essays he wrote for the *Tablet* in 1967 and 1968 (Oliver 119). Similarly, problems with sexuality, such as feelings of sexual loss and betrayal, though they inspire some powerful mythological and symbolic female figures in his verse, are only treated episodically in prose (Oliver 94–96). Finally, his mystical revelation of a higher destiny through the call to Jerusalem, emerging as a form of political activism, undermined the need for self-writing to shape his life's meaning: instead it led to a new departure in his poetry. Nevertheless Baxter's self-writing of the sixties does demonstrate an urge to shape his life in prose, using his poetry for added insight – even though the attempts are often meandering, fictionalised and incomplete, possibly affected by the limiting factors of time and freedom to write at length, as much as by his own lack of enthusiasm to bring the projects up to the present day.

'Notes on the Education of a New Zealand Poet' can be described as a 'spiritual autobiography', an inner pilgrimage and peregrination to the present day, although the metaphor of a journey and the outlines of a chronology are only visible in the first two sections, focused on schooling and education. Baxter's poetics of self-fashioning blend dream, fantasy and reflection with critical comment and poetry. His self-education as a poet through his early love of classical mythology and Norse and Irish legend, his interest in Jungian psychoanalysis and archetypes of the unconscious, and his identification with socially marginal figures and Māori ways of knowing provide him with anecdotes, symbolic forms and mythological archetypes with which to counter the western system of learning. They also confirm he was unable or unwilling to 'demythologise' his life (2. 217). Writing his life is associated with fragmentation and incompleteness. Of 'Notes on the Education of a New Zealand Poet' he says that they constitute 'the *corpus* of an unfinished autobiography, which I have no intention whatever of finishing' (2. 130) – with a possible pun on *corpus*/corpse. Indeed, he intends that they be merely a 'counterpoint' to the lectures from which they originally derived.

Baxter's oppositional education in poetry begins with the 'exact mythological record' of his genesis and birth, described in a poem that concludes with the private joke 'poets are born with three balls' (2. 218; see also 2. 195).[9]

9 Besides the obvious implications of poets having powerful sexual

It continues with another poem that mythologises his childhood self as Prometheus (2. 220–21), resistant to social and parental pressures, the 'Calvinist ethos' that '*work is good; sex is evil; do what you're told, and you'll be all right*' (2. 220), waiting for his true destiny to present itself. There is no middle ground for Baxter:

> As soon as [the education process] came near me, I instinctively slipped my mind into neutral, became passive, inert, allowed myself to be pushed around mentally or physically, and . . . came as near as I could to a state of suspended animation. (2. 223)

Becoming 'de-educated' by reading A. S. Neill, Jung and other 'alternative' writers convinced him of the need to trust in 'a kind of subconscious wisdom' (2. 223–24), and this anti-education myth culminates in the image of the suffering poet whose duty is to explain to himself this state: 'A writer cannot avoid the task of exploring and understanding the private hell which lies just below the threshold of his own mind' (2. 222).

The autobiographical impulse is never far from the surface in the restless voice of these monologues, and Baxter continues within his oppositional binary structure rather than finding a temporal momentum through narrative. Yet various substitutions and self-displacements suggest that he also seeks to identify alternative points of reference. The second section addresses his sense of a gap between himself and others by finding a compensatory ethnic identification with 'the mythical Maori', a phrase that refers to an old Māori man in a joke he has just told (2. 223) (having already seen himself as like a 'Jewish boy in an anti-Semitic neighbourhood' in the first section). Anecdotes about ancient Māori wisdom, and praise of indigenous educational values for a unity of imagination and the use of symbols to

drives and/or enhanced sex-driven perceptions, Baxter may also allude to the three balls symbol of pawnshops and the joke that 'two to one you won't get your money back'.

explain the invisible world, anticipate his later conversion to a Māori way of life and spirituality.[10] This affinity with deep wells of intuition also includes the natural world, valued because of its revelatory powers: 'Waves, rocks, beaches, flax bushes, rivers, cattle flats, hawks, rabbits, eels, old man manuka trees' (2. 226). Being out of touch with 'the natural contemplative faculty' that guarantees such appreciation and that 'involves an entirely primitive movement of the intellect' (2. 225) is the basis of Baxter's critique of the four schools he attended (two of which were Quaker, including a boarding school in the Cotswolds in England when he was nine). In honing his argument with a poetic prose style, Baxter returns to his opening theme of gestation and birth – 'the school days were mainly a blank period, a time of waiting – waiting for what?'(2. 223) – and introduces the alternative birth metaphor of the dinosaur's egg, the hatching of which is associated with the writing of poems. A cohesive device that links the two opening sections of 'Notes on the Education of a New Zealand Poet', this metaphor identifies his anarchic self with the unconscious sources of creativity: 'I was already unconsciously erecting my defences around that core of primitive experience, that ineducable self which I like to call a dinosaur's egg' (2. 225; see also 223, 229).

The techniques of using poetic devices in prose found in these two sections resemble the genre of 'autobiography as poetry', described as 'symbolic studies of the psyche', and as uncertain and tentative portraits which articulate a degree of anxiety and dislocation.[11] This text also shows 'the poetic act of continuing self study' (Howarth 104), the puzzlement over identity, the return to the past in order to explain present uncertainty, the lack of clear answers; for example, the question of what would have been a better education

10 Newton points out that Baxter often wished for a Māori guide, a tuakana, when he first decided to enter the Māori world in 1968 (*Rainbow* 13).

11 Writers who write this kind of autobiography include Yeats, Goethe, Wordsworth, Henry James, Rousseau, Thoreau and Whitman (Howarth 104).

yields these speculations: 'Perhaps – till ten years old, on a farm in the South Island mountains or the Urewera country . . . then, for a year or two, during puberty, in a Maori pa; then perhaps on the coastal boats' (2. 229). Baxter openly confesses his limits to working in this genre: his memory is unreliable, and life writing has an element of provisionality or invention, undermining any claims to objectivity and 'factual truth':

> All mental reconstructions of those early events seem likely to be false – not deliberate lies, but an improvised and artificial childhood tidied up for others to look at. I am one of these people who can't give a clear account of what happened the day before yesterday . . . and while this is usually a great blessing, it cramps my style in autobiography. (2. 217)

When Baxter moves away from his schooldays and the mythological constructions in his poetry, he makes no attempt to sustain narrative coherence, and the image of the ineducable self is carried through in a more Rabelaisian way in the following four sections which cover the next phase of his life. In any event the informal, anecdotal style of sections three to five of 'Notes on the Education of a New Zealand Poet' can be traced to their origins as separate sketches published in 1949 and 1955. These recreations of adventures in late adolescence and new freedoms as an ex-university student, dominated by conflict such as fighting in 'the wars of Venus' (2. 241), drinking bouts, and rootlessness, are presented episodically: indeed, the themes of sexual betrayal, alcoholism, unemployment, the fleeting temptation to go to sea, and the unregenerate poet, are all incorporated into *Horse*.

### *Horse: an unpublishable novel*

*Horse*, Baxter's only novel, began as a series of prose sketches written in 1962, for he wrote to John Weir that he was writing a tragi-comic novel with a certain element of 'self-portrait' (McKay 191). Considered at first to be unpublishable, *Horse* appeared in print posthumously in 1985 with an Afterword adapted from comments Baxter made in the lecture 'Conversation with an Ancestor' (2. 135–37). Baxter returns to the image of the ineducable protagonist represented in the birth metaphors of 'Notes on the Education of a New Zealand Poet', the opposite of his outwardly respectable self, holder of the Robert Burns Fellowship in 1966 and 1967 (when he delivered this lecture) and a 'teetotal, moderately pious' family man (2. 135). His premise, that 'Art . . . is not bred by culture but by its opposite – that level of hardship or awareness of moral chaos where the soul is too destitute to be able to lie to itself' (2. 135), suggests that rather than continue his semi-poetic, mythological account of the poet's education, he now aims to celebrate the untamed, 'unredeemed self' (Oliver 97). This is dramatically represented as a conflict between bourgeois and Bohemian values (2. 138).

The novel's basis in the life story means that *Horse* can be read at one level autobiographically, according to current theories of autobiography that stress the fluidity of the boundaries between the genres of life writing and fiction. Such theories see both as narrative arrangements of reality; autobiography or life writing is a 'deliberate fictional construction of the self for public purposes' (Ang 24) and 'inevitably constructive and imaginative in nature, and as a form of textual "self-fashioning" [it] ultimately resists a clear distinction from its fictional relatives . . . leaving the generic borderlines blurred' (Schwalm 1).[12] Interpreting autobiography as closely aligned to fiction dispenses with the need for truth claims based on facts, dates and chronology, and stresses the unreliability of memory, the links between emotions and subjectivity, so that certain events assume more importance than others, often of a symbolic nature. Such broader interpretations of the genre thus make it possible to attribute some autobiographical status to

12 For a fuller discussion that distinguishes between the two genres see Smith and Watson 9–12.

Baxter's fictions of himself in *Horse*.

Resemblances between episodes in *Horse* and the sketches in sections three to five of 'Notes on the Education of a New Zealand Poet' suggest that the novel may have been planned as a revision and extension of those sketches and an attempt to bind them together through developing the figure of the ineducable self into a full-blown fictional character, 'my collaborator, my schizophrenic twin, who has always provided me with poems' (2. 135). This divided figure is a 'natural man', that is, the everyman, fallen Adam (2. 138); his public name is Timothy Harold Glass, while his alias, 'Horse', refers to the fact he is constantly 'ridden' by others (2. 135). In Jungian terms Horse is the 'shadow', represented as an archetype, the 'unconscious side of the human psyche' and '"the lower part of the body and the animal drives that take their rise from there"' (McKay 191, citing Jung 29).

A fictionalised account of the year after Baxter left university in 1945, the novel deals with his sorrow at the loss of his first love, a medical student at Otago University, Jane Aylward (McKay 95–97), his rejection of his parents' ambitions for him in leaving university, his departure from the family home and work in an iron foundry, his Bohemian lifestyle of drinking binges and gambling bouts with friends and workmates. This corresponds to one of the most turbulent periods of his life: about the time his first book of poems, *Beyond the Palisade*, was published in 1945. The novel is influenced in style and composition by Dylan Thomas's ribald *Adventures in the Skin Trade* (written 1938, published 1955), a flamboyant, semi-autobiographical story about a young man's leaving home for the city, alcoholic excess and unexpected sexual adventures.[13] As in Thomas's novel, continuity of action, reminiscent of the picaresque novel, is provided by the deeds and thoughts of the protagonist as he plunges further into social outrage and inner chaos.

The novel's mix of narrative, dialogue and poetry gave

13 Baxter reviewed *Adventures in the Skin Trade* for the *New Zealand Listener* in 1956, praising its 'strong wind of rebellious laughter' (1. 269).

Baxter scope for linguistic invention and play with the demotic idioms of the Kiwi vernacular, suggesting his continuing engagement with the sounds and inflections of the human voice, a concern that first emerged in the plays for radio and stage he wrote in the late 50s: *Jack Winter's Dream* (1958) and *The Wide Open Cage* (1959). He introduces narrative techniques, including self-reflection and mockery, doubling, and criticism of his protagonist through the voices of those he has offended, in telling of the profligate years before he gained acceptance as a poet and settled down to married life. The raw, unfettered account of living rough can also be seen to anticipate the 'new realism' (McKay 191, 196) of the poems of 'Pig Island Letters', as appears in the conversational, epistolary style of address to his friend and recipient of the letters, the writer Maurice Shadbolt.

Framing the crisis with which *Horse* opens is the representation of a split personality through the device of the double or doppelgänger, now linked to the disturbing forces of the imagination and the protagonist's precarious psychic balance (due to vulnerability to alcohol and distress over sexual betrayal).[14] The dualism of Timothy Glass is reflected in his semi-conscious state, waking with a hangover, then dreaming of losing Fern (his beloved) to a rival. The mention of his nickname 'Horse' marks the self-division and the novel's conceit: that the unruly Horse will run amok, allowing Baxter to imagine a chaotic but creative universe in which poets and poetry are idolised for their determination to *épater la bourgeoisie*. The story climaxes in the budding poet Horse's encounter with a caricatured older version of himself, the dead drunk poet Grummet, whose scandalous performance at a literary society gathering run by a young couple mockingly called the Virtues and success in

14 Baxter's alcoholism led him to associate with poets like Dylan Thomas, while his grandfather, John Baxter, also an alcoholic, was 'my looking glass twin'. His self-analysis while a member of Alcoholics Anonymous explains this inner division as Jamie 2, 'a pathological deadbeat', and Jamie 1 (without booze), 'no beauty but functionally sound' (McKay 145).

apparently seducing Fern, blends dissolution with charm in a way that enchants Horse.[15]

The novel's entry into its fictional world hinges on the imagined death and burial of the protagonist. The narrator overcomes the psychological fear of defying family expectation by first staging the drama of his own death, witnessed as if outside himself. Upon seeing his public, respectable face reflected in the mirror as the meek, self-effacing Timothy Glass, Horse triggers the crisis, symbolised by a hail of bullets which fell Timothy, leading to his burial: 'Six feet underground a young man's bones lay quiet until the ending of the world' (*Horse*, 1. 532). As in 'Before Sunrise', metaphorical death allows for a singular reincarnation that releases the protagonist from conforming to the moral principles of his upbringing. 'Horse, the redhot stovesitter . . . had hurled the grenade', that is, the decision to leave university, catalysing the dreaded quarrel with his mother, while Timothy Glass, 'the good son', puts his hands over his ears (1. 533); later, like a 'ghost in trousers', he had 'dissolved into thin air', leaving only Horse alive (1. 535).

The line of influence between *Horse* and 'Pig Island Letters' has been noted by Baxter's biographer, Frank McKay,[16] and the self-image as internally conflicted poet was one that Baxter clung to during these middle years and developed through growing intimations of his own mortality. 'The poet as family man' of letter nine, whose true self is the 'undercover convict', 'incorrigible, scarred / With what the bottle and the sex games taught' (*CPoems* 282), recalls Timothy Glass who lives in the cellblock in the basement of my mind . . . incorrigible, ineducable, unemployable' (1. 136). In the same way Baxter's confession to Shadbolt of a similar mid-life crisis to his, framed by considerations of his own

15 Grummet's 'purple and gnome-like' face (1. 571) suggests this may be a caricature of Denis Glover; I owe this insight to Kevin Ireland.

16 McKay argues that Baxter needed to come close to the chaos of the unconscious in order to write with truth, referring to the image of the plank over the lion's den in 'Pig Island Letters 9' (203).

death, burial and afterlife, now moves from his ritualistic death and burial in both *Horse* and 'Before Sunrise' into contemplation of death's presence in his everyday world, an essential component of the creative sphere. These reflections approach the topic of his mortality in personal and mythical ways. Not only is this perception evident in every poem in one form or another, but the collection is framed by two poems that together project death as a process that infiltrates life: letter one relates death to the 'little death' of the sex act, and hints that it is a going into the dark, 'the gap itself' (276), while letter thirteen is a semi-comic dialogue on the afterlife between the poet and the 'Great Mother of God' (284). In between are pervasive hints of the imminence of death. Using these life–death tensions, as if a psychomachia, the collection proclaims the survival of the unregenerate Baxter of *Horse* and explores how to keep him alive (Oliver 97).

*

Baxter seems to have abandoned all further attempts at telling his life story in a discrete prose narrative form after 'Notes on the Education of a New Zealand Poet' and *Horse*. This is not just because he continued to shape his changing outlook on life predominantly in poetry, but because he also saw through the illusion of narrative self-determination, that the psychological losses it commemorated could not be brought back to life. In Ricoeur's terms, he had taken on authorship of his narrative by centring himself in it, but not authorship of his life (Ricoeur 32). The 'Pig Island Letters' sequence carries further the implication of *Horse,* that the anarchic, creative self still needed to rebel against the social constrictions of New Zealand's secular Calvinism. Baxter's departure from writing in prose about these endeavours appears in the confession in section 6 of 'Notes on the Education of a New Zealand Poet' that he is unable to account for his life beyond the age of about twenty: 'As I grow older I cease to know who or what I am' (2. 241). The perception of being engulfed by the unfathomable sadness of the world that frames this admission points to a romantic view of life, which is partly explicable in terms of the Fall. Just as likely, though, is that Baxter, in seeking how to conclude his disconnected recollections, borrowed Dylan Thomas's subversive mode in *Adventures of the Skin Trade*. Thomas's novel terminates abruptly, as *Horse* does, and its severance from the fictional world is anticipated by the narrator's comic determination not to be in control of his narrative, evident in comments such as 'I don't want to make anything happen' (Thomas 47).[17] Just as Thomas undermines the conventions of the narrator as artist or author of their self-narrative (as in the Bildungsroman), Baxter points to the fruitlessness of the autobiographical endeavour when self-identity is unknown, so subverting the generic expectations of self-writing and the assumption that identity becomes more defined with age. If his confession about not knowing himself is read alongside the abrupt termination of *Horse*, it points to a more radical break from that self-image as unredeemed poet at odds with society than the text alone suggests. His lack of conclusion might be read as evidence of his psychic self 'signing off' from that social milieu.

17 Other such comments are 'I don't know what I expect to happen' (44); 'I'm not going to choose anything' (49).

## *Works Cited*


Allen, Jason. 'The Underworld as Mythical Decor of Modernity in Aimé Césaire's *And the Dogs Were Silent.*' *Journal of Postcolonial Writing* 53.4 (2017).

Ang, Ien. *On Not Speaking Chinese: Living Between Asia and the West.* London and New York: Routledge, 2001.

Derrida, Jacques. *Of Grammatology.* Trans. by Gayatri Chakravorti Spivak. Baltimore, MD: Johns Hopkins University Press, [1975] 1997.

Folkenflik, Robert. 'The Self as Other.' In: *The Culture of Autobiography: Constructions of Self-Representation.* Ed. Robert Folkenflik. Stanford CA: Sanford University Press, 1993.

Genette, Gerard. 'Boundaries of Narrative.' *New Literary History* 8.1 (Autumn 1976). 1–13.

Howarth, William L. 'Some Principles of Autobiography.' In: *Autobiography: Essays Theoretical and Critical.* Ed. James Olney. Princeton N.J.: Princeton University Press, 1982.

Jung, Carl. *Modern Man in Search of a Soul.* London: Kegan Paul, Trench, Trubner and Co. Ltd., 1934.

Newton, John. '"By Writing and Example": the Baxter Effect.' *Ka mate ka ora: A new zealand journal of poetry and poetics* 1 (2005). http://www.nzepc.auckland.ac.nz/kmko/01/ka_mate01_newton.asp. Accessed 27 December 2015.

Olney, James, ed. *Autobiography: Essays Theoretical and Critical.* Princeton N.J.: Princeton University Press, 1982.

———. *Memory and Narrative; The Weave of Life Writing.* Chicago: Chicago University Press, 1998.

Ricoeur, Paul. 'Life in Quest of Narrative.' In: *On Paul Ricoeur: Narrative and Interpretation.* Ed. David Wood. London and New York: Routledge, 1991. 20–33.

Rushdie, Salman, 'Outside the Whale.' In: Salman Rushdie, *Imaginary Homelands: Essays and Criticism 1981–1991.* London: Granta/Penguin, [1984] 1991. 83–101.

Schwalm, Helga. 'Autobiography.' In: *The Living Handbook of Narratology.* Ed. Peter Hühn, et al. Hamburg: Hamburg University Press, 2014. hup.sub.uni-hamburg.de/lhn. Accessed 3 January 2017.

Slaughter, Joseph R. 'Life, Story, Violence: What Narrative Doesn't Say.' In: *The Social Work of Narrative: Human Rights and the Cultural Imaginary.* Ed. Gareth Griffiths and Philip Meade. Stuttgart: Ibidem-Verlag, 2017: 15–37.

Smith, Sidonie and Julia Watson. *Reading Autobiography: A Guide for Interpreting Life Narratives.* 2nd ed. Minneapolis: University of Minnesota Press, [2001] 2010.

Spender, Stephen. 'Confessions and Autobiography.' In: *Autobiography: Essays Theoretical and Critical.* Ed. James Olney. Princeton N.J.: Princeton University Press, 1982. 115-22.

Thomas, Dylan, *Adventures in the Skin Trade.* London: Putnam, 1955.

White, Hayden. 'The Value of Narrativity in the Representation of Reality.' *Critical Enquiry* 7 (Fall 1980): 5-27.

# *'Women are all mothers to him': Displacing Fear in James K. Baxter's Short Stories*

Sharon Matthews

James K. Baxter's short fiction – by which I mean his short stories, prose poems, prose dialogues, semi-autobiographical fragments and parables – makes up a relatively small but significant part of his oeuvre. The bulk of these pieces were written between 1942 and 1960, although he continued to weave allegorical fables into his lectures and more informal talks until the end of his career. Baxter neither could nor wished to separate his life from his work; hence much of this 'fiction' examines the human condition through the lens of self-experience. So marked is this slippage that the stories 'Blue Peter' (1949), 'Some Time Ago' (1955), and 'Venus in Her Western Bed' (1955) were republished with the more clearly autobiographical 'Beginnings' (1965) and 'Recollections of School Days' (1966) in 'Notes on the Education of a New Zealand Poet' (1967), as what the poet calls his 'unfinished autobiography' (*Complete Prose* 2. 129–243; 130).

The short stories develop themes underlying much of Baxter's work: the debasing constraints of social institutions such as marriage, the family and the Church, and the sexual hypocrisy and spiritual bankruptcy of neo-Calvinism and Puritanism in the New Zealand society of his time. In Baxter's interpretation of the 'domestic tragedy of Pig Island' (3. 64), it is the destructive female figure who suppresses the sexual and emotional life of the individual and destroys the creative potential of the artist. Men in this society are crushed under the 'hand of the castrator' (1. 289), from which they seek refuge in 'the birth cave', which is also the 'death cave', of the pub (2. 179). Here, as in much of his work, Baxter's broad gestures towards social reality direct the reader instead towards his 'large subconscious corpus of personal myth' (cited Weir, *Bone Chanter* 5–6) and to the 'affective pressures' of autobiographical memory (Fox 97).

The characters playing out these themes draw on aspects of the poet's own life – his alcoholism, his various manual jobs and his compulsive sexuality – which suggests, in W. H. Oliver's words, that they can be read as split-off parts of a 'multiple self-portrait', with the female characters being barely disguised versions of the significant women in Baxter's world (92). The importance of these stories for Baxter may therefore lie in how they bring opposing parts-of-self and parts-of-'other' into relations with each other, enabling the playing out of long-held inner dramas at a displaced symbolic remove. I would argue that, in this, the stories serve perhaps as precursors to Baxter's plays and the translation of his concerns into the 'more externally dynamic medium' of theatre (Millar, *Selected* xx).

These female characters are predominantly maternal figures. To borrow a phrase that Baxter himself uses to describe his protagonist in 'Henley Pub' (1961–65), 'Women are all mothers to him' (2. 179). Baxter consistently portrays 'woman' split (in Kleinian terms) into the antithetical archetypes of, in the poet's own words, the Blessed Virgin, the 'good mother' who 'rules over the spirit', and the Temptress, the 'bad mother,' who governs the flesh (2. 182). Reading the short stories, it becomes apparent that these figures are also 'monstrous' mothers, in Barbara Creed's terms – rejecting mother-wives and abjected temptress-mothers – with their relations to the male protagonist both castrating and uneasy. This tension between self and female 'other' infuses Baxter's work. Sex, alcohol and the transformative aspects of religion are shown to be both appealing and frightening in that they all involve the surrender of the self; in psychoanalytic terms, they offer a potential regression to a period when the individual was continuous with the mother. Linked to this ambivalence is Baxter's iterated portrayal of the maternal imago who both nurtures and rejects. Addressing the New Zealand Universities Arts Festival in 1966, Baxter told his audience that:

> Many writers, like Yevtushenko, tend to symbolise their country in female terms. . . . Metaphorically I tend to think of my own poems as semen deposited by me in the sad barren belly of this society. She is determined to bear no children – that is, she won't allow any living acts or thoughts to survive inside her.

The poet expresses an uneasy dependence on 'Mother New Zealand' that is consequently resented. He goes on to say: 'But deep in the marrow of my bones I still have an agonised despairing affection – all the stronger because it hurts so much – for this poor old maltreated bitch' (2. 32).

Baxter's 'problematic' and 'appalling' portrayal of women is well known, yet something beyond the habits of his rhetoric seems to pull him back to these figures (Millar, *Selected* xix; McNeill 4). As John Davidson rightly comments, Baxter's female characters can be seen as problematic if 'viewed as statements about the nature of women; but that is not necessarily their function'. Considered as 'statements about Baxter's mental landscape, about the human (male) condition, and about the forces which goaded or scourged him into poetry', these figures sit 'very close to the heart of his creative process' (Miles et al. 116). Critics have clearly established how Baxter continually returns to certain figures, sometimes in 'deeply ambiguous and contradictory' ways, to 'represent his own experience and wrestle with his own inner conflicts' (Miles 234). It is to a consideration of the psychic underpinnings of this wrestling match that I address myself in this essay. Using Baxter's short stories as exemplars, I draw on psychoanalytic theory to explore how Baxter's female characters may be seen as relational 'objects' which act to displace and project troubling emotions within the imaginary. The remarkable consistency with which Baxter returns to plot configurations of death, suicide or flight from reality and tropes of male potency broken or violently amputated, suggests that beneath the conscious processes of the creative work lies the fantasy of the rejecting 'bad' mother that is Baxter's emotional response to his difficult relationship with his own mother, which he 'recognised, struggled with in various guises, but never resolved' (Wilson 48). The recurring figures of the castrating mother and her apparent antithesis, the loving, betraying temptress, point to underlying fears of being unloved, which he articulates in his wider oeuvre through tropes of childhood loss and endlessly deferred utopias and Edens. In defence against fears of being rejected, the mother figure is constructed as 'monstrous' and castrating so that she, like the 'maltreated bitch' referred to above, may rightfully be rejected. This form of scapegoating enables control over fears, if only in symbolic form, while attacking the fictive version of mother or wife protects fragile parts of the self from having to directly face these fears.

Baxter spoke to friends often about his mother's lack of physical demonstration and his belief that 'he had not received enough love from her' (McKay 281). Throughout his life Baxter looked for the 'good' mother in alcohol, in various communities and in multiple lovers, both male and female. After converting to Catholicism in 1958, Baxter invested the Virgin Mary with those qualities of unconditional love and acceptance that he felt his own mother did not provide (2. 290–92; see also McKay 223). As one of Baxter's creative masks, the character Horse, puts it, the 'misunderstanding' between mother and son was 'more profound than any communication', stretching right back to 'the cotton wool and enemas and foreskin-clipping doctors of a Karitane nursing home' – an image potent with castrating potential and phallic violation by literal assaults on penis and anus

(1. 532). Indeed, Baxter's writing is notable for the level of explicit anatomical and poetic detail he gives to masculine psycho-sexual anxieties and longings.

Theorists such as John Bowlby and his associates argue that perturbations in early attachment relationships recreate themselves in 'internal working models' that make up one's inner reality and define the way we live our lives (Eagle 14). This 'emotional legacy', Alistair Fox contends (122), plays a part in determining the metaphoric condensations and symbolic networks found in fictional representation, such as Baxter's repeated imaging of lovers as 'distant or absent' and loving relationships characterised by 'reluctant dependence' (Millar, *Spark* 22). Psychoanalyst Brett Kahr posits that one of the functions of fantasy is to help the individual maintain emotional 'equilibration' in the face of the lingering affects of childhood disturbances (335). For Kahr, fantasy, whether articulated in dreams, daydreams or the creative work, functions in a similar way to the 'transitional object' of infancy which bridges gaps in the continuity of the caregiving experience. D. W. Winnicott theorises that the infant learns to relate to the external world through the use of symbols – 'transitional objects' such as a blanket or a toy – that merge both inner and external reality by representing both the intimate relationship between caregiver and infant and their separateness (4–5). As such, forms of creativity, such as fiction, serve as part of an individual's ongoing process of psychic regulation and self-reparation. The creative work can thereby facilitate a number of purposes: rework disturbing emotions or experiences, offer a forum for trial action, communicate inner conflict, discharge aggressive impulses and master trauma (Kahr 311–36). We may see this process playing out in Baxter's case through his repeated return to fictive 'objects' that stand for specific emotionally invested experiences.

Considered in this light, Baxter's depiction of 'woman' cannot be dismissed as simply misogynistic – though, at some level, it certainly is – but as representing attempts to come to terms with conflicting desires related to autonomy and secure attachment within the relatively unchallenged 'transitional space' of fiction (Winnicott 53). Psychologist Margaret Mahler has indeed proposed that this struggle is common to all individuals:

> One could regard the entire life cycle as constituting a more or less successful process of distancing from and introjection of the lost symbiotic mother, an eternal longing for the actual or fantasised 'ideal state of self', with the latter standing for a symbiotic fusion with the 'all-good' symbiotic mother, who was at one time part of the self in a blissful state of well-being. (338)

Julia Kristeva's concept of the abject perhaps helps illuminate Baxter's depiction of woman as monstrous, especially 'in relation to her mothering and reproductive functions' (Creed 7). Drawing on Kristeva, Barbara Creed identifies a 'deep-seated attitude of extreme ambivalence' towards the mother who nurtures, but who also 'helps bring about the most painful of all separations', namely that of mother from infant (7). As such,

> The abject represents a 'primitive terror of maternal engulfment' that threatens the psychological and physical boundaries of the infant 'almost before those boundaries come into being' in other words, whilst the individual is beginning to conceptualize him or herself as distinct from both the mother and those fluid, excremental inputs and outputs of his own body (shit, milk, urine, the maternal embrace, etc). (Marshall 201–202)

Yet, as Kristeva explains, the process of continuously rejecting the abject – our connection to the mother – paradoxically brings it into back in existence: 'Repelling, rejecting; repelling itself, rejecting itself. Ab-jecting' (13). The uneasy relation between Baxter's 'monstrous' mother and the protagonists of these stories is in this sense abject. The assault of emotions she causes 'disturbs identity, system, order' within their self-sense (Kristeva 4). The maternal body is the site of conflicting desires, as in the story 'To Have and to Hold'. It is shifting and fragmented: grotesquely formless and sexless, as is Mrs Matheson in 'The Mathesons at Home' and abject and 'above all' ambiguous, as is Celia from 'The Blue Divan' (Kristeva 9).

In what follows, I focus on a group of stories written between 1949 and 1960, a period in which Baxter struggled to balance the demands of family life with the needs of that 'doubtful treasure', namely the poet's sense of self (2. 130). Baxter's bleak view of family life is manifested in these stories using repeated characters and images. He writes: 'I do not think we men ever emerged from the adolescent torture room . . . We regarded women as authorities whom we had to placate, not even remotely as fountains of hope or understanding'. Boredom and 'violence' are 'endemic' in marriage. What we call 'maturity', he states, is 'commonly amputation', again, an image signifying a violent loss of potency (3. 64). The multiple identifications that can be made between the recurring figures of the castrating mother, the rejecting wife, the tormented adolescent, the 'young unhappy married man' (*CPoems* 385) and Baxter's own life, indicate how the fiction may also alleviate areas of psychic distress through complex processes of projective identification, reversal and displacement.

The clear parallels between Jack, the five-month married protagonist of 'The Name and the Game' (1949), and the newly married Baxter illustrates how contradictory and ambiguous emotions may be so displaced.[1] Jack is twenty-three, like Baxter was at the time of his writing, and works in the gutting room of the local freezing works; Baxter worked in an abattoir in Ngauranga to pay rent and bills after his marriage (4. 36). Baxter gave up drinking during this period – again, like Jack – realising that 'it was time I stopped playing the fool' (letter to Charles Brasch, 8 April

1 According to the Oxford English Dictionary, 'Jack' is the generic proper name for a man of the common people.

1949, cited in McKay 121). Frank McKay comments that life for Baxter and the pregnant Jacquie was 'suddenly very grim', which came as a 'shock' for Baxter (120–21). Baxter's mixed emotions regarding this 'struggle for survival' and the resulting enforced dependence on each other infuse the otherwise simple story (McKay 157). Baxter draws on his experiences as a drunk and his rueful self-awareness of the 'emotional patterns' below addictive behaviour (2. 22). Jack avoids having a drink after work (although, tellingly, his wife Brenda does not mind), for 'the need had left him with the loneliness from which it had sprung', indicating how addictions serve as an equivalent to maternal security (1. 47).[2]

Jack and Brenda are saving his pay to furnish their house. Jack's older co-worker, Harry, genially mocks Jack for taking all his paypacket 'home to Mum, eh?' and encourages him to join his work mates at the weekly Crown and Anchor game (47). At first Jack wins, then loses heavily. Although he worries about what to tell his wife and resolves to never gamble again, his final thought is: 'if I'd stuck to the diamond I'd be sitting pretty' (49). Jack's external world, in which the working man 'tear[s] gut from paunches' and the placid married man digs the garden or does 'odd jobs around the house', is vividly contrasted with the heightened affect of his inner world in the company of men. When he wins, the 'fever and unreality of the game' lifts Jack 'like a rising tide'. The crown seems to 'stand out from the rest of the board, red and magical'. When he loses, his head sings and his 'heart pound[s]', the directly corporeal and sensual nature of this testing of male potency jumping from the page (48).

Jack's paypacket signifies the conflict underlying his seemingly unruffled reality. Jack feels pride and enjoyment at throwing the unopened envelope 'down on the kitchen table as if it were a gift' (47). His gambling, paradoxically, places this money – earned, like the poet's, through hard physical and 'muck[y]' labour – under Jack's control. In

2 Unless otherwise noted, all further references to Baxter's short stories are to volume one of the *Complete Prose*.

this way, Jack, the fictive self, serves to externalise hidden resentment incurred by the discovery that married life depends less on 'gifts' and more on meeting one's obligations. At the same time, a key image of the freezing works' killing chain unsettles our view of Jack's equilibrium. Walking to the 'butchers' dining room' to join the game, Jack hears the 'crying of sheep' and feels the horror of their change from 'live struggling animals to dangling carcasses'. Those who escape are 'always recaptured and hauled back to the knife' (48). Jack's empathy causes him, and hence the poet, to identify with these helpless animals and it is they who have been captured by the woman-dominated domestic sphere that Brenda signifies. The gutting room that Jack works in both represents Baxter's own life and symbolically – through the connection with the maternal abject – externalises emotions of being consumed by the demands of being a husband.

Jack's heightened emotions while gambling can be linked to those experienced by the central character in 'The Kite' (c. 1942), a small boy 'perhaps ten years old'. In this unpublished story, the boy watches kites flying 'almost to the curved yellow sea-beach' (a classic maternal image) and yearns to own 'one of these miraculous things that rose twisting in their will to be free'.[3] To hold one is to be granted 'power and sureness', and when he does so, the boy feels himself 'changed, felt the wind blowing in him' (2). The kite represents, John Weir notes, 'freedom from the constraints of family' (4. 89). Seeking such freedom, the boy takes old bottles from the washhouse and sells them to buy a kite. His theft is discovered by his parents. He is punished, and again, the tool of potency – the kite – is 'broken'.

In 'The Mathesons at Home' (1956), an 'ungainly' adolescent is driven to suicide by family pressure. The story

3 In her maternal guise, the sea threads her way through many of Baxter's short stories. Her rejecting aspect is clearly portrayed in 'The Sea Stayed' (1944), in which the narrator watches a man (a hypermasculine Burnsian 'buirdly chiel') test his strength against the sea. He drowns, but 'the sea stayed' (1. 10).

takes place in the 'early summer of '55' (274), hence shortly after Baxter joined Alcoholics Anonymous late in 1954, and features two versions of Baxter's split-off selves. The narrator, Mr Gantry, is the newly sober family man, a schoolteacher-poet who has had to 'lay off the grog six months before' (274). The second is John, a 'slight, fair youth' clad, despite the heat, in a 'gabardine overcoat', a garment much favoured by the poet himself (278). This doubling establishes a parallel between the emotional state of John, the adolescent who is crucified by the Puritan Devil, and the poet's struggle with both the 'massive disturbances and irrational fears' of the drying out alcoholic and his acute awareness of the damage his drinking and its related sexual irresponsibility had done to his marriage (2. 271; McKay 143–45).

John's parents, Mr and Mrs Matheson, are devout Methodists 'blanketed' by a 'negative spirituality' (278). Arthur Matheson – a retired schoolteacher with a 'thick, androgynous body' – embodies Baxter's disgust with the education system, here also figured as an emasculating influence. His 'hard, dead bird's eye' stares at the flowers he waters as if 'they were children whom he suspected of talking in morning assembly' (275). Mrs Matheson is also described in terms that emphasise her grotesque, sexless physicality. She is a 'shapeless shadow' with a 'heavy, spade-square face'. Her lips are pale and moustached and her eyes have an 'irritable needle brightness' like that of a 'broody hen'. In these characters, masculine and feminine become confused in a grotesque caricature of the patriarchal family.

John writes poetry and brings Gantry two 'grubby school exercise books' full of verse (278). He asks Gantry to call him 'Jack', which is his name at school – only his parents call him 'John'. Articulate, and even brilliant when he talks about his own poetry or that of Wilfred Owen, on all other matters Jack is 'as naïve as a ten-year-old' echoing 'his mother's pious dogmas'.[4] Visiting one afternoon, Jack finds Gantry in the company of an effervescent friend, the friend's 'lush thrush'

4 The young Baxter also read Owen, reviewing his poems in *Critic*, 20

of a girlfriend and a half empty bottle of gin. The 'lushness' of the thrush presumably distinguishes her from the bird-like qualities of the Mathesons, although the secondary meaning of 'thrush' suggests the abject quality sexually active women often have in Baxter's work. Looking up from his inefficient attempt to make the 'thrush' sit on his knee (accompanied by recorded 'obscene army songs'), Gantry notes Jack's shock at the apparent 'pagan Saturnalia' (280). A week later, Arthur Matheson confronts Gantry. 'John's dead,' Arthur says. 'Dead. Come and look at your work.' They walk together to a 'very tidy' army hut at the back of the Mathesons' house. Jack lies 'curled on the bed with bare feet and the muzzle of a shot gun inside his clenched jaws'. Jack's suicide note reveals his sexual guilt and fear. He writes: 'Dear God – I can't go on the way I am. You know I've prayed again and again for you to take this terrible thing away from me . . . I would rather die now than go mad when I am older' (281). Above the head of the bed hangs an enlarged photograph of Mrs Matheson splashed with blood. His masturbation – 'this terrible thing' that Jack has 'tried again and again to stop' – is explicitly linked to his relationship with his mother.[5]

Mrs Matheson incarnates all the negative aspects that Baxter identifies with Puritanism. Jack's physical frailty, the 'dark hollows' under his eyes, is contrasted with her deformed vigour: her 'broad, misshapen, almost dwarfish body gave a sense of huge vitality turned in against itself and continually jarring' (276–77). She places emphasis on 'moral integrity', criticises Gantry's borrowed house (a 'sad state of disrepair'), disapproves of drinking and stiffens 'visibly' when told of his slovenly habit of sleeping wrapped only in a blanket on the floor (277). Signifying the 'bitter core' (278) of a society that distrusts pleasure and believes in the inherent

July 1944 (1. 8–10).

5 Janet Wilson notes that Millicent is 're-incarnated' in Baxter's poetry as 'the cold-hearted, bitch goddess who symbolises both temptation and negativity' (51): '[m]y mother in the kitchen sunshine / Tightens her dressing gown / Chops up carrots, onions, leeks' (*CPoems* 237–38).

depravity of man, she then ironically elicits such depravity from her son. In terms of Baxter's underlying personal myth, it is notable that depending on the mother figure as Jack does ('Mother is a very good woman. People think she is a saint') is shown to be destructive. Rather, Jack's 'continually anxious' expression in his mother's presence (277), and the image of her enlarged photo staring down at her son's dead body, illustrates the poet's thesis: the constraining mother's 'legacy of sexual imprisonment and self-doubt' will destroy her children (*CPlays* 336). Attempting to 'break through the crust' and 'reach the real boy behind the intricate defences', the narrator asks Jack whether he has a girlfriend and makes a crude remark about 'lively little pieces'. Jack's face goes blank. He replies that his mother thinks that 'people shouldn't go out together' until marriage. Only his hands 'desperately gripping the edge of the table showed that the remark had any meaning for him' (279–80).

The castrating mother-wife also incarnates a form of the abject: the fear of maternal authority. In this story, the fictive pairing of the monstrous mother and tortured adolescent simultaneously exemplifies Baxter's version of family life and externalises for the poet a complex cluster of anxieties relating to sex, alcohol and creativity. W. H. Oliver comments on how Baxter mythologises his mother into 'a figure of menace' and recounts an anecdote in which Baxter, his cousin, and another small girl were caught by Millicent while they were showing each other their bottoms (24, 28). The poet's memory is of overwhelming fear: 'God and all his bulldozers were on the march . . . [the fear] was, quite honestly, the most extreme I have ever felt' (3. 193). Psychoanalyst Karen Horney argues that man's experience of women as powerful mothers leads him to fear and resent her for her imagined powers as castrator. Man 'strives to rid himself of his dread of women by objectifying it. "It is not," he says, "that I dread her; it is that she herself is malignant, capable of any crime, a beast of prey, a vampire, a witch"' (349).[6] The male child's fear of the

6 See also Patricia McLean who reads the dominance of the monstrous

father 'is more actual and tangible, less uncanny in quality' and does not need to include the shameful admittance of dependency (Horney 352). What is expressed here is the fusion of one image of the mother – that first formed in childhood by the son fearful of the mother's potential power over him – and his sexual desires, seen as transgressive.

Baxter writes vividly of his adolescent years tormented by 'subconscious terrors' and dreams of being dragged to Hell in punishment for his 'auto-erotic practices' (2. 220). Jack is a fictive version of 'that / sad boy' who hid in his upstairs bedroom, wrote poems, masturbated and 'wish[ed] to die' (*CPoems* 309, 237–38). Looking back, Baxter remembers placing a loaded .22 rifle used for shooting rabbits in his mouth. The feeling of 'hard, cold metal' on his tongue was a 'bit too real'. He blames his adolescent 'hopelessness' on his education at home and school that made him feel that 'whatever was wrong with me must be entirely my own fault' (1. 603–04). Baxter's present guilt and his memories of being overwhelmed by sexual fears and flirting with death via a .22 rifle are converted into the objectified form of the adolescent. Attached to this figure is a knot of protective associations related to the young Baxter's experience as a member of a pacifist family in a country at war. Two early stories, 'The White Gull' and 'Before Sunrise' (c. 1941–48), use the image of a small creature shot with a .22 rifle – gull and rabbit respectively – to emblemise the destruction of the innocent and, through their connection to the 'primitive paradise of childhood', childhood loss (*Horse* 1. 553). White gulls also symbolise, for the poet, 'an undivided being' (1. 28).

The adolescent figure and his associated motifs not only bring a particular self-experience into being again, but also, by incorporating the idea of innocence under attack by external forces, objectify the poet's sense that psychic continuity (artistic fertility) is threatened by being 'forced'

Puritan mother-wife motif among provincial and post-provincial writers as masking 'discomfort with the domestic sphere as the place where male power is disrupted' (62).

to give up drinking, with the resulting loss of the addictive structures necessary to create the experience of self-care (McDougall 82–3). At the same time, these symbolic patterns express opposing desires for acceptance and rejection. Baxter associates the 'disturbing' elements within his personality – his 'incorrigible, ineducable, unemployable' and *drunken* twin-self – with the psychic energy from which the poems grow (2. 136). Returning to the image of the dead rabbit late in the 1960s, Baxter calls the 'rabbit with its guts blown out . . . [the] other self, the dirty soft warm dark self' that 'had to die' (2. 403). The abject rabbit-self reflects the 'lousy pit of adolescence', in which the adolescent, feeling 'repulsive' assumes that he is repulsive (2. 31). This, again, links the adolescent figure to the poet's present feelings of guilt. Insofar as Jack stands in for Baxter himself, his suicide is a fantasmatic self-punishment for both real and imagined crimes (Kahr 324).

If Mr Matheson is a distorted version of Baxter that has introjected the social values he so despises, Gantry is the 'sober' Baxter which the poet both wants and does not want to be. Consequently, on some level, Gantry *has* killed Jack by submitting to the demands of 'Mother New Zealand'. The story begins with Gantry basking in summer sun like 'molten steel' (1. 274), seemingly an image of hard, phallic potency, but also carrying connotations for Baxter of the 'sun-drugged' security of institutional life he rejected (*CPoems* 417–18). It ends with Gantry walking away from 'the plaster gnomes and penguins and dogs' – emblems of despised suburban domesticity – into the falling rain (281). Beneath the image of falling rain is Baxter's most prevailing myth, and the one that Vincent O'Sullivan argues that he most identified with, the journey of 'separation, death, and rebirth' towards renewal (9). Adolescence is 'a grave and equally a place of birth' (2. 31). At the core of these recurring symbolic patterns is the belief that change demands sacrifice.

Although 'The Story of Butch' (1956) is a slight, light-hearted satire, it is of interest for the way that it similarly expresses Baxter's conflicted embrace of sobriety through tropes of castration and suicide. Butch, a rabbit, miraculously sprouts wings after a fall. He loses his job after zooming around the factory like a 'jet bomber' and subsequently his girl rabbit. Jobless and girl-less, he starts drinking, is arrested, and then committed to a mental hospital where his wings are amputated. Seemingly cured, Butch recovers his 'status in the rabbit community', is forgiven by his girl rabbit, and his marriage is rescheduled (273). Yet Butch sleeps badly, 'climbing out of bed and shouting angrily at no one'. Unable to accept society's amputation of his freedom (which is also the creative self) or to escape the shackles of family life, Butch leaps from the quarry's rim 'like a sack of greens' and dies (274). It is notable that alcohol is here invested with the emotional projections attached to the idea of the 'good' mother (McDougall 97). After Butch gives up drinking, he lacks any defence against his dominating mother and fiancé and must resort to self-violence in order to relieve the 'strain of relating inner and outer reality' (Winnicott 13).

'To Have and to Hold' (1956) is a far more complex dramatisation of Baxter's 'domestic anguish' (McKay 158–59). It is set in the 'calm, bird-thronged bush' of the Collingwood home that the Baxters bought in 1955. Although, as McKay notes, the story expresses Baxter's contemporary anxieties regarding sex, alcohol and the state of his marriage, the family unit it describes – a couple with a baby girl – looks back at the first year of his marriage. Repeated images, metaphors and motifs that speak of exclusion and rejection are paired with tropes signifying the search for the ever-elusive maternal ideal, articulated through Jack's retreat into the refuge of the pub and his futile attempt to imaginatively recreate his wife within a mythic model. The overdetermination of these tropes suggests that in addressing current anxiety-laden material, Baxter may also be responding to the emotional legacy inculcated by what Janet Wilson calls the 'emotional exclusiveness' of his parents' relationship (51).

The protagonist, Jack, is sent out on his wedding anniversary by his wife to buy 'green vegetables'. Jack feels that their marriage is dying and contrasts their awkward, uncomfortable intimacy with the freedom of their early illicit relationship: the 'shifting leaf-patterns' on the wall of the room 'where they lay together, alive in the unrespectable night'. An unplanned pregnancy forecloses this freedom, signified with a typically violent image: 'The axe had fallen: for a life a death'. They are hustled into marriage, relatives whisper with 'gravestone faces' (289). Feeling trapped 'like a dog in a kennel,' he drops in to the local pub (290). Returning home, he finds that his wife has been waiting for him. She has laid the table with a clean cloth and 'brightly coloured earthenware' (291). Realising he has been drinking, she leaves the room, telling him: 'Oh I hate you! You spoil everything, everything' (292).

'To Have and to Hold' is narrated solely from Jack's point of view. The impression conveyed is that of a couple locked in an unvoiced struggle for control. When Jack feeds his child, Beth, his wife critically comments, 'you'll never feed her at that rate' and picks the child up, 'expertly' sliding the teat into her mouth. Money for domestic expenses is kept in her 'purse' (290). A link is easily made between the wife's control of her purse, a common symbol for the vagina, and Jack's view of their sex life as locked in a joyless routine. He thinks of how she hates to be touched except at the 'expected moment. And with that strangling of desire, a hot band tightened on his forehead'. Watching her, he feels that she grows 'calmer' once the moment of potential contact is over. He feels a 'vacant coldness' that she is able to respond to the beauty of the irises she picks, but not to him. Anger moves 'obscurely' in his mind that she 'could walk lightly in the sun, unmoved by the violence of his own pain and desire' (288). A central trope is the opposition between tamed gardens and wild nature. Flowers, a rose and a bunch of irises, signify respectively Jack's oscillation between hope and frustration, and castrating domesticity.

Jack's sense that he is excluded from the 'closed world of maternity' violently disturbs his sense of self. He is seized by fits of 'savage depression' in which he chops wood or flies into 'pointless rages'. Racked by 'leaden irritability', Jack turns to alcohol as a defence against feelings of loss, taking refuge in the local pub in an act of what Baxter explicitly calls a form of 'rebellion against the hand of the castrator'. There, he soothes his wounds by joining in the exclusively male 'small talk' that reduces 'every wife to a comic antagonist and moral censor' (289). Within Baxter's mythology, the pub stands as an 'approximation' for the 'foetal condition . . . the birth cave which is also the death cave' (2. 179). Jack finds relief in contemplating the sea, which is also a retreat to the archaic mother. For Baxter, the sea is 'the image of death, the separating void, which nevertheless is the source of my joy' (2. 142). As the train pulls out of the station, Jack watches 'the harbour waves rise and fall beyond the circle of his own dilemma'. In a complex mingling of eroticism, aggression and love, Jack relives 'erotic episodes in his single life; and then turn[s] back in shame to the image of her calm face bent to the feeding child' (289). Baxter's portrayal of a protagonist seeking the attention of a maternal figure whose loving attention lies elsewhere can be read as 'displaced expression' of patterns in his relationship with his mother (Fox 124).

Similarly, the anxiety and guilt arising from Baxter's 'failed romantic expectations' and his 'sexual frustrations' are projected onto the fictive wife's body, so that it becomes the 'monstrous' site of conflicting desires, negatively transformed by pregnancy and birth and redefined as the site of shame and exclusion (McKay 158). From their 'few sexual encounters during her pregnancy', Jack comes away 'bitterly ashamed', feeling that he has forced himself on a 'tired and ailing woman'. He develops 'the habit of suppression', so that when his wife does initiate sex it brings the opposite of relief. He perceives the act as a 'solitary spasm' which leaves 'his inward hunger unsatisfied'. He asks himself, '*Will we always lie like this, rock beside rock, and communicate only through our angers?*' (289). His wife's impenetrable body becomes as impossible for him to imagine as that of the lost mother object that haunts it. He attempts to discharge mingled anger and shame arising from her control of his body – like a mother controls the body of an infant – by attempting to rouse her later that night, 'but she was fast asleep' (289).

Her 'tiredness and irritability' towards him while nursing the child increase his conviction 'that his sexual need' is a 'parcel delivered at the wrong door' (289). Jack contrasts the way that her body is open and nurturing to their child, but closed, rejecting and dangerous to him. Much as Mrs Matheson is depicted as sexless and grotesque, the wife is objectified as 'the Sleeping Beauty', inaccessible behind her 'wood of briars'. Her presence is 'tormenting'. 'Rigid' with anger, she is the 'enemy' – 'sharp, sensitive, locked in her own sufficient world where an iris was lovelier than a phallus' (289–91). These penetrative motifs associated with the wife imply that not only does she reject his masculine 'phallus', she possesses her own. In comparison, he is 'tongue-tied, inept', a beer-breathed 'stumbler all the way'. The iris stands here for nature that has been, like the husband, domesticated, castrated, and by being encased in a vase, taken from the mythic world (the 'bush gullies', the 'young earth') into the emasculating mundane (291).

Walking home from the pub half-drunk, Jack constructs an imaginary scenario of mutual 'harmony'. The wife walks 'swaying before his mind's eye'. Transformed into the antithesis of her prickly real self, she is the 'Wild mare of Scythia, fertilised by the wind'. By invoking the romantic idealised feminine at one with the natural world, he flees from the 'dreadful' reality of women (Horney 351). In doing so, Jack's longing for freedom and the shame and guilt tied up with pregnancy and childbirth are projected into the wife, objectifying her as the avatar of nomadic freedom whose impregnation by the non-phallic 'wind' displaces anxieties associated with her body. He imagines their love-making as powerful, restorative: 'peeling black leaves from the young earth'. Stumbling home he realises however that 'No magic tree had grown up to cover them with its healing branches'.

At the end, the rose he carries, which has come to signify in his mind his fluctuating emotions, will not fit in the vase with the wife's irises, reinforcing his sense that there is no room for him in the marriage. The ending offers no resolution to the tension set up between Jack's longing for a mythic sexual union and the demands of the domestic bond. Moreover, it is Jack's own actions that destroy any positive outcome and provoke the expected rejection.

'The Blue Divan' (1960) is one of a series of prose sketches that become Baxter's semi-autobiographical novel, *Horse*. Jack and Celia's affair materialises the affective experience of the seventeen-year-old Baxter who, as Weir puts it, was 'determined to find love' and so sought sexual experience. Weir notes that while Baxter's occasional conquests 'gave him a measure of satisfaction and pleasure', the experience 'also (and always) brought him pain and guilt' (*Glass Woman* 36). In psychoanalytic terms, 'The Blue Divan' models how the addictive search for sex may be used to compensate for the absence of an inner soothing mother.

Jack here is the young, drunken poet from Dunedin in the 1940s, when 'parties kept going till dawn / And saveloy skins [condoms] were left on the lawn' (Baxter, 'Reflections' 2). Sheltering in a phone box as much from the 'eddying wall of hangover' (422) as from the 'fury of negation' loosed from the grey winter sky, Jack visualises 'somewhere' with 'company and light and colour – and girls, girls with sweaters on or off' (421). Seeking refuge from loneliness, he calls a girl, Celia, seen briefly at a party, 'Ugly and bored and wanting a man.' His friend, Tony, calls her a 'sure thing': 'Half the Art School have been through her'. He wants, but does not want, to see her, linking desire with fear, a 'vague sense of enormity' struggling to the 'surface of his mind'. He thinks of 'bees crawling in a smoked hive', an image signifying for Baxter humanity's Fall (see Jones 68). Celia remembers Jack from his ignominious drunken stumble, fully clothed, into the river. He feels that she is mocking him, her tone that of 'the women's gang . . . chewing the cud of male deformity'. Anger strengthens his resolve, and he arranges to meet her at her parents' house while they are out (422).

Jack's aggressive pursuit of Celia displaces the troubling coexistence of guilt and need into anger. Reproducing Baxter's characteristic binary, Jack experiences women as both transformative source of delight and rejecting 'other': 'Hanging gardens. Doorways into the cave of Aladdin. Clueless bitches' (421). In defending against fear of rejection, Celia becomes the object of scorn Jack imagines himself to be. He feels the 'briskness of lust moving in his belly. She was a bag all right, but a man couldn't be choosy' (422). Her grey eyes are 'enormous behind glasses', her face 'reddened and shining' (424). Imagining woman as ugly or monstrous brings the dangerous sexual impulses she embodies back under control. After he arrives, she pours him what she calls her 'Ophelia drink', gin with a 'long cool splash of water to drown it' – suggesting the idea of oblivion, which is also the looked for fusional ideal (423). He rests his hand on her arm, stroking it gently. She responds physically to his lovemaking, but asks, 'Do you really like me, Jack?' (424). In her longing to be loved, her 'awkward[ness]' and 'strained smile', Celia can be read as Jack's double. Indeed, Celia also echoes Jack from 'To Have and to Hold' with his 'rabbit's smile, a baring of the teeth while the eyes did not change' (288). Celia's ambiguous, difficult love for the Church that has cast her out for playing the 'bedroom game' (422) – signified by a cloth scapular hidden under her clothes – parallels the affective state of Baxter's split-off fictive selves, as well as that of the poet himself. Celia tells Jack, 'I can't go back and yet I can't let it all go'.

As Jack rides the 'dolphin of Arion, a woman's body, through the dead sea of the afternoon', he looks down at her face with a 'mixture of anger and complacency. It was for the moment all but beautiful, a primitive mask of desire'

(424). Jack has, within his imaginary, remade the grotesque body as the ever-sought idealised feminine. More, the sexual act itself enables Jack to purge 'anger' and violence through 'riding' (subjugating) Celia's body. On a mythic level, she rescues him (as Arion is rescued from drowning by a dolphin) by breaking up and temporarily dispersing painful affect – symbolised by Jack's sense of being 'old and empty', and the images of the 'dead' maternal sea and the inescapable doom of the 'dead afternoon hung around his neck like an albatross' (423) – much as the maternal figure soothes the infant. The 'blue divan' they lie on is the ever-moving maternal sea reborn through their union. Jack's compulsive search for sexual experience can be read as a 'magical' attempt (like alcohol or gambling) to fill the void in the inner world in order to 'restore, if only briefly, the primitive dyadic ideal, in which all affective arousal ceases' (McDougall 82).

When they dress after sex, the sense that something is 'lacking' disturbs him. He kisses her 'as a man might kiss a prettier girl who was his sweetheart'. The 'explosion of tenderness' this gesture evokes from Celia remains 'sunk' in Jack's memory, long after he had 'forgotten her name' (424). Celia's emotion echoes Jack's own 'lack'. Cast out from the Church and emotionally destitute, Celia is both abject and ideal. For Baxter, it is the 'Women who think they have ceased to be Christian [who] shack up with dying alcoholics and wash their piles with warm water' (*Jerusalem Daybook* 3. 298). On the other hand, the way that Celia's name vanishes from Jack's memory indicates that no permanent inner change has been made. While the ending implies a 'good' outcome in that Celia's abjection enables her to 'save' Jack, her absence from his subjectivity unsettles. Celia's 'explosion of tenderness' sinks into Jack's memory like a 'buried fragment of a meteorite'. Yet the source of that emotion – the feminine 'other' – is 'unexplained and inexplicable', thus 'at the boundary of what is assimilable, thinkable: abject' (Kristeva 18).

The ambiguous ending of 'The Blue Divan' is common to Baxter's short stories. We are implicitly or explicitly left with a sense of failure and loss, suggesting that the affective meaning these figures have acquired cannot be contained within, or dispelled by, the process of creative displacement. This is precisely why the monstrous mother-wife is never exorcised. But in exploring the vital role that she, in all her fictive guises, plays in displacing affect into fictionalised scenarios, we extend our critical appreciation of the subjective signifiers underlying the poet's wider oeuvre. As the poet himself puts it: 'In any given poem there are many levels of symbolism; and each level when recognised makes clearer the contours of that reality which the symbol reflects' (1. 183).

## *Works Cited*

Creed, Barbara. *The Monstrous-Feminine: Film, Feminism, Psychoanalysis*. London: Routledge, 1993.
Eagle, Morris N. *Attachment and Psychoanalysis: Theory, Research, and Clinical Implications*. New York: The Guildford Press, 2013.
Fox, Alistair. *Speaking Pictures: Neuropsychoanalysis and Authorship in Film and Literature*. Bloomington: Indiana University Press, 2016.
Horney, Karen. 'The Dread of Women.' *International Journal of Psychoanalysis* 13 (1932): 348–60.
Jones, Lawrence. 'The Mythology of Place: James K. Baxter's Otago Worlds.' *Journal of New Zealand Literature* 13 (1995): 65–96.
Kahr, Brett. *Sex and the Psyche: The Truth about Our Most Secret Fantasies*. London: Penguin, 2008.
Kristeva, Julia. *Powers of Horror: An Essay on Abjection*. Trans. Leon S. Roudiez. New York: Columbia University Press, 1982. Trans. of *Pouvoirs de l'horreur*. Paris: Editions du Seuil, 1980.
Mahler, Margaret S. 'On The First Three Subphases of the Separation-Individuation Process.' *International Journal of Psychoanalysis* 53 (1972): 333–38.
Marshall, Jonathan W. *Performing Neurology: The Dramaturgy of Dr Jean-Martin Charcot*. New York: Palgrave Macmillan, 2016.
McDougall, Joyce. *The Theatres of the Body. A Psychoanalytic Approach to Psychosomatic Illness*. London: Free Association Books, 1989.
McLean, Patricia. 'The Prior Family Drama: A Kristevan Reading of Maurice Gee's In My Father's Den.' *Journal of New Zealand Literature* 23 (2005): 62–78.
McNeill, Dougal. 'Being a Bard.' Review of *Selected Poems* by James K. Baxter, ed. Paul Millar. *New Zealand Books* 91 (Spring 2010): 3–4.

Miles, Geoffrey. 'Three Calypsos: Baxter's Variations on a Mythic Theme'. In: *Still Shines When You Think of It: A Festschrift for Vincent O'Sullivan*. Eds. Bill Manhire and Peter Whiteford. Wellington: Victoria University Press, 2007: 234–48.
Wilson, Janet. 'Archie, Millicent and James: The Baxter Autobiographies'. *Journal of New Zealand Literature* 13 (1995): 47–64.
Winnicott, D. W. *Playing and Reality*. London: Tavistock, 1971.

# *'There May Be Something Wrong with My Mind': The Difficult Journey of James K. Baxter's 'Ghost in Trousers'*

Paul Millar

In 1958 James K. Baxter began making notes towards his major piece of prose fiction, a short novel which he completed in 1962, but which was only posthumously (and reportedly reluctantly) published as *Horse* by Oxford University Press in 1985, with John Weir acting as the book's editor. The work was called in its first early draft 'The Adventures of Harry Glass', and Weir notes faint debts to both Dylan Thomas's *Adventures in the Skin Trade* and James Joyce's *Ulysses*, 'for JKB intended to parallel his "Harry's" exploits with those of "Hercules" and drafted a list of these' (*Complete Prose* 4. 291). In its final draft, Baxter retitled the work 'A Ghost in Trousers', referencing Russian futurist poet Vladimir Mayakovsky's major early work 'A Cloud in Trousers'.[1] This poem, while opposite in tone to Baxter's determinedly comic novel, shares certain themes, in particular the experience of 'pain-filled, unrequited love' and a visceral urge to 'revolt against injustices' (Jangfeldt 60). In both works these themes are encapsulated in a

1 Grateful thanks to Professor Stephen Burt of Harvard University for alerting me to the Vladimir Mayakovsky source for Baxter's working title 'A Ghost in Trousers'. I was aware of Baxter having read Mayakovsky as early as 1944, because he refers to him in the long poem 'Janus Unheard' (see *Spark* 325), but I hadn't associated the novel with the poem.

central character oscillating between revolt and surrender, a dichotomy established in Mayakovsky's prologue:

> If you wish,
> I shall rage on raw meat
> – or, as the sky changes its hue –
> if you wish,
> I shall grow irreproachably tender:
> Not a man, but a cloud in trousers!
> (Jangfeldt 61)

It was as 'A Ghost in Trousers' that in late 1962 Baxter sent his manuscript to some publishers, boosting it as a straight-up comic yarn of the sort not generally well written in New Zealand, and admitting it probably trod a thin line when it came to acceptable sexual content. None of the publishers was interested in the novel and Baxter's hopes for it faded quickly. To his mother he explained this failure as some sort of deficiency in himself:

> Recently I wrote a series of prose sketches which could hardly be called a novel about a character named Horse whom everyone will think is me, though he is not me. I had intended it to be comic; but the couple of people I showed it to tell me it was tragic. And the publisher I showed it to told me he didn't feel like having to fight a court case. It seems I am coarse without trying to be coarse: either coarse or vacuous. There may be something wrong with my mind, but I don't think it can be laid at your door or Daddy's. (Letter to Millicent Baxter, 7 November 1962, Hocken MS-0975/210)

The conundrum Baxter faced throughout his life was that whatever was 'wrong' with his mind was inextricably connected with his creativity. Although his 'poem-writing habit began when [he] was seven' (1. 723), his adult conception of the 'poetic self as a composite of opposites dwelling within in a state of perpetual poem-producing tension' (*Spark* 102) he attributed directly to the 'adolescent crisis' in his essay 'The Creative Mask':

> Adolescence is the cradle both of delinquency and of creativity. The secret joy in the act, say of smashing the windows of an empty house, and the joy in that act of choice which lies at the core of the creation of an art form, sprang from the same root (though one act is fruitful and the other demonic) – *It is I who choose to do this.*' (1. 176–77)

Whether or not there was something 'wrong' with his mind, Baxter was haunted by the way his perception of the world had altered at adolescence, and what this meant for his art. Nowhere is this fixation more evident than in his novel *Horse* and in certain seminal works of prose fiction leading up to it.

Unlike poetry, writing prose fiction never came easily or naturally to Baxter; turning to writing prose fiction in 1944 at the age of seventeen required a conscious effort of will and intent, while ceasing almost completely to write prose fiction after his failure to publish 'A Ghost in Trousers' in 1962 seemingly took little effort and cost him nothing. Ceasing to write poetry, on the other hand, proved impossible. Twice in his life he set out to quit, and both times he failed. The second time he tried to quit was for the sake of poverty. The first time was for the sake of prose fiction.

The second time was the late 1960s, and Baxter was trying to step out of the role of 'bourgeois family man – ape in an overcoat, donkey with a crown of thorns' (3. 304), and onto the path 'of poverty and detachment from material possessions' that would lead him to the commune at Hiruharama (3. 215). His dilemma, as he saw it, was that if he continued to write poetry 'for money and kudos' it would become 'absurd to say I am really a poor man while I keep on putting words together. Words set in order are mental possessions.' But his compulsion to write poems was as difficult to master as his compulsion for the cigarettes he chainsmoked through the day, having found that 'laying off smoking' caused 'several gruelling withdrawal symptoms – dizziness . . . nausea, insomnia' (3. 454). Similarly unable to quit poems, the nearest he could approach mental poverty was to 'write my words, and then forget what I have written' (3. 304).

Baxter's early attempt to quit poetry for the sake of prose fiction might seem more germane to this essay, if a little unusual, but both efforts, though separated by twenty-five years, have an important element in common: each occurred at a point of major, life-altering change and transition. His late 1960s decision to leave home and family for poverty and life in the commune, being so ostentatious, might appear the more major. But what happened around March 1944, when Baxter was seventeen, was as significant, possibly more so. The year offered Baxter the beginnings of escape from a painful and alienating wartime adolescence as the son of notorious and derided pacifists. The ostracism of the preceding four years of high school had delayed and distorted his passage to adulthood, turning him into a solitary figure, living mainly in his head with a thousand overwrought poems for company. Now, with school behind him, this stuttering rite of passage through adolescence became transformative as he enrolled at the University of Otago, a life now staged in lecture theatres, dances, public houses, student flats and the like, on boards trod by a more diverse cast of characters, though not at first the longed-for 'girls at university who want you to sleep with them' whom his mother admonished him against:

> I was seventeen still, and a strange glamour rested on those grey pseudo-Gothic arches. On a lawn that resembled Dante's Limbo one could sit and watch the waters of the Leith Stream sliding endlessly over weirs. And one of those grave, charming, untouchable nymphs might appear and sit down on the green grass and say, 'Hullo'. (1. 482)

Encountering a different and diverse world, less constrained by parents and teachers, with new experiences of all sorts on offer, afforded Baxter the opportunity he seemed to think necessary to become adult, in life and in writing.

His March 1944 letter to his friend, imprisoned pacifist Noel Ginn, declared, 'I have come to a point (I think) that others come to later, the necessity for broadening. Later on I'll come again to poetry maybe, but never the same way. Poetry is an attitude, not verse or rhyme, and will go into prose instead. Poetry is of the child, prose-poetry of the adult' (*Spark* 346).

Baxter's conclusion that writing in prose was more 'adult' was shortlived in practice, primarily because where poetry was effortless, prose was a struggle. But it is significant that the impulse to write prose fiction arose after experiencing the early short stories of one of his most profound influences, Dylan Thomas, the writer he most closely identified with and strove to emulate throughout his life. 'I . . . read Thomas with joy and awe that so great a thing could happen in our time', he wrote in 1956. 'In the moment after birth and before death, in the gulf of our unquiet nature, [Thomas] stands with us, and "the soul walks the waters shorn"' (1.311). In 1970, more experienced as a writer, and closer to the moment of his death than he might have imagined, Baxter could concede, 'I have only to read a poem by Dylan Thomas . . . to know the narrow unchanging limits of my own intellect and imagination' (3. 111). Back in 1944 he offered Ginn this rationale for admiring Thomas's prose:

> It is impressionistic; and to my mind there are only three types of readable prose: journalistic; fact-statement; impressionist. The first jars, and wins by trading on ignorance. The second is the birth of literature; though of course there is no pure fact-statement, it must sway to the word-bolsters of journalism or the subjective truth of impressionism. The last is the natural development of prose as an individual medium: into it come the tricks of style which depart from objective truth for the sake of emotional effect . . . (*Spark* 345)

But what fiction by Dylan Thomas could Baxter have been reading in 1944, that he should classify Thomas as an impressionistic prose stylist? It can't have been *Adventures in the Skin Trade*, Thomas's unfinished, posthumously published, semi-autobiographical novel, which is mentioned above as one of the models for *Horse*. Though begun in 1941, *Adventures in the Skin Trade* wasn't published until 1953, with a later edition reviewed by Baxter in 1956 for the *New Zealand Listener* (1. 269). Is the most obvious candidate, then, Thomas's other celebrated prose collection, the one Baxter called 'that rum, racy little book, *Portrait of the Artist as a Young Dog*' (1. 139)? Yes, to an extent, but not entirely. Ann Maher's detailed explanation of ways in which the ten stories in *Portrait of the Artist as a Young Dog* represent Thomas's 'abandonment of subjective, experimental, or surrealistic convolutions in favour of simple realism' (Maher 87) affirms my belief that Baxter's early prose emulated the stories of *Portrait* alongside those of an even earlier work, Thomas's first collections of poems and prose, *The Map of Love* (1939) 'that he intended to be unified with related poems and stories that reflected each other' (Maher 4). There is evidence that Baxter had access to this collection by 1944, because it was the first volume to include one of Thomas's most celebrated poems, 'We Lying by Seasand', of which Baxter had remarked to Ginn in June 1944, 'I agree about Dylan Thomas, an objectionable specimen of introversion – yet would I give worlds to have written his "*We lying by seasands . . .*"' (*Spark* 360).

That said, the stories in *The Map of Love*, while they likely account for the young Baxter's description of Thomas's prose style as impressionistic, and for his own attempts to work into his own stories and prose poems various 'tricks of style which depart from objective truth for the sake of emotional effect', don't fully account for the themes and content of his six earliest pieces of fiction, which in the *Complete Prose* are dated between 1942 and 1944. This is because Baxter was reading far more widely than simply Thomas, and a lot of what he was reading was interacting at the level of the Gothic with the difficult adolescence I have described above.

> At puberty the door had opened into some kind of cellar of the subconscious mind. A number of sensational ghost stories which I read at this time helped to give shape and body to the subconscious terrors. The one which impressed me most was about a lad who dabbled in black magic, or something of the sort. At the end of the story the moralistic narrator observes him at dusk running and crouching among the long grass of the churchyard, and finally scrabbling vainly at the heavy closed door of the church while large black supernatural dogs drag him down. I think it stirred up in my mind the Calvinist image of reprobation. I had only to substitute auto-erotic practices for black magic, and there I was in the centre of the tale. (2. 220)

Masturbation, indeed sex of any kind, is almost as entirely absent from Baxter's earliest stories as it is present in Thomas's. The common theme in Baxter's stories is the progression towards death. The boy in 'Before Sunrise', for example, who is as complete a loner as the young Baxter was on his Central Otago holidays with his parents, wandering 'among the broom and gold-claims' making up 'moral codes' (*Spark* 313), inhabits a threatening, pantheistic world of 'vast lands of silten rivers . . . swollen and swift from the lake, home of the abyss-monsters' (1. 5). As the boy dives off the jetty into the chill lake, the reader is plunged into the familiar, submerged realm of the Baxterian unconscious:

> . . . under water where the lake floor lies out of perspective; pressure blankets me fish-like; are there coins below? Under the wooden girders I swim, below sea-storm, my mer-hair swims suspended and rippling; I reach in the unknown element, see secrets unnameable, then rise by the rotted quay – beware snags – to the flash of sunrising.' (1. 6)

This impressionistic little vignette certainly owes a debt to the prose of Thomas, but the underwater transition in the boy's mind to memories of the shooting of the rabbit the preceding day opens the gates to the supernatural dogs of reprobation: 'It shrieks, it is agony, the sound cuts my eyes. I run and it crawls to its burrow . . . I run and hold the rabbit.

Its head droops and wobbles at the rabbit-punch; like corn rain-flattened its white belly-fur and brown side draggled where blood drips. Blood drips from its mouth but the eyes are brown and deeply sad.'

Whereas the boy in 'Before Sunrise' has a caring and interested father, the father of the small boy in 'The Kite' is a more vindictive version of God. The child's metaphorical purchase of freedom by procuring a kite with proceeds from the sale of his father's store of old bottles invites one of the early Baxter's favourite classical motifs, the doom of Icarus (see Miles et al. 307–08): 'he dreamed that he was flying the kite from the top of a high cliff. The wind grew stronger and stronger till he was lifted off his feet and carried out above a shining sea. Strangely, he had no fear' (1. 3). But the boy's father is no supportive Daedalus, he is a bookkeeper, tallying both bottles and childish transgressions. The father, not the sun, deprives this fledgling Icarus of flight: 'The father's face grew more red with anger. A little vein stood out on his temple. He put the kite over his knee and broke it. Twice' (1. 3).

In 'The Kite' the son's transgression culminates in broken wings and a beating. In the stories that follow, the hounds of reprobation turn upon the generation of the fathers. A man absorbed in an erotic daydream of 'Judy and a few others' in a 'mohammedan heaven' jaywalks and slips beneath a truck that amputates his legs (1. 8). In 'The Sea Stayed' a 'thick-set, fleshy' butcher with 'an air of vitality; and the blood vessels dark in his cheeks' drowns at sea, and is retrieved as an ignominious corpse 'hanging . . . like a sack; so much lime, so much phosphorus . . . a trace of copper' (1. 10). In the parable '[In those times when the Church had grown rich in the goods of the world]' a mineowner, a Bishop and a Socialist, each recently dead, appear before God to account for their lives. All three have fallen short, but the Socialist, in his efforts to champion the oppressed, has failed the most egregiously by neglecting the Gospel's fundamental tenet. '"Love one another",' Christ observes, 'is a bitter necessity' (1. 15). The last story from this period, 'Enlightenment', owes much to 'The Visitor', Dylan Thomas's disturbing, surrealist account of a dying mind learning 'the mysterious and inarticulate unity of man and nature in death' (Ackerman 171). In 'Enlightenment', Brown's delight in a flood of epiphanies that flow through his day – the uniqueness of others, the importance of art, the value of his wife – gives way to horror when he learns he has died and is a ghost, without agency or opportunity to ever do the things that might have given his life real meaning.

The most striking and significant piece of early fiction for the purposes of this essay is the story 'Mood', in which a boy is trapped, ghost-like, in the limbo-world of adolescence, ensnared by a 'net of unreality' (1. 8). It is significant because Baxter will spend the next fifteen years in recurring attempts in prose and poetry to liberate the boy from that net of 'adolescent crisis' without, in the process, destroying him as an artist. The following passage, though long, is thus important as a description of the exact moment when the child realises he has been cast from Eden; the moment which initiates Baxter's obsessive idealisation of the prelapsarian that he and Thomas share; the moment in which the individual divides, and the artist discovers he has a second self, an opposite to the conforming public self only partially alive, who in the novel *Horse* will be represented by Horse's more respectable alter ego, Timothy Harold Glass. While the boy in 'Mood' has no name, the thing that catches him is the same thing Baxter will attempt to free Horse from years later in his novel :

> Then the music, the voices, the smell of the fish and chips, all lost their reality. It was very odd. And when I went out into the street again it, too, had become unreal. It hadn't been like that before. But it was now. It was as if I was in a dream. It was cold, too, and the air was very still. The long lines of the street lights seemed to stretch for miles and miles in a glittering fantastic chain. Nearly all the people had gone. How strangely

> my footsteps echoed in the stillness. Then a tram clanged past and the noise of it lingered behind, poised in the silence that there had been. The shops were empty now; empty and dark. It was like a dream walking along under their verandahs in the dark and I walked on and on and on. All I could hear were my own footsteps. All I could see was myself reflected dimly in the darkened shop windows. And the silence and the darkness increased and clung closer round me. It was all me, and yet it wasn't me. I didn't understand it, but I felt it and accepted it. I no longer existed, nothing existed, nothing was real, nothing at all, save the footsteps and the shadow, the darkness and the sound-imprisoning silence. The net of unreality had caught me and held me. (1. 7–8).

So much of Baxter's writing returns to the moment when the child reaches puberty and his conception of the world and the self change. The ghostly town in 'Mood' is the first of many versions of pre-pubescent Baxter's Edenic hometown Brighton, lost beneath the waves in the poem 'The Town Under the Sea', when 'At puberty, / Or the first deadly sin, the sea rose up in one / Pounding night and swallowed the land' (*CPoems* 253). Any poem or story that references bells or music under the sea recognises the enduring influence of the ghostly inspirations from that idyllic first world. Later in life, in a series of notes on his early poem 'The Unicorn' (1943), Baxter uses the fabulous creature to explain emblematically how the artist – 'Over and through the wind / Sea-music moves his mind' (*CPoems* 10) – becomes a divided self at adolescence. The unicorn, 'a hybrid creature, beast and spirit inhabiting the universe of the adolescent mind' exists 'in a double solitude', he writes. '[A] natural contemplative solitude, resonant with the correspondences of nature, and the terrible solitude of the boy himself, a child becoming a man and regarding himself as a monster' (*Spark* 536). As with the stories of reprobation, the boy's horror at his monstrous postlapsarian metamorphosis is infused with guilty pleasure in the knowledge gained when innocence is lost. The irony that art cannot arise without the fall, that paradise must be lost before art can mourn it, is treasured by Baxter for the creative tension it generates:

> . . . loss is a precious stone to me, a nectar
> Distilled in time, preaching the truth of winter
> To the fallen heart that does not cease to fall. (*CPoems* 83)

Thus, Baxter regularly cautions himself against forgetting the adolescent crisis, because to do so is to lose track of the source of creativity:

> The seedtime, as it were, of creativity occurs in adolescence, that time in the life of modern man when he moves furthest from the influence of social custom, propelled by the newly weakened force of his critical faculties, and the pressure of his sexual instinct. He recognises then for the first and often the last time that he is an individual, a free agent; for a child is unconscious of its freedom, an adult generally conscious only that he has somehow lost it. (1. 176)

Obviously, as Baxter concedes, the 'adolescent crisis in itself does not make an artist', but, he proposes, 'in an artist's life it is invariably perpetuated in some way' (1. 177).

Baxter's next focused efforts at writing prose are a number of short impressionistic pieces labelled as 'prose-poems', which he published in 1948 in the Canterbury University College student magazine *Canta* while serving as the editor of its literary page. Again, the influence of Dylan Thomas's early stories is evident, the pieces are dense with Baxter's personal symbolism, and a strong strain of nihilism permeates the whole, most evidently in the appositely titled 'Ex Nihilo':

> Let the clock toll in its boarded tower.
>
> I too have known the City of Man and the anarchic Tree of Knowledge – where the great Tyrant is thrown down from his rock of clouds and the lion waves roar on the beaches.
>
> And I may yet live to see Queen Venus cross the Dead Sea in a witch's sieve. But I am now in the crypt of the City of God:

green stalactites hang from the roof, the sole voice heard is that of the arid scorpion, blood in circle of fire. (1. 28–29)

There is not really a lot else worth saying in the context of this essay about the prose-poems published in *Canta* (and some later in the *Salient* literary issue of 1952), other than that they stand largely alone as a body of work that captures a mood and an attitude, and harks back to the densely symbolic poetry of his isolated adolescent period mentioned above. They are interesting as emblematic of a phase, but are of less interest and relevance than the story 'Stone Lions', written around the same time, which deals realistically with a young man's first, intimate relationship with a woman, and which anticipates the characters and subjects of the novel *Horse*. Shorter than 'Stone Lions', but similar in subject matter, and interesting for bridging in style the impressionistic and realistic, is the hitherto unpublished story 'Encounter'. Form, style, content and handwriting all suggest to me that this story was written around 1948. Discovered only after the publication of the *Complete Prose*, it is here reproduced in full, both to ensure that it is properly associated with Weir's heroic edition, and because it provides a compelling link in the chain of argument I am attempting to make in this essay.[2]

2 The discovery of 'Encounter' and the reason it is not in the *Complete Prose* deserves some explanation. It is yet another of many uncanny coincidences that have punctuated my research on James K. Baxter. Over the course of a number of years I have collected large archives of Baxter papers from various sources. During the Canterbury earthquakes many boxes of such papers were tumbled from shelves, hastily re-stowed, and placed in storage. Earlier this year, well after John Weir had published the *Complete Prose*, I finally found time to begin sorting some of these boxes. The first one I opened was full of old newspaper cuttings and articles about Baxter, apart from a single, flimsy, sheet of paper stuck between two reviews, with the story 'Encounter' handwritten in black ink. The degree of shock of recognition that this was an original story in Baxter's handwriting, with Baxter's initials affixed, was almost as great as my degree of bemusement at where the story had come from.

Encounter

She looked much the same as when he had last seen her. That full firm mouth and nose slightly tilted; the air of calm integrity and perfect balance she always carried, a woman with a child's innocent sensuality. Even now unwillingly he could feel warmth stirring round his heart.

She smiled at him apologetically. The eddying music flowed out of the window of the small room, into the cool night, to mingle with the sound of trains and slap of waves along the wharves. The air smelt of tobacco smoke and stale beer. Fifteen in a room the size of a dog kennel. Yet under the babble there was no one there. They were all animated puppets – the automatic sexual laugh, the clown's mask over a face of scalding tears.

Tears. As if it were something he had read in a book, he remembered the blind desire, the helpless frozen grief soaking into a wet pillow. Though in a way her leaving him had been a relief. Physical possession but mental loneliness; only in a rare moment of compassion could he join hands with her.

In her yellow dress she was flushed and virginal. The blaze of bodies under rough blankets, nights of drowning, the shared peace of light over low hills or music in a quiet room – these had slipped from her, leaving her remote.

What was it St. Augustine said? That when a friend has died he had preferred the loss of his friend to the loss of his grief. Without a tremor he looked at her. A delicate glass wall divided them; though deep under sea came the echo of a bell tolling. He was himself again, painless, desireless, indifferent and quite dead.

J.K.B

Perhaps the most unusual thing about this story is the description of the former lover's 'calm integrity'. Integrity is a noun Baxter rarely uses in poetry, and when he does it is to refer to an individual (rarely a woman) who represents some sort of ideal, such as his father Archie, whom he idealised as a 'rock of passionate integrity' (*CPoems* 65). I believe that in the late 1940s Baxter's ideal lover was an amalgam of two charismatic women he had been in brief relationships with in the preceding years: musician and composer Dorothy Freed, with whom he shared the peace of music, and medical student Jane Aylward, upon whom Fern in the novel *Horse* is modelled. Fern, tired of Horse's drunkenness, abandons him at Zoe Virtue's party. Like the narrator of 'Encounter' he observes at a distance her flushed innocence:

> Jock Saunders was present; and with him, Fern. She had removed her lambswool overcoat, and after three heavy doses of punch, was entertaining a small group of males in an alcove. Gloomily Horse heard her singing her favourite number. . . . Her face flushed and innocent, her limbs moving in an impromptu solo dance, she gallivanted in a separate orbit, as remote from Horse as Arcturus.

But the most relevant part of 'Encounter' for this essay is the ending, which revisits the moment the world transforms in 'Mood' and a 'delicate glass wall [divides] them'. Despite ghostly inspirations from drowned Eden – 'deep under sea came the echo of a bell tolling' – the narrator is trapped by the net of unreality: 'He was himself again, painless, desireless, indifferent and quite dead.'

After the hectic output of 1948 there is a hiatus in Baxter's fiction writing, with only three stories of any significance written between 1949 and 1954, all of them exercises with little relevance to my argument. In 'The Name and the Game' (1949) a young freezing worker gambles away the pay his family needs to get through the week. A drunken youth in 'Blue Peter' (1949) is nearly inveigled into disappearing off to sea on a merchant ship, only sobering up and backing out quickly when he meets the vessel's intimidating crew. 'Apple Mash' (1954) is a moral fable based on *Animal Farm*, in which a community of pigs feast illicitly on apples sneaked from the orchard, scapegoating one weak sow for the collective crime in what seems a critique of patriarchal hypocrisy.

Why did Baxter write so few stories during this period?

Primarily because he was a parent with a young family, who needed money, and whose writing was therefore focused on reviews and the like for the 'clique that pay me for my pen' (*CPoems* 72). However, a short visit back to Dunedin, the city of his youth, rekindled a need to write about the life he had led in the late forties: 'I stood again in the bush belt above the town where I came to life and died again. . . . The hot, live, ringing town had gone as if it had never been, with girls in overcoats and boys in corduroys, the night's manna and the day's longing. The old bludgeoned core of knowledge under my singlet woke and winced again' (1. 251).

Baxter's 'bludgeoned core of knowledge' was the recognition that in his struggles to escape adolescence's ensnaring net of unreality he had become one of those men for whom, as the critic Wallace Fowlie said of Rimbaud, 'it first is necessary to act, to explode, and to vituperate, before they can discover the reasons which prompted their deeds and explosions and vituperations' (1. 177). With this in mind, Baxter wrote:

> The huge discovery of the adolescent, which brings with it a torment that most are glad to shrug off in conformity, consists in his knowledge that freedom is not an ideal to be attained but already a human condition, like a ruby in an old ring, that has been taken for a garnet. Significance in poetry depends largely on the poet's capacity to make a free and entire response to the world in which he lives: a capacity of which he first becomes aware in adolescence. How to maintain creative freedom without its demonic counterpart is a problem of each person's destiny – often a tragic one, for artists are generally less efficient in their lives than in their art. (1. 177)

Writing in 1968, Baxter asks, 'how – to use Martin Buber's unforgettable words – can the buried power to enter into relation with others re-assert itself while an active ghost tramples continually on the ruins? One has to learn to master the incubus by knowing its name' (2. 661). Mastering the incubus by knowing its name is, I would argue, the explanation for the next few intensive years of writing prose fiction about that seminal period in Dunedin, which culminates in the novel *Horse*, and in which Baxter deals fully with the particular and peculiar dichotomy that is Timothy Harold Glass and his demonic counterpart. It is a period of writing that serves in part as a penitential admission that, for Baxter, creative freedom wasn't maintained without its demonic counterpart, and that his task in prose is both to exorcise ghosts and exercise therapeutic healing. It is in the service of this dual purpose that Baxter arrived at his creation 'Horse': 'my collaborator, my schizophrenic twin who has always provided me with poems' (2. 135).

The story 'Venus in her Western Bed' is Baxter's first effort to co-locate these two figures of the self in a single narrative. Jimmy, the narrator, is the 'dead respectable self' who struggles through a life half-lived in the nets of unreality and wakes up 'like a zombie and walk[s] woodenly to the hall. Although '[s]ea-bells' from the town under the sea ring 'in the holes in [his] head', he is 'stone cold sober' (1. 249). Jimmy is also the keeper of drunken, belligerent Jack, who disdains every social consensus that Jimmy might be tempted to conform to. Only in the final paragraphs does Jimmy begin to comprehend the ties that connect them:

> By the time we reached the railway tracks, where a white eye shone down from a signal tower, Jack had grown maudlin. His arm was heavy round my shoulders and his feet tripped on the clinkers. 'You're a good sort, Jimmy. You wouldn't let a cobber down. It's a great thing for a man to know that he's got a real cobber. You and me, Jimmy, we make a good pair.' And clambering on through the acrid haze of the railway yards I seemed to see a vast tragic meaning in his babble.

'Walking up Castle Street' picks up in the same locale a decade later, with the narrator, 'a fat man of thirty' on a pilgrimage through the streets of central Dunedin on the heels of the strong ghosts that have haunted so much of his life's writing:

> A girl ghost stood on the kerb, brisk as a nanny goat, with check coat and skirt and orange lipstick. The tram screeched to a stop. With a backward smile she skipped on board.
>
> My floral shirt and the spare tyre under it were blown off me in a magician's moment. Lean as a poker, nimble and blushing, I scrambled on to the moving tram and sat down beside her, afraid to say a word. (1. 308–309)

For the fat Baxter of thirty, this return to the streets of Dunedin, still haunted by his troubled youthful self and his first loves, was the catalyst for beginning work on 'A Ghost in Trousers'. While to his mother he may have blamed some deficiency in his own mind for the novel's failure, he was far less circumspect in a letter to writer Ted Middleton, laying the blame elsewhere:

> I have written a short novel called A GHOST IN TROUSERS which describes a young man boozing and shagging and punting his way round the fringes of Otago University – not wholly autobiographical – I meant it to be funny, but the few people I've shown it to tell me it's really tragic; and the one publisher I've shown it to so far tells me he'd be up on a dozen charges of obscene libel if he brought it out. I find it annoying that by simply putting down what one knows one runs bang up against the grannies of the tribe. (Letter to O. E. Middleton, 22 November 1962, VUW Library, MS McKay 15/7/77)

Whether or not the 'grannies of the tribe' were to blame, 'A Ghost in Trousers' was never published during Baxter's life, and apart from quoting from it in some lectures and prose, the work remained in manuscript form.

Whatever Baxter may have hoped or intended, his readers were correct that 'A Ghost in Trousers' is far more tragic than comic. It exists on a continuum with the stories already mentioned which deal with the importance of the adolescent crisis, the need to exorcise ghosts and the need for an artist like Baxter to find ways to deal with his demonic other self. *Horse* is of additional interest for its detailed, loosely autobiographical version of Baxter's life in Dunedin in the late 1940's, though it would be an error to take that all too literally. It is also possible to go through *Horse* and discover echoes of Thomas, Joyce, Frank Sargeson and other prose writers, which help give the novel a distinctive character. Of further interest is the relationship between this novel and other traditions that Baxter the polymath was so quick to borrow from, such as the classical association of Horse with Hercules (Miles et al. 129–131), and the debt to the Haitian voodoo belief that Baron Samedi, the Loa of the Dead, used zombies as his vehicles from time to time and that any zombie so used was known as his 'Horse'. Some years later, in justifying his decision to accept the Burns Fellowship at Otago University, Baxter would claim the Baron's special protection:

> I travel under the protection of Baron Saturday, the voodoo god of graveyards, coarse, truculent, tough-minded, who has a special weakness for drunks because he himself likes to drink rum flavoured with a number of different kinds of pepper. I used to pray to him during drinking bouts.' (2. 615)

One of the most interesting aspects of Baxter's failure to publish 'A Ghost in Trousers' is that it signalled the end of any focused efforts on his part to again write fiction. Leafing through the pages of the *Complete Prose* that follow *Horse*, only three more pieces might be considered fiction; these are described as parables and they stand apart thematically from the works discussed here. Baxter's 1967 comments about *Horse* in 'Conversation with an Ancestor' suggest that, even though unpublished and unpublishable, the novel had served a valuable function as a way of managing the demons and dealing with the fallout from everything engendered by the adolescent crisis:

> The publishers apparently did not find this work either funny or instructive. That doesn't really matter much. But it would be very dangerous for me to forget Timothy Harold Glass. He has done the suffering and I have done the writing. Occasionally I

> visit the cellblock in the basement of my mind where he still lives, incorrigible, ineducable, unemployable; and through the bars he will pass me a message written on the back of a tobacco packet. Something like this – 'Look out, you bloody fool! What will happen if I die? I'll tell you. One by one you're going to lose your sex, your art and your sense of humour. All the Fellowships in the world won't make up for that. I am it; and you can't do without me . . . .' (2. 136–37)

This is not to say that the difficult dichotomy between the respectable Baxter and his skull-faced twin was ever resolved. Even in his 'Jerusalem Journal', written towards the end of his life, he was still dealing with the familiar conundrum:

> The dead body, the one that stinks in the ground. This is the man who retains his possessions, who expresses his opinions as if they were worth hearing, who orates about art and society, who gets money to keep the community pot boiling. The students and the businessmen's wives think a lot of him. They read his verse and ask him what it means. This poor man, Hemi, is the live one, and the other is the dead one. It is unpleasant to have a corpse for a twin. (3. 290)

## *Works Cited*

Ackerman, John. *A Dylan Thomas Companion: Life, Poetry and Prose*. London: Macmillan, 1991.

Jangfeldt, Bengt. *Mayakovsky: A Biography*. Chicago: University of Chicago Press, 2014.

Mayer, Ann Elizabeth. *Artists in Dylan Thomas's Prose Works: Adam Naming and Aesop Fabling*. Montreal: McGill-Queen's University Press, 1995.

# *'Conversation with an Ancestor': James K. Baxter's Prose Exploration of His Personal Poetic Situation, 1966*

Lawrence Jones

Reviewing James K. Baxter's 1967 collection of essays, *The Man on the Horse*, James Bertram noted that it added up to 'the most substantial prose work Mr Baxter has published', but went on to say that 'to call it a book of prose is misleading: it is really a comment on the development of a poet's mind, in a particular time and place, appropriately illustrated at key points by passages of verse' (20). An analysis of 'Conversation with an Ancestor', the text of a public lecture Baxter gave in 1966 and which he placed first in the book, bears out Bertram's point in that the essay includes five poems and it certainly deals with Baxter's poetic development as he saw it in 1966, but it is mostly in prose, combining a variety of prose genres – autobiography, literary criticism and theory, theological discussion, a scene from a novel, and, in the section that gave the essay its title, an 'imaginary conversation'. All the genres and modes come together to form a coherent exploration of his personal poetic situation; both the verse and the prose are recognisably the expression of a single sensibility with a powerful metaphorical imagination, capable of expressing itself well in both prose and verse.

In 'Drama among the Faceless (An interview with Arthur Baysting)' in 1969 Baxter referred to *The Man on the Horse* as 'fairly subjective stuff' but with 'a bit of polish' (*Complete*

*Prose* 3. 19), and at the opening of 'Conversation with an Ancestor' he acknowledges its subjective focus on himself as poet in this time and place:

> In this talk I will be speaking as much about myself as about the standards and problems of art – that is, I will speak about the situation of being Robert Burns Fellow; about the implications for me of a return to the town in which I grew up; and about those changes which one is obliged to face at the beginning of the second half of life.

He is careful, however, to make a distinction between being 'self-centred' and being 'self-involved', arguing that the self is 'an artist's baggage, his burden, his doubtful treasure, which he must come to understand on his own terms under pain of losing his gift' (2. 130), implying that a poet to be true to his gift and vocation must be involved with himself.[1] To carry out this self-exploration and 'polish' it, Baxter uses many of the techniques of the creative writer rather than exclusively those of the conceptual analyst. These include the invention of the imaginary ancestor with whom to have a conversation, and the imagery, figurative and literal, shared by verse and literary prose, while over a quarter of the space in the printed text is allocated to five of his own recently written poems and an extract from his unpublished novel to illustrate points in his argument.

In the 'Foreword' to his book, Baxter points to the central aspect of that personal poetic development he discussed in 'Conversation with an Ancestor': '. . . the search for the tree of Jesse, the sense of ancestral continuity, which the modern way of life tends to cut down and destroy' (129–30). By the end of the long first paragraph of the published lecture Baxter is well into that theme in relation to his poetic vocation by way of a comparison of the artist to the Trappist monk. Both the monk and the artist serve society by being 'useless', in terms of practical utility, but creative: the monk in descending in

1 All subsequent quotations from Baxter, unless otherwise noted, are from Volume Two of the *Complete Prose*.

silence into 'the abyss of his own soul' to find first-hand 'the source of holiness and the meaning of creation'; the artist by descending into the self to gain a 'first-hand intuition into things and the relation between things, which Aquinas tells us constitutes the creation'. In 'the modern world of noise, falseness, staleness and repetition', the 'natural contemplation' of the artist is as much a 'vital necessity' as the 'supernatural contemplation' of the monk, for the artist can be seen as 'a tribesman, cut off from his tribe', one who intuits and hungers for the tribal awareness of the 'sacred relation between themselves, as a local and interdependent group, and the life of nature, the other half of the creation that actively or passively confronted them' (130–31).

Baxter's argument up to this point is constructed on an abstract plane, with traditional theological terms such as 'sacred', 'soul' and 'creation', but the language becomes more sensuously concrete with literal and figurative images as he evokes a personal imaginative vision:

> I have seen inwardly my first ancestors in this country, those Gaelic-speaking men and women, descending with their bullock drays and baggage to cross the mouth of what is now the Brighton river: near to sunset, when the black and red of the sky intimated a new thing, a radical loss and a radical beginning, and the earth lay before them, for that one moment of history, as a primitive and sacred Bride, unentered and unexploited.

Defining the spiritual function of the artist in the modern world and relating his Scottish ancestors to the tribal terms he uses, he applies his definition and imaginative vision to himself as an artist in New Zealand:

> Those people, whose bones are in our cemeteries, are the only tribe I know of; and though they were scattered and lost, their unfulfilled intention of charity, peace, and a survival that is more than self-preservation, burns like radium in the cells of my body; and perhaps a fragment of their intention is

> fulfilled in me, because of my works of art, the poems that are a permanent sign of contradiction in a world where the pound note and the lens of the analytical Western mind are the only things held sacred. I stand then as a tribesman left over from the dissolution of the tribes. The Bride, however, the earth itself, is still there to keep me company. (131)

Of course Baxter's 'sacred Bride, unentered and unexploited', like F. Scott Fitzgerald's 'fresh green breast of the new world' at the end of *The Great Gatsby*, is not all that virginal, for the Scottish settlers were not the first people to view Brighton any more than the Dutch sailors were the first to view Long Island – there was another tribe there before them. But for Baxter in 1966 his return to Dunedin had helped to reawaken his sense of his Scottish ancestry, and his father's ancestors became his lost tribe. The Hemi of Jerusalem several years later was to see things differently, but the speaker is the Baxter of 1966, and the remainder of the lecture works out the implications of this eloquent first paragraph for Baxter as new Burns Fellow.

Before turning to his personal poetic situation in 1966, Baxter introduces an anecdote about a work of art he possesses that is 'a permanent sign of contradiction' to contemporary New Zealand culture – a painting given to him by its creator, Drew Peters, of an old possum trapper bending over, eagerly attempting to drag the body of a dead female possum from a trap, against a background of 'the smashed mutilated trunks of trees, green and black, with ferns among them: the kind of desert swampland which we so often create in this country'. The painting, which he so vividly describes, he sees as 'the New Zealand version of the juxtaposition of man and nature', capturing 'the solitary vitality of man joined to nature only insofar as he can use her', presumably for pecuniary profit. Baxter is, in evocative prose, attempting to communicate verbally a sense of the symbolic image of New Zealand made by a visual artist of a similar sensibility, 'the man who is able to look on the Bride' and communicate to those who have the eyes to see what

New Zealand society was doing to her (131–32). The vision of both poet and painter of the exploitative pākehā relation to the natural order is darker than those of any of the previous generation of New Zealand writers except possibly Roderick Finlayson and his mentor, D'Arcy Cresswell. Baxter knew Cresswell's work, liked the prose but had mixed feelings about the poetry, while he knew and respected Finlayson, serving as the School Publications sub-editor for a series of *School Bulletins* Finlayson wrote between 1955 and 1960 which were collected as the historical novel *The Springing Fern* (1965), and conducting a serious correspondence with the older writer (who was also a late convert) concerning Catholicism.

After that brief excursion into visual art, Baxter moves to 'speak simultaneously as a Robert Burns Fellow and a New Zealand writer', to explore whether the first role compromised him in carrying out the second. The first question he confesses he faced as Fellow was whether that position compromised him in his primary task. The university, he argues, may be a patron of the arts, but it is also an institution of a state that builds prisons and maintains an individualistic, capitalistic economic system that denies tribal values. He considers it his 'chief function, as a man and a writer, to struggle . . . against the devil of acedia who . . . inhabits, like an honoured guest, our Government Departments, our business offices, our churches, our schools, our places of entertainment, our art galleries and our homes'. He admits he feared that 'by accepting this Fellowship' he would 'give an inch of ground in that lifelong battle; because there is always a connection, however tenuous, between the University and the administrative machines which act out the fantasies of the dull, man-killing brain of Caesar . . .' (133).

He illustrates his 'sense of unease about this connection' by reading his poem 'On Possessing the Burns Fellowship 1966' (the first poem in his poetry notebook for 1966), a poem of multiple ironic contrasts. He, who had four years earlier written in a poem (unpublished), a plea to the 'dear ghosts' from his past to let him '*abandon / What cannot be held against / Hangmen and educators, the city of youth!*', should be returning of his own volition to the city of his youth – not to the rebellious Bohemia of that youth but to a setting of which no respectable educator or hangman (an ironic pairing) would need to be ashamed, a setting in which he could

> Drink fresh percolated coffee, lounging
> In the new house, at the flash red kitchen table,
> A Varsity person, with an office
> Just around the corner – what nonsense!'

The only 'culture' in that setting of bourgeois consumer society may be the black south wind / Howling above the factories' which could be 'the voice of an oracle . . . a blood transfusion / From the earth's thick veins', the leaves and clouds which it blew appearing like 'A dark mocking funeral wreath' marking the death of the 'Caesar' who ruled a New Zealand society which had lost touch with the forces of nature (133–34).

Baxter's personal unease at holding the Burns Fellowship, which the poem expresses in its densely metaphorical language and its layers of irony, he then explores in a variety of prose modes, circling around the image of New Zealand prisons, 'those monasteries of pain' occupied mostly by the outcasts and failures of society, as instruments of Caesar that respectable New Zealanders accept but do not want to know much about. After an anecdote about an imprisoned man pointing out mounds in the prison yard that he thinks are the graves of earlier prisoners, he turns to a fiercely ironic analysis of a piece of prose quoted from the *New Zealand Weekly News* concerning 'the prospects for good fishing on the Tongariro Prison Farm' as an example of the subtlety of 'the devil of acedia'. The passage skims quickly over the rules, which allow no contact of the fishermen with inmates, to focus on the use of the dry or wet fly in the fishing, leading Baxter to comment that he could imagine nothing so terrible within that prison as 'the man outside, wading the stream in gumboots, using the wet fly and the dry fly, justified by the approval of Caesar, while the devil of acedia reduces his mind to nullity'. The implicit question is whether his accepting the Burns Fellowship from the university, an institution of the state that builds the prisons, so that he can make poems, is analogous to the fisherman's acceptance of the prison and its institutional rules so that he can catch fish. The discussion of his possible complicity he raises in his confession that 'by accepting any gift, honour, or public position, one may appear to condone our society, the clumsy nurse who smothers the children committed to her care' – with the sober, generalised language heightened by the final metaphor (134–35).

With the question of whether holding the Fellowship involved complicity with that 'clumsy nurse' at least faced, if not definitively answered, Baxter, with no explicit transition, turns to a related question: whether possession of the Fellowship might lead to his being so absorbed into the role of playing the public self within the social system that he could lose touch with the independent inner natural man who is the source of his art. This topic he approaches through a kind of playful paradox:

> In a sense the Fellowship was awarded to the wrong man: my shadow, my enemy, my monster: the public person who would destroy whatever gifts I possess. Art, the mainstay of culture, is not bred by culture but by its opposite: that level of hardship or awareness of moral chaos where the soul is too destitute to be able to lie to itself. Thus the Fellowship should have been awarded, if at all, not to me – a family man, teetotal, moderately pious, not offensive to sight or smell, able to say the right thing in a drawing-room – but to my collaborator, my schizophrenic twin, who has always provided me with poems. (135)

Baxter turned forty in 1966 and was aware that if a 'new self' is to emerge in middle age, for the poet it must be one that remains in touch with the 'schizophrenic twin', as he states in 'Pig Island Letters 9' when he contrasts 'the simple caption of success, / The poet as family man', with

> . . . the other
> Convict self, incorrigible, scarred
> With what the bottle and the sex games taught,
> The black triangle, the whips of sin.

Instead of a simple dichotomy, he there sets up a dialectic:

> The first gets all his meat from the skull-faced twin,
> Sharpening a dagger out of a spoon,
> Struggling to speak through the gags of a poem:
> When both can make a third my work is done. (*CPoems* 282)

The poem was first published in the volume *Pig Island Letters* in 1966 during Baxter's tenure as Robert Burns Fellow, but the title sequence of that volume was written as early as September–October 1963, directed to the holder of the Fellowship then, Maurice Shadbolt.

The 'skull-faced' twin, then, he saw as a necessary presence, to be integrated into the self of the poet as independent seer with 'first hand intuition'. If acceptance of the Fellowship meant losing touch with that part of himself, it would be a disastrous error. As he puts it in 1968, looking back at the Fellowship time in a contribution to a *Landfall* symposium,

> the Muse, that primitive and prejudiced old Lady, does not smile on Fellowship holders. . . . She goes away from us to whisper in the ear of a young poet with a raging hangover and three mistresses and no money at all, who inhabits a blanket-shrouded bedroom in a flat above a wineshop in Greater King Street. (614)

Now he represents the 'schizophrenic twin', not with the young poet living above the wineshop but rather with the protagonist of *Horse*, which he calls his 'unpublished and unpublishable novel' (135) – Timothy Harold Glass, known as 'Horse', a young poet living with his family in Brighton, a man with an equally raging hangover but with only one mistress, a female student at the Medical School who lives in a flat on Castle Street. She was based on Jane Aylward, with whom Baxter had carried on a passionate affair in 1946–47, celebrated at the time in the poem 'Let Time be Still' and viewed retrospectively in the fourteen-poem Catullan sequence, 'Words to Lay a Strong Ghost', one of the major works of 1966 but not published until 1973. Glass, he said, was his 'Pig Island version of natural man, that is, in theological terms, the fallen Adam who remembers, as if in a dream, his first state' (138).

Probably inspired by Dylan Thomas's *Adventures in the Skin Trade,* Baxter had begun taking notes for an autobiographical novel in 1958–59, then had put the project aside until 1962, when he added to the draft. But, he now comments, 'the publishers apparently did not find this work either funny or instructive' (136), and it remained unpublished until 1985, thirteen years after his death, when it was an unlikely but welcome addition to Oxford University Press's short-lived reprint series, 'New Zealand Classics'. In it, he projected two versions of himself – Timothy, the nineteen-year-old anti-hero, the young man he had been in 1945, and John Grummett, the kind of man Timothy might become, a middle-aged, alcoholic visiting poet who recites to Timothy some lines from Baxter's 'Poem in the Matukituki Valley' and who probably seduces Fern, Timothy's girlfriend. Now in the lecture Baxter publishes a later addition to his draft, showing a guilty hungover Timothy having a waking dream in a friend's kitchen in which he is accused of being a 'drunkard', a lustful voyeur, a 'constitutional psychopath', and a 'sexual maniac' by figures from his waking life, but then has a vision of a Japanese girl from the greengrocer's calendar on the wall who smiles at him without 'a shadow of accusation in her gaze' and claims to be '*eternal*' and '*at the heart of the world*' as his accusers 'melted away' (136).

The Baxter who wrote the draft of that novel in 1962 had in 1966 been married for fourteen years and had two teenage children, had been eight years in Alcoholics Anonymous and three years a baptised Roman Catholic, and had recognised that he could not have continued living Timothy Glass's kind of life. However, he also recognised that

> . . . it would be very dangerous for me to forget Timothy Harold Glass. He has done the suffering and I have done the writing. Occasionally I visit the cellblock in the basement of my mind where he still lives, incorrigible, ineducable, unemployable, and through the bars he will pass me a message written on the back of a tobacco packet. Something like this –
>
> 'Look out, you bloody fool! What will happen if I die? I'll tell you. One by one you are going to lose your sex, your art and your sense of humour. All the Fellowships in the world won't make up for that. I am It; and you can't do without me . . .' (136–37).

The value to Baxter of his inner Timothy Glass he illustrates in the lecture with a poem that he had built from a phrase supplied by that presence – '*Suffer the autumn of the succubus*'. That poem, 'The Succubus', written in 1965 but first published in the lecture, is difficult, and Baxter admits that he cannot interpret his own poems 'infallibly', but he reads it as providing a gloss on the scene from the novel: 'the Venus of the greengrocer's calendar who gives life becomes in the long run the succubus who gives death.' The middle-aged poet, in the autumn of his life, can remember the Timothy Glass days of his youth and how he 'toiled' at the 'cloven anvil' of the young females' genitalia and felt 'unfit for other work', but now he can see that Venus is becoming the succubus, that sex and death are inevitably parts of the individual life-cycle that must be 'suffered' and accepted. Baxter's point in introducing the poem is that 'this kind of knowledge would escape me if I were to nail down the trapdoor and never visit my collaborator in his kennel under the stairs' (137).

Baxter then uses that knowledge to explore the 'conflict of bourgeois and Bohemian values' to show that 'complete adherence to one or the other is probably fatal for the artist' (138). He had said in his essay 'Beginnings', the fourth in a *Landfall* series by writers telling how they began to write, published in the issue of September 1965 (and later turned into the opening section of 'Notes on the Education of a New Zealand Poet'), that he had decided in his youth, 'with no hesitation at all', that his life 'would flow like a river into the gulf of Bohemia'. That would be his way to resist the pressures he had felt since childhood to 'accept the Calvinist ethos which underlies our secular culture like the bones of a dinosaur buried in a suburban garden plot – work is good; sex is evil; do what you're told and you'll be all right; don't dig too deep in yourself' (1. 727–28; cf. 2. 220–22). 'After twenty years of doubt and fumbling', he had seen that he could not live in Bohemia, but if he lived entirely in the bourgeois world he would cease to be a poet. He saw that bourgeois values, too much influenced by 'the Calvinist thesis that the Fall is absolute and the natural man totally depraved', had assumed 'a deep reliance, torn still by an anguish of uncertainty, on the civilising influence of education, culture and the power of the state – as if these could eradicate the turbulence of the passions and put in their place an abstract social benevolence'; thus the bourgeois values would put aside the natural man. On the other side, the Bohemian 'values too much his contact with the natural man, *l'homme donné*, to sacrifice him to an abstract benevolence', a position that has 'the best authority' on its side:

> If, as the Catholic thinkers have always taught, the Fall was not complete, and the natural man, though wounded, is still the earth lamp who holds the oil of grace – then the only viable solution is a difficult humanism which works towards an understanding of the passions without being overthrown by them. (138)

Both the bourgeois and the Bohemian are 'half-men . . . because each turns away from some essential aspect of life.' Both are needed by the poet, not in a permanent stable synthesis so much as in a dynamic tension. Looking at the lives of other New Zealand writers Baxter describes discovering that 'nearly every capable writer in this country has passed through a time of radical revolt of cutting the apron strings of the social nursery, and that their later balance, if they achieve it, includes a direct knowledge of those aspects of human nature which a neo-Calvinist would ignore or repudiate.' Such writers 'work continually with two sides of the life of man – the instinctive and the social, the wild and the domestic, the passionate and the rational – and their art is the fruit of this radical tension' (Baxter may have been drawing on Allen Tate's seminal essay 'Tension in Poetry' for that concept). Creators of such art must see Timothy Glass and those like him not as 'enemies who endanger an otherwise satisfactory order', but as 'their difficult *alter egos*, emblematic of the natural man, the living proof that no temporal order is ever satisfactory; and to this extent a writer is obliged to be Bohemian in thought, not moralising but mythologising, rediscovering his or her own buried natural self' (139).

Baxter then includes the poem, 'The Girl in Yellow Jeans', which was written in 1962 but first published in the final issue of the *New Zealand Poetry Yearbook* in 1964. It had been one of the six poems (including two others by Baxter) that he thought his 'fellow members of the New Zealand State Literary Fund Advisory Committee felt they could not accept as part of an anthology to be sponsored by public money, because it would not meet with the approval of all members of the public.' In the poem, which he calls a 'modern fairytale', the girl of the title enters a tourist bureau office, sees the poster proclaiming 'Let's love', and thinks 'there could be no harm / In paying a visit', and lets herself be guided by the 'nice' clerk through a dark tunnel behind the poster, thinking '*Soon . . . I'll know what it means*,' and then emerges into a familiar coffee bar where two young men she knows are playing in the band. Her guide disappears, the band stops, service is slow, but she simply wonders when 'the telly show' starts; then when she looks into her coffee cup it is full of blood and she screams. Early in the paragraph that ends with the poem, Baxter asks his audience how they regard a young man who loudly drives his motorbike much too fast or 'the girl who seems to be unaware of the dangers of sex?' (139). The poem is Baxter's portrait of that girl, mythologised by a writer in touch with 'his own buried natural self'. The poem takes a mythical rather than a realistic form 'because this is the only way in which the conscious mind can assimilate' such 'crises, violations and reconciliations of the spiritual life' as she has when she discovers that the loss of virginity is not a tourist pleasure trip to a new experience but rather involves blood and all it can symbolise – from hymeneal blood to the blood of initiation and sacrificial rites and even to the blood of the Holy Eucharist. Baxter hypothesises that the members of the committee who disapproved of the poem because it was 'pornographic' or 'unsuitable' 'understood obscurely that it presented the loss of innocence as if in a dream' but that they thought that 'by writing the poem, [he] was the violator, the Satan in their Garden of Eden' (140). Perhaps he saw them as reacting to the kind of personal denigration of Baxter that I heard five years later from a Wellington policeman – that he was a dangerous, manipulative middle-aged man who used his fame to seduce younger women. At any rate, the poem's place in the controversy over the State Literary Fund's refusal to fund the 1964 *New Zealand Poetry Yearbook* served him as an example of the conflict of bourgeois and Bohemian values and the necessity of the poet's keeping in touch with his younger Bohemian self, which could feel sympathy for the girl instead of viewing her from the middle-aged bourgeois perspective as 'a kind of plague' or one of 'the enemies who endanger an otherwise satisfactory order' (139).

Thus Baxter in the first half of his lecture outlines his situation as a middle-aged writer cultivating an individual but traditional vision that is opposed to the bourgeois values and secular Calvinism of his society; a writer who feels cut off from his tribal matrix, uneasy about accepting a Fellowship that might compromise that vision and enmesh him more in bourgeois society, and thus cut him off from the erratic, self-indulgent but vital buried natural self who had been powerfully present in his youth and who was the source of his poetry. In his discussion of Timothy Glass he begins to outline how he could attempt to deal with the difficulties of his position by keeping in contact with his buried natural man, trying to achieve a radical tension between the natural and the social man. In the second half of his lecture he focuses more on the positive forces that could help him to keep this radical tension.

In his reading and discussion of one of the earliest of his poems written as Fellow, 'At Aramoana', first published in the lecture, Baxter points to three of those positive forces – his contact with the natural creation, his awareness of death, and the teachings of the Catholic Church. On the surface the poem is a narrative of part of a day spent by Baxter and his wife at Aramoana, the beach on the northern head of Otago Harbour where a long jetty reaches out into the South Pacific. But the commentary that follows the poem reveals that at a deeper level it is a narrative of a spiritual journey; it does this by making 'more explicit' 'certain intuitions in the poem', 'especially intuitions about death'. The narrative moves through six stages, each focusing on different Aramoana images. The first image is of godwits taking off from the jetty on their long seasonal flight to Siberia, as the speaker imagines that some will fall into the 'void white thundering wilderness' and 'melt like ash or salt', so that he interrupts what Baxter calls 'the logical structure of the poem' to cry out *'Abba, / father!'* Baxter comments that the words are from St Paul, but while Paul in his two uses of the words (Romans 8.15, Galatians 4.6) associates them primarily with the cry from the hearts of those who through Jesus have become true sons of God, Baxter comments that the cry here comes at 'the point where the ground fails under one's feet', so that the speaker cries out in pity for the fallen birds (hence the exclamation point). In the commentary Baxter remembers 'the words of my master Dylan Thomas', and quotes the lines from 'Over Sir John's Hill' where Thomas cries out for God to have mercy on, save and hail the 'led astray birds' for their 'breast of whistles' and their 'soul's song'. When the cry appears again in the fifth stanza without the exclamation point there is no element of pity, including self-pity; it is a call for reassurance in his faith that whatever the power of what he calls 'the negative side of God's mercy', those who approach God through belief in Jesus and acceptance of all that God offers, including death, will find the answer to their prayers in 'the serenity of God's silence'. The rest of the poem shows the speaker arriving at a reaffirmation of that faith in the remaining five stages of his Aramoana experience.

The second stage of his spiritual journey involves the speaker observing the 'prodigies of nature' more positively, as he had in his youth. He can see that the 'sheaves' of the waves 'bow', as if to the sickle that will cut them down, 'an image of the obedience of nature that does not resist death'; and the inner Timothy Glass in him can sympathetically observe boys watching a girl on a surfboard and building their youthful sexual fantasy, imaged as a 'goatskin ark' because it is a response to the 'sacred' sexual force, seeing in her a 'Venus not rising from the sea but going out into it'. But he is a forty-year-old veteran of the sexual wars, and has his own way of 'hiding from death' – as he moves on to the third stage in his journey, constructing his own dream of union with 'the least demanding and most supporting reality, Gea, the earth herself', the 'symbolic ground of existence' who 'speaks in parables of rock' and in 'her changing and austere testament of sand' messages that are unconnected with the 'acedia' of his unhappy, dissatisfied society. He constructs his own image of her with the cone of sand her breast, the cutty-grass mats her pubic hair. Gea, however, because 'all people die', 'can only comfort, never save'. Thus the speaker goes on from that comfort to face in the fourth stage of his journey the 'black swells' of the sea which 'swamp, pound and hurt the land', and which elicit from him his second cry of '*Abba, father*', a cry for strengthening in his faith. He then goes further on the fifth stage of his journey, going in his imagination to 'where the serpent current / flows out of the harbour gates . . . strongly tugging at / the roots of the world' – an image of the natural force that drives all creation towards inevitable death or dissolution. The sea, Baxter observes, is 'the image of death, the separating and dividing void, which nevertheless is the source of my joy', for the current 'betrays the world by delivering it into the hands of God; yet we are not creatures of earth, our renewal can come only out of the storm, out of the void, out of the depths of God.' Thus the speaker arrives at the final stage of his journey as he observes the night sky, which tells us that 'after singing / silence is the only voice.' Baxter comments that 'the serenity of God's silence is the answer to our prayer' (140–42).

Perhaps sensing that his interpretation of his poem was not self-evident, Baxter explains that his statement that the images from the natural world could comfort but not save is not meant as a contradiction to the 'Christian revelation' but rather to place them as the objects of natural contemplation that can stand in contradiction to 'the work of lucre and boredom by which we continually poison the waters of our own souls' (142). To further develop the point, he tells how when his wife once said she was disturbed that the boulders of Aramoana would still be there when she was dead, he had answered that man would still exist when the earth had gone back into the sun, but then had realised that she was speaking from the knowledge of what she could see and feel while he was speaking from belief. 'The certainty of death' may be 'the subconscious problem of every man who is lucky enough to reach the age of forty', but 'the austere and loving voice of the Church tells me that to live is to die – that is, to live is to accept all things willingly from the hand of God, including death – and that no man can escape this issue by fantasy or art.' Pointing out that the certainty of death can provide 'the spirit of destitution' necessary if 'one is to remain untroubled in this century of massacres and empty miracles', Baxter goes on to quote Teilhard de Chardin about how death is necessary for the next existence, for in order to 'assimilate us in him, God must break the molecules of our being so as to re-cast and re-model us' (143).

Baxter then uses Teilhard's words as a bridge back to the theme of 'ancestral continuity' with which he began, saying that 'in the light of the truth behind them one comes to see the dead as one's destitute brothers and sisters, hidden in the silence of God, to whom one may speak, and receive an imperceptible reply.' He acknowledges that such a sense of continuity is difficult for modern man compared to tribal cultures such as the pygmies of Gabon, whose 'chant above their dead' he quotes, but he has found that the knowledge of death was making him 'reach out to the tribe that no longer exists', and he constructs a twilight meeting with the ghost of an ancestor at 'that gully where the clan built their houses, washed their linen, made their music, harvested their crops, bore their children and watched over the dead', behind Brighton. 'The ancestral face is very familiar to me,' Baxter said in his 'Recent Trends in New Zealand Poetry' lecture in 1951 (67), and the ghostly ancestor with whom he carries out his conversation and whom he calls Chennor seems to have been based on the elder Duncan McColl, the Gaelic-speaking paternal grandfather of his paternal grandmother Mary McColl Baxter.

The conversation is a kind of stocktaking that determines whether he can go on in his life as poet with an ancestral blessing from the tribe, and consists of five questions Chennor asks him and his answers. The first question, '*Do you still wear the Tartan?*' he states he can answer only by interpreting it metaphorically. He admits to not having any publicly recognisable identity as a member of the clan nor owning any tribal family land, but if he interprets the tartan symbolically as a sign of 'the coloured cloth of individuality' involving the 'mutual working of the conscious and subconscious mind, the coat woven from the four coloured strands of reason, feeling, sensation and intuition', then, although he knows his coat is often threadbare, he can answer carefully that he either wears it or he goes naked. His answer implies that if he had not fully achieved an integrated individual identity, he was making an effort for it and had not accepted the ready-made bourgeois identity offered him by his society, and Chennor was content with that answer (144–45).

To the second question, '*Have you ever taken the Queen's money?*', Baxter offers an answer to show that he is carrying out in the modern world the spirit of resistance to unjust domination by the state that his ancestors showed in eighteenth-century Scotland, demonstrated by his public opposition to New Zealand's participation in what he considered to be an unjust war in Vietnam against a peasant tribal culture. That opposition was very evident in his Burns Fellowship years in poems, both in the satirical ballad mode of 'The Grand Tour' and in the sober metaphorical free verse of 'To Speak Truly'. It was also evident in his public speeches: I remember how all of us on the organising committee for a seminar on the ethics of the Vietnam War were impressed with his eloquent discussion of the war in the light of Catholic ethics, and how beneath the statue of Burns at a rally in the Octagon following an anti-war march he stated that if Burns were alive he would oppose the war. The unmistakable tones of Baxter the public speaker were so familiar around the university in those Fellowship years (including his public reading to students in 1967 of his 'A Small Ode on Mixed Flatting') that when a student production of *Ubu Roi* opened with King Ubu rising up out of a giant onstage toilet to speak his scatological opening lines, the appreciative audience reaction indicated that everyone recognised that the student actor was imitating Baxter's speaking voice. That voice was heard often enough opposing the Queen's government (or in 1967 the university's policy on mixed flatting) that it would have been difficult to view its originator as selling out for the Queen's money. To Chennor, Baxter did admit that 'Perhaps the man who works for the state in a civil capacity, has in a sense been bought by the Queen's money', but he makes a distinction between the soldier 'who sells his life and power of moral choice', and the civil employee (such as the Burns Fellow?) who 'may choose how much he sells', and states that he (who had worked for School Publications and had been a postman) has sold as little as he could – 'the use of the hands and a little of the brain'. Thus he could answer with a 'provisional *No*' (145–46).

He is able to give an affirmative answer to Chennor's third question, *'Can you hide from the keepers in a bush?'*, because again he translates it into modern terms. He speaks of an ancestor, John McColl, who had been a keen poacher in Scotland, sought after by the keepers, and had been brought to New Zealand by his parents because they 'feared he might shoot a keeper and be transported or hanged' (McKay 3). Reasoning that, for his ancestors in Scotland, 'poaching was a legal fault, not moral' and that hiding from the keeper thus 'signifies the cunning and protection of himself and others necessary for the man who recognises the great gap between legality and morality', he declares that for 'the tribesman who has no tribe', such as himself, who recognises that gap, 'it is necessary . . . to learn to hide himself and his friends from the hard hand of Caesar; to ignore the regulations; to give no information; to keep a blank face' (146–47). Thus again he carries out the spirit of his ancestors in a modern situation.

Chennor's fourth question – *'Have you got a woman with child and then left her?'* – Baxter considered 'the hardest of them all for any man who is not a eunuch or a saint'. He looks for the spirit behind it, concerned not with 'a fault against chastity' but rather with 'a fault against the ancient tribal charity and responsibility', and decides that, whatever the sexual excesses of his youth, as a middle-aged man he had learned more pity, so that possibly 'the protective decisions of family life, even though ruthless at times in a love that excludes responsibility to the rest of the world, are sufficient to allow me to answer, *No*' (147).

The 'unexpected' last question – *'Can you bait a hook to hide the barb?'* – Baxter again answers by taking it metaphorically: in his 'craft of verse-making' he has learned to hide the barb of 'boldness [of] matter' with the 'prudence [of] form' (147–48), as he did with 'At Aramoana' with the 'prudent' 'formal strait-jacket of seven syllables to the line' (140), as well as six lines to the stanza with irregular rhymes and half-rhymes, enclosing a 'bold' message.

Although Baxter acknowledges 'the five questions of Chennor had not been well answered,' he senses that his ancestor is 'satisfied' and has given him the ancestral blessing of his hand on the poet's shoulder and his breath on his forehead, so that Baxter can go ahead as Burns Fellow strengthened with tribal protection:

> And when I go from the place, the breath of the ancestor goes with me, before me, behind me, around me, to defeat the enemies of the heart and give me strength at the hour of death. With that protection, under God, I do not require any other. (148)

The 'under God' is significant, for in the final poem, 'Ode', written in Wellington in 1964 anticipating his return to Otago and first published in the lecture, Baxter focuses on the need for the spirit of Christ to be born in our society, which has spurned it. Through natural contemplation of the teachings and sacraments of the Church, the lost, uprooted souls of the modern secular world must learn 'the vowels of human speech' to bring them back from their culture's death wish. The speaker imagines, first, the modern unbelievers coming to what was once a Māori burial cave and then a pioneer cattle stall, part of the earth they have 'desecrated', deaf to the Holy Spirit, desiring not the 'second birth' of Christ's spirit in them but 'the sleep of the unborn'; then, he imagines a drunk on the way to the Scroggs Hill farm seeing in a sod hut (Archibald Baxter was born in his grandfather's sod hut in the vicinity) a young Māori woman and her child, a vision of 'mercy to swamp despair / At the gorgehead of grace, / Where the Christ of fire is born'. For the drunk, the imagined result was that he could return to Brighton and 'praise the living scene / With an unwounded tongue' (148–50).

Unlike the other four poems in the lecture, 'Ode' has no accompanying commentary. In his brief closing remarks, Baxter merely states that he has said 'enough . . . for one man in a single talk', that he does not think he has 'spoken with an unwounded tongue; but to speak at all from the place where the poems and the dream begin becomes increasingly difficult' so that he would 'prefer to be silent and let the younger ones do the talking' (150). The poem has its own system of symbols that might have gained from commentary, such as the sun and the midnight sun, being burnt black and white, or the 'furious Christ', the 'Christ of death' and the 'Christ of fire', while the two Māori references imply a view of Māori culture rather like Finlayson's, anticipating his Jerusalem writings. Despite his semi-apologetic conclusion, the echoes between the first and last stanzas imply a parallel between the ex-alcoholic Baxter and the drunk, and a desire to write in his Fellowship term poems 'In the land where I was born' that 'praise the living scene'. As a virtuouso prosodic performance, with its seven stanzas, each made up of ten trimeter lines rhymed in an intricate abacbdecde pattern, the poem speaks for itself, while 'born' as the final syllable in each stanza makes the verbal music underline the theme.

The lecture-essay as a whole is a successful prose exploration of Baxter's poetic situation and a justification to himself as well as to his audience of his acceptance of the Burns Fellowship. There were doubts and difficulties during his term, but he thought it successful enough that he applied for a second year in August 1966, pointing to 90 poems completed by then. In John Weir's edition of the *Collected Poems* there are 113 poems (filling 80 pages) that Weir dates from 1966 or 1967, and more exist in manuscript. As well there was *The Man on the Horse*, with its four lectures of 1966 and a memoir (including some sections written earlier), and the shorter *Aspects of Poetry in New Zealand* (1967). Those works, as well as essays in the *Tablet* and the often revised or combined versions in *The Flowering Cross* (1969), reviews, unpublished talks, interviews and other miscellaneous items that Weir dates as written in 1966–67, make up 492 pages of Volume Two of the *Complete Prose*. Howard McNaughton's edition of the *Collected Plays* is made up mostly of works dating from late 1966 to late 1967: three radio plays written for the NZBC, a full-length play written for a student group, and six full-length plays and three mimes written for Patric Carey's Globe Theatre. No other Burns Fellow has been so productive.

The return to Dunedin had been successful enough for Baxter and his family that, although he had originally taken only a year's leave of absence from the Post Office to take up the Burns Fellowship and then had stayed an additional year as Fellow, in 1968 he took a position for a year with the Catholic Education Office in Dunedin. But his dream vision of a call to Jerusalem in April of that year led by early 1969 to his taking a radically new direction – not finding his tribe in his Scottish ancestors but building his own tribe as an elder of the Ngā Mōkai, the young rebels and seekers who rejected the bourgeois New Zealand world for a radical commune, under the aegis of the Ngāti Hau of Jerusalem and the Catholic community there; becoming Hemi, not James; making his poetry out of that experience in the present, the poetry a by-product of that experience rather than a primary vocation. The understanding he reached in 'Conversation with an Ancestor' had served him well, but it was time to move on to what proved to be his final phase as man and poet. However, in the process of reaching and expressing that understanding he had created a prose piece of lasting interest as autobiography, as literary criticism and theory, and as a *sui generis* prose piece containing some of his most eloquent writing and most suggestive images.

### *Works Cited*

Bertram, James. 'A Considerable Myth.' *NZ Listener*, 7 October 1967: 20.

# *Baxter, Academia and Academic Writing*

John Davidson

The juxtaposition of the name James K. Baxter with the concepts of academia and academic writing may seem anomalous. Throughout his adult life, Baxter tended to take swipes at academic learning and the institutions associated with it.[1] Even while he was still at school, he was sounding a note of caution. Thus in his last year at King's High School in 1943, when speculating about possible future professions, he wrote in a letter to Noel Ginn: '. . . if I see any chance of a job as lecturer or literary critic I'll go for it. The ideal, of course, is Professor of Poetry – but after all, that might lead to narrow-mindedness even more than law.'[2] In hardening this embryonic anti-academic attitude, he was running counter to what he records had been envisaged by his family as a suitable career for him. In the earliest available account of this, he speaks of his parents presenting him with a proposal for his future – 'with their generous support, I was to obtain a New Zealand degree in English, go to Oxford or Cambridge, obtain an English degree, and then become a scholar and lecturer in English literature' (*Complete Prose* 1. 352).

In later accounts, however, it is specifically his mother to whom he attributes this vision of a son's future, and it is

1 My remarks about Baxter's life are principally indebted to Frank McKay's *Life* and John Weir's *Complete Prose*, 4. 1–151.
2 Letter to Noel Ginn, 14 March 1943. See Paul Millar, *Spark* 200. When he first enrolled at high school in 1940, Baxter had chosen a 'professional' curriculum with a view to going into the law.

hardly surprising to learn that she in fact would have been the driving force in such a connection. Daughter of well-known Canterbury University College professor John Macmillan Brown,[3] she had a distinguished academic education herself. In a 1961 piece, Baxter puts it like this: 'My mother was a graduate of Newnham college, Cambridge. She studied Old French for her M.A., and enjoyed punting on the Cam. I think she hoped that some day I would climb the ladder of academic distinction, and go there too, go and get some manners, and come back to be a Senior Lecturer' (1. 482). Although he refers again, perhaps with an underlying sense of pride, to his mother's Newnham MA degree (1. 724), Baxter himself was more drawn to the example of his autodidact father who was no academic but who clearly possessed a love for and understanding of poetry, and it was towards a career as a poet that he inexorably progressed. Despite this, as we shall conclude, there seems always to have been in Baxter's psyche a hankering after success or at least acceptance in the academic world, a hankering that he tried to mask by his constant and exaggerated criticism and mockery.

Even as a young schoolboy, Baxter was already a voracious reader of literature and a writer of verse, and his knowledge of literature at an early age was quite exceptional. After leaving school, where he performed with distinction in English, he did enroll at the University of Otago in 1944, taking English along with Latin, French and philosophy. However, his real interests, namely his poetry and love life, not to mention an addiction to alcohol, severely limited any chance of academic success at this stage. Although he was later to comment that '[a]t university you learn more in three months than in three years at school' (1. 25), this first year at university

3 Baxter had planned to edit Macmillan Brown's memoirs during his tenure of the Burns Fellowship at the University of Otago in 1966, but was unable to do so. (See *CP* 4. 328.) An Introduction to the memoirs, which he did work on, can be found in *CP* 2. 127–29. Here, Baxter describes his maternal grandfather, with undisguised pride, as 'a prominent and influential educator' (128), referring to the great respect and appreciation held for him by former students.

rapidly turned sour. While enjoying philosophy, which at that level had a strong dose of psychology, he was not at all happy in general, complaining that '[a]t varsity my mind is blurred and cramped. I am sensitive to the attitudes of those around me, and unconsciously absorb those attitudes: and at varsity most are neurotic, even those whom one would least expect to be so, such as footballers' (1. 10–11). His attendance at lectures was often sporadic as he reacted against the discipline of tertiary study. He completed an undistinguished year, passing English and philosophy but failing to gain terms in Latin and French, and then shook off the academic dust from his sandals for the time being.

Baxter later wrote a parable about a fictional student named YZ, whose experience of an initial year of university study closely resembled his own. The quasi-autobiographical content of the account is palpable:

> In his first year at university, YZ became a member of the Literary Club, the Debating Club, and another less formal society known as the Frothblowers' Association. At any of these gatherings he was prepared to speak at a moment's notice on any topic. His examination results, however (he was studying for a B.A. in English), were less promising. He regarded the lecturers in the main as fools, and their view of him was no more charitable. He was floored in three subjects in Finals (Philosophy; Education; Greek History, Art and Literature) and passed English I with a mark of 52%. His parents were disappointed. He lost his Bursary. (1. 212)

After several years punctuated by, among other things, periods of casual employment, Baxter moved to Christchurch at the end of 1947. This change of scene, he tells us, was supposedly so that he could resume his university studies there, though in fact it was to consult a Jungian psychiatrist (1. 484). However, he was drawn to Canterbury University College, which acted as his central base. He was not enrolled in any courses, but attended lectures from time to time in 1948, and was heavily involved in campus literary life, even becoming literary editor for the student newspaper, *Canta* (McKay 105).

After his marriage to Jacquie Sturm he moved again, this time to Wellington. Frank McKay, in the course of his chapter 'The Young Married Man' (120–50), provides details of his resumption of university studies at Victoria University College, leading to his graduation with a BA in May 1956. Baxter himself offers a typically ironic version of events:

> Ever since I had failed in Otago to master the Higher Learning, a sense of incapability had gnawed like a rat at my diaphragm. To quiet this rodent, I acquired extra-murally a unit in Greek History, Art and Literature, while working in the Wellington abattoir . . . This period is a trifle foggy. I gave three Macmillan Brown Memorial lectures. I passed Stage II Latin with the help of an admirable tutor . . . and passed Stage III English, after two failures, with the help of a tutor in Anglo-Saxon . . . Well, I got my B.A. and have it still. (1. 484–85)

The last statement seems to point to what might be termed his secret ambition to achieve academic success in the long run and his pleasure at attaining his goal.

McKay points out that Baxter's enrollment in Greek history, art and literature in 1950 was, in fact, part-time rather than extra-mural. In 1951–52, since he had decided to become a primary school teacher, he attended the Wellington Teachers' Training College, but when the course was completed he was able in 1953 to go full-time at Victoria where he passed Latin I and Philosophy II, but failed English III because he was unable to apply himself to the work required for success in the compulsory paper in Old English. He commenced his teaching career at Epuni School in Lower Hutt in 1954, the same year that he delivered the Macmillan Brown lectures at Victoria. Studying part-time at the University, he passed Latin II but again failed English III, for the same reason as previously. He finally jumped the English III hurdle in 1955 and completed his degree, which was conferred in May 1956. He then enrolled for an MA but did not pursue this. As a footnote to this account, it is worth noting that he also enrolled in Greek I early in the 1950s, but dropped out after a month. Like so many, he found that the reality of learning the language of Homer and Sophocles is rather different from the idea.[4]

Baxter's own less than enthusiastic account of his university career is reinforced by a number of negative comments about the academic approach and about academics, which can be found scattered throughout his prose writings. For example, in writing about how poets of the Left had, in his view, lost contact with the wellspring of poetry after World War II, he commented: 'the weakest (Spender among them) retreated nervously to the library and locked the door' (1. 262–63; 4. 235–36). In the same year, while recounting a 'moral fable', he put into the mouth of a monk the statement 'All Professors are proven heretics' (1. 264).[5] Then again, in defending Louis Johnson's poetry, he wrote, 'I have been astonished to hear university men of good standing wipe Mr Johnson's achievement off the slate with a single phrase' (1. 703). Similarly, in discussing lines of a poem by R. A. K. Mason, he imagines how a *Landfall* critic 'bred in the varsity stable' would have savaged them if they had been written by Louis Johnson (2. 332).[6]

A more extensive broadside aimed at 'academic' criticism can be found in a short and uncompleted paper perhaps written in 1966. Baxter has just mentioned with approval the large number of new books of New Zealand verse published in the previous few years. He then launches his assault:

> If one were to put on the totem mask of a critic of our local academic cult, the task of just comment on the works of

4 I personally saw the details of Baxter's enrollment in Greek I in the relevant Victoria University Classics Department mark book, which has sadly long since been thrown out.

5 This was first broadcast as a talk from National Stations of the New Zealand Broadcasting Service. See 4. 236.

6 Interestingly, an early draft of this entitled 'The Innovators', Hocken MS-0739/009, does not contain the conditional clause referring to Johnson. See 2. 46–71, at 55.

> seventeen poets would become negligible. Glover and Brasch would receive a somewhat clammy handshake, as veterans surviving from the legendary Thirties. The ghost of Mulgan would be ignored, as in life, because he fought on the wrong side in those old skirmishes. Rawlinson and Adcock are both women – I doubt if they would get a leg in, though Adcock might get a small pat on the rump for being able to read Latin. Sinclair might get past the electronic eye – at times he reads like a translation from Lorca, and there is an air of sound scholarship about his footnotes on the cargo cult. Bland, Challis, Doyle, Packer – no, they have made their bed in Wellington, and they must lie on it, though Doyle is physically in Auckland, he is still a spiritual émigré from the dark and dirty South. Campbell and Ireland – well, perhaps there is some codicil to Leavis's last will and testament, a special dispensation for Romantics, leaving them an old pair of suspenders to share between them. Tuwhare – go carefully, brother, Tuwhare is undeniably Polynesian – perhaps we can link him to the canoe-building chants. Weir and Hooper – we can ditch them at the start – they haven't waited the requisite ten years before getting their verse published. And Johnson – bring out the tear-gas, boys! – the anti-academic dragon is at the gates. This leaves Stead, a good lad and true, with all his tropes in order, who can load ten lines with twenty-eight literary echoes. For him alone, a small sliver from the Laureate's crown of thorns . . . (2. 117).

This typically trenchant piece of criticism is followed by a reluctant admission that academic critics 'do contribute a touch of intellectual stiffening', though he then immediately claims that one can infer 'two highly dangerous premises held by members of the academic cult'. These two premises are that 'good poems' can only be written in one way, and that a metaphor that cannot be evaluated à la Leavis is not a 'true' metaphor. Baxter goes on to say that he himself is unable to 'wear that totem mask' and has no wish to wear any other – 'for in my estimation critics should interpret and assess the work of poets, not make blueprints to indicate the way poems should be written'.

Baxter once described himself as 'a lifelong fugitive from all forms of Higher Learning'.[7] Indeed, he seems at times to have felt a certain uneasiness when entering territory also inhabited by academics, pointing out on one occasion that 'I am not a lecturer by profession' (1. 618).[8] He also makes a number of remarks about Latin. Thus in one discussion of metaphor, he notes (offering a contrast to how poetry works), what he could do to explain the roots of certain verbs and nouns bearing weak metaphorical charge if he were 'a scholar of Latin' (1. 104).[9] In one 'letter to the editor' too, he takes a correspondent to task for 'trying to bamboozle me and himself with heavy Latin' (1. 229). And in a review of *The New Jerusalem Bible*, which appears in *The Flowering Cross* (1969), he offers a stereotypical *apologia* for having 'no knowledge of Hebrew – and little enough of Latin . . .' (2. 245).[10]

It is, in fact, useful to remember that Baxter himself had a reasonable grounding in tertiary-level Latin, from his studies first at Otago and later at Wellington. Thus he can point out that the poet Ronald Duncan 'has tried to imitate Catullus' (1. 428), and he can identify Latinisms in the verse of Ursula Bethell (1. 109). We have already noted his acknowledgement of Fleur Adcock's ability to read Latin. All this can be seen too in the context of his own composition of a sequence of poems adapting Catullus, 'Words to Lay a Strong Ghost' (which was written, for the most part at least, in 1966)[11] in which the Lesbia figure becomes Pyrrha,

7 Draft (1) of 'Shots around the Target' (1966), Hocken MS-0975-104. See 2. 13–16, at 13. This has been edited out of Draft (2), for which see 2. 16–19, and from the full manuscript text of the talk with this title which he gave at the opening of the New Zealand Universities Arts Festival, May 1966 (Hocken MS-0975/123). See 2. 20–43.

8 'Further Notes on New Zealand Poetry'. Hocken MS-0975/115. This was apparently a talk to the English Association Winter School, August 1963. See 4. 295.

9 'Modern New Zealand Poetry', Hocken Misc-MS-0682. This is the second of two lectures given as part of an adult education discussion course. See 4. 208.

10 This is a slightly revised version of a review for the *New Zealand Tablet*. See 4. 331.

11 *CPoems* 356–63. While Burns Fellow, Baxter discussed Catullus with

a name which he took from the fickle subject of Horace, *Odes* 1.5, and which he had already used for his girlfriend in 1957. Both Catullus and Horace were normal features of Classics Department curricula when Baxter was a student. He will also have read Virgil, part of the fruits of which can be seen in the early poem 'Aeneas' (*Cold Spring* 3). His study of Greek history, art and literature will also have reinforced his childhood knowledge of classical myth, which plays such a prominent part in his poetry.[12]

Given Baxter's negative feelings in general about academia, however, it is somewhat ironic that he applied for, was awarded, and accepted, the Burns Fellowship at the University of Otago. He did, of course, have greater financial security for himself and his family, with the salary of a full-time university lecturer. He also had considerable opportunity to write without having to expend energy on his occupation of postman, was provided with a study at the university and was able to interact with colleagues. He was also close to his parents and other family members. Furthermore, returning to Dunedin in 1966 to live (his Fellowship was extended for the further year of 1967) gave him the chance to encounter and possibly exorcise ghosts from his former period of residence in Otago and his unsuccessful time as a student at the university two decades earlier.[13]

Baxter himself was, of course, aware of the irony. A report on the new Fellow's return to Dunedin by Kevin Cunningham states that, given Baxter's belief in the 'sterilising effect of university life on original writing', his acceptance of the Fellowship involved a compromise which,

Kenneth Quinn, who had recently taken up the Chair of Classics at the University of Otago and who was an internationally recognised scholar of Catullan poetry (Quinn once phoned me about this connection with Baxter). Baxter had already experimented with adaptations of the Latin poet, having written the poem 'Catullus at the Grave of his Brother' (*CPoems* 47) as early as 1946.

12 See Geoffrey Miles, John Davidson, and Paul Millar, *The Snake-Haired Muse: James K. Baxter and Classical Myth* (VUP 2011).

13 For accounts of his years as Burns Fellow in 1966–67 as well as the following year in Dunedin, see McKay 208–38 and *CP* 4. 71–88.

however, he saw as only slight (2. 9–10). In this, he seems to be downplaying his convictions, since Cunningham goes on to repeat Baxter's objection to academic life on the grounds that it tends to teach students the ideas of other people rather than encouraging them to develop their own, that academic 'success' is tied to examinations, and that financial dependence on families cramps individual talent. Moreover, in his view, poets teaching poetry end up with 'deadness in expression and technique'. A poet should rather be 'a man talking to men, rather than to professors' (2. 9).

Once established in his position as Fellow, Baxter had no hesitation in beating his anti-academic drum. Thus in Draft (2) of 'Shots around the Target', a revised version of which (without the passage about to be quoted) he was later to deliver as a talk at the opening of the New Zealand Universities Arts Festival, he claims that when he was a student at the University of Otago '*nothing* ever happened inside those walls to help me grow in the way I needed to grow'. He goes on to say that any significant experiences happened elsewhere, and that he sees the Festival as 'either a non-academic happening within the academic region or else as something useless to me and to people of my kind' (2. 17).

In 'Conversation with an Ancestor', one of the Burns Fellowship lectures he gave, later to be included in the 1967 publication *Man on the Horse*, he lays bare his soul for all to see as he reflects on his position:

> Perhaps, by accepting this Fellowship, I gave an inch or two of ground in that lifelong battle [i.e. against 'the devil of acedia']; because there is always a connection, however tenuous, between the university and the administrative machines which act out the fantasies of the dull, man-killing brain of Caesar – a connection which university men themselves would deplore and attempt to diminish. (2. 133)

And he proceeds to quote from a poem he had recently written expressing something of his unease about this connection. Two of the stanzas included in the poem are as follows:

And I who wrote in ’62,
*Dear ghosts, let me abandon*
*What cannot be held against*
*Hangmen and educators, the city of youth!* –

Drink fresh percolated coffee, lounging
In the new house, at the flash red kitchen table,
A Varsity person, with an office
Just round the corner – what nonsense! (2. 133)

Perhaps his most interesting statement on the subject, however, comes shortly after this passage in the same lecture:

> In a sense the Fellowship was awarded to the wrong man: my shadow, my enemy, my monster: the public person who would destroy if he could whatever gifts I possess. Art, the mainstay of culture, is not bred by culture but by its opposite: that level of hardship or awareness of moral chaos where the soul is too destitute to be able to lie to itself. Thus the Fellowship should have been awarded, if at all, not to me – a family man, teetotal, moderately pious, not offensive to sight or smell, able to say the right thing in a drawing-room – but to my collaborator, my schizophrenic twin, who has always provided me with poems. (2. 135.)

And he goes on to see this ‘twin’ as the man who was in Dunedin two decades earlier, the man portrayed in his at that time unpublished, quasi-autobiographical novel *Horse*, on which he had begun exploratory work in 1958 but had substantively written and completed in 1962, whose hero hovers drunkenly around the environs of the university.[14]

Baxter continued to muse in print about his tenure of the Fellowship. In September 1968, *Landfall* published a series of short reminiscences by holders of the award, including Baxter. What he says is most revealing, pointing as it does to the last and most famous period of his life. Here are extracts:

14 The novel was published in 1985, well after Baxter’s death. See 1. 529–89, and Weir’s notes, 4. 290–92.

When I applied for the Fellowship I was tired of pounding the Wellington streets on a postman's round, and a bit of leisure seemed a good idea. Thirty-nine was a stopping place: a place to sit down and think about the road ahead. And I had heard others say that if a man had leisure he could write, at least without tiredness, perhaps with a new drive. I've never planned more than a year ahead if I could help it; and the Fellowship would last a year. But when I got the Fellowship I thought: 'Man, you're mad.' Others had gone down to Dunedin to drink from the big gravy dish. They had come back boozed or haunted, needing longer to recover from their leisure than others do to recover from work . . .

The main trouble is of course that the Muse, that primitive and prejudiced old Lady, does not smile on Fellowship holders. Our good morals seem to bore her. She goes away from us to whisper in the ear of a young poet with a raging hangover and three mistresses and no money at all, who inhabits a blanket-shrouded room in a flat above a wineshop in Greater King Street. She says to the Fellowship holder: 'All right, mate. You've made your choice. You want money and status – well, you've got them. Don't ask to have me as well, thrown in to make up the full bundle.' . . .

So I came down to Dunedin. The first year I wrestled with the ghost of an ancient mistress who came back to haunt me, and got a number of written lectures and some grim, dry poems out of the encounter. Sitting half asleep in that sun-soaked Trappist cell in the English Department, I began to think that I had the Fellowship by the short hairs. But there were harder times to come. In some ways I am sorry that I did not receive the Fellowship while I was still an active alcoholic. To spend a year roaring drunk – the committee that administers the fund would of course in those circumstances never have granted me a second year – but to do this would have truly honoured the Muse, who likes a rumpus better than she likes omelettes, and it would have left a hairy legend of the Abominable Snowman to gladden the hearts of the young and offend the nostrils of the old . . .

> And I received the Fellowship for a second year. And the thought stuck with me: 'O.K., mate. But what'll you do when you have to get out of this Old Man's Home . . . ?' . . . And I could feel the death trance beginning . . .
>
> I wonder how much of the death was my own and how much came from the Fellowship. Lately it has seemed to me that God was trying to say something to me . . . '. . . The Fellowship was a conditional mistake. You knew that all along. Why don't you use your radar? I'm not angry about it; I'm only sorry . . .'
>
> Something like that. The Fellowship hadn't exactly done me in. But my asbestos suit had worn through in a few places. (2. 614–17)[15]

The irony is that the Fellowship years in no way diminished his creative spark, since he produced a significant amount of poetry of high quality, and indeed a new poetic trajectory was taking shape. Thus his complaint that the Fellowship was a mistake and his disparagement of his tenure seem unjustified.

Leaving Baxter on the path leading to the North Island once more, Jerusalem and beyond, we come to the difficult task of assessing those of his prose writings throughout his career that have serious academic content. And here we immediately encounter a problem of definition. As well as a range of prose types such as talks to student audiences and other educational material, parables, dialogues and letters to editors, he wrote numerous book reviews, especially reviews of collections of poetry, for a variety of publications, including regular contributions to the *New Zealand Listener* from 1950 onwards. Most importantly, on the basis of his own wide reading and practice as a poet, he outlined his views on criticism and the role of the critic, as well as displaying his own talents as a critic of poetry in particular, in a series of lectures over the years which were later published – *Recent*

15 For further brief, not exactly complimentary remarks by Baxter about the Burns Fellowship and his view of academics, along with comments by the author about his performance as Fellow, see Oliver *passim,* esp. 103–05.

*Trends in New Zealand Poetry* (The Caxton Press, 1951), *The Fire and the Anvil* (New Zealand University Press, 1955), *The Man on the Horse* (University of Otago Press, 1967) and *Aspects of Poetry in New Zealand* (The Caxton Press, 1967).[16]

The question is the extent to which any of this material can be called 'academic writing'. Baxter himself was very much aware of the issue. In one letter to the editor of the *New Zealand Listener*, he responds to criticism from another correspondent about the principles of critical reviewing. He says that in some circumstances it is not necessary for a reviewer to have 'a full, scholarly, bibliographical knowledge of the background of the book he reviews' (1. 451). He adds, however, that this depends on what kind of periodical the review appears in. If it is an academic journal, then the review of an academic book would have to be 'exhaustive and scholarly'. The same book, however, when reviewed in the *New Zealand Listener*, 'might be scholarly, but would not have to be'. And he goes on to say that his own qualifications for reviewing the book in question (on the subject of James Joyce) were 'a full knowledge of Joyce's writings, not scholarly but literary'. Baxter is clearly differentiating between the approaches required for scholarly or 'academic' writing on the one hand and 'literary' writing on the other. However, there seems to be no reason for a well-written piece of criticism, based on knowledge and sensitive appreciation, not to be included under the label 'academic' even if it lacks the support of secondary reading on the subject and a proliferation of footnotes.

This issue of a 'scholarly' approach versus a 'literary' one that is somehow freed from academic strictures rears its head also in the controversy about Allen Curnow's editorial principles, in which Baxter was heavily involved. He, like a considerable number of others, had objected strongly to Curnow's 'prescriptive' model for New Zealand poetry and his resulting choice of poems (and indeed poets) to be

16 The page numbers in the *Collected Prose* are 1. 65–77; 1. 145–98; 2. 129–243; and 2. 325–53 respectively.

included in the 1960 anthology *Penguin Book of New Zealand Verse*. Baxter provided his own analysis of the development of New Zealand poetry in two lectures, identifying first a group of 'Innovators' and then a group of 'Broadeners' as the two important movements up to that time after the so-called Georgian phase. These lectures were originally designed as Otago Burns Fellowship lectures, but were in the event not delivered. Instead, they were amalgamated, compressed and significantly rewritten, to be delivered at Victoria University of Wellington in July 1967 and published as *Aspects of New Zealand Poetry*, the 'Innovators' and 'Broadeners' becoming the 'transitional poets' and the 'post-transitional poets' respectively.

In the draft of 'The Broadeners' (2. 71–76), Baxter in fact seemed to be playing down the concept that had been developed by some dissatisfied with the Curnow line, who saw 'Romantic' writing about poetry diametrically opposed to the 'academic' criticism practised by Curnow. He argued that the word 'academic' had generally been used in a social rather than literary sense, and that 'academic criticism' really meant criticism associated with the universities, the implication being that 'Curnow and certain *Landfall* reviewers have regarded poems and books of poems as texts for linguistic analysis, [sc. and] have been limited in fact by a special university conditioning'. He concluded that the accusation had some justification, given the close university associations of most of the 'Innovators', but was hard to prove.

Baxter's discussion of the issue in this initial handling of it is a little unclear, and it is undoubtedly a good thing that it was more or less edited out of the final version in *Aspects of Poetry in New Zealand*. Here he simply commented: 'Many critical problems that should have been settled remain unsettled. At the present time the main divergence seems to lie between the university critics who favour an impersonal and academic mode and the various poets who progress to an anti-Romantic Romanticism' (2. 339). The way in which he expressed the contrasting approaches echoes the formulation of W. S. Broughton (in an article in *Salient* of 5 October 1964) which Baxter had quoted in 'The Broadeners' draft. There, Broughton spoke of 'the rather artificial distinction that a number of poets and critics assume exist between regional-University-academicism and universal-bardic-Romanticism'. Baxter had stated that he shared Broughton's hope that this turf war would end so that any serious devotee of poetry could assess New Zealand literature without becoming involved in feuding (2. 72). This is a rather complex issue, made more so by the fact that there seems to be a contrast not only between 'academic' critics on the one hand and poets on the other, but also between 'academic' critics and those poets who are divorced from a university context turning their hand to criticism.

Returning to the four key publications by Baxter that we have mentioned, we can, I believe, safely suggest that at least parts of them contain criticism of a standard that would be the equal of passages of criticism by academics in academic contexts. When he wrote the last two, he had a BA and significant university experience. At the time of writing the second, he was well on the way towards his BA, while the first was written when his degree completion was several years in the future. This makes *Recent Trends in New Zealand Poetry* all the more remarkable, since it is a very clear and coherent analysis of the subject, even if he himself calls it 'a somewhat rambling address'. He was already touching on issues that he was to develop more fully in later lectures. He noted that the 'new movement' [involving what he was later to call the 'transitional poets'] began in the universities and interestingly, in the light of his usual hardline approach, said that '[t]here is no reason why a poet should not earn his living as a rabbiter or as a University lecturer, so long as he does not develop a split personality' (1. 75–6). Given the clarity of the writing, it is no wonder that as a lecture it made such an impression at the New Zealand Writers' Conference held at Canterbury University College in May 1951. McKay discusses it and records some of the adulatory comments made about it by eminent critics (McKay 131–34; also 4. 202–04).

Even before this, however, he had shown unusual maturity as a critic of literature. For example, his review for *Landfall* in 1950 of Allen Curnow's *At Dead Low Water* and *Sonnets* (1. 57–59) is characterised by perception and clarity of writing. Weir comments, '[t]his review is the most carefully argued piece of critical prose which JKB had yet written. His argument and analysis are carefully considered and developed because he was writing about a man who seemed to want to be his patron' (4. 198). This was, of course, well before he took issue with Curnow over the latter's editorial and critical approach to New Zealand poetry. The many other reviews he wrote in the 1950s and 1960s usually display a similar acumen and clarity of expression.

The Macmillan Brown lectures of 1954, which were published the next year as *The Fire and the Anvil*, are each longer than *Recent Trends* and deal with criticism, inspiration and symbolism respectively. In the first two, we find included some discussion of technical aspects of poetry such as metrics and nomenclature. He was later to have a field day on metrics in a piece for the *New Zealand Listener*, which was his contribution, along with contributions from some academics, in response to a correspondent's criticism that a poem by Peter Bland published in the *Listener* was prose rather than poetry (2. 106–08). Weir's comment is most apt: 'It seems as if in the company of academics JKB needed to be more academic than the others. They preferred to comment on the language used (based on images, not scientific), on the necessity of rhythm, but not metrics, and the key distinction between poetry and verse' (4. 326).

The second lecture of *The Fire and the Anvil*, entitled 'The Creative Mask', is somewhat discursive, but is generally again most perceptive and makes a good case for the importance of 'heart over mind' and 'creative freedom', as well as advising an element of 'tykishness' for poets. The third lecture already criticises the neglect of Louis Johnson and others by Curnow in his 1951 updated *Book of New Zealand Verse*, a criticism that was to become even harsher, as we have seen, after the publication of the *Penguin Book of New Zealand Verse* in 1960. Baxter himself was not one to 'straitjacket' or be prescriptive.

McKay comments that Baxter laid down a challenge with his judgements in these lectures, but he 'did not sustain an argument in the manner of analytical criticism', instead adopting 'an impressionistic approach'. He goes on to say that the 'weakest sections were those where he assumed the mantle of an academic, the strongest, those where he gave his personal response' (McKay 140). This is certainly justified to an extent and reinforces what he had said earlier in the Introduction to his edited selection of Baxter's critical works, namely that Baxter was 'an intuitive not an analytical critic' (*Baxter as Critic* vi).[17] It must always be remembered, however, that intuition can often offer insights lacking in straight analysis and can therefore be said to make a significant contribution to academic discourse. McKay records both positive and negative responses to the lectures, along with part of Baxter's typically self-deprecating inscription on the personal copy he gave to John Weir: 'This confused and sincere book still expresses a good deal of what I feel about the artist's vocation . . . and most of it was written between or during savage drinking bouts' (McKay 141).

The four Burns Fellowship lectures published as *The Man on the Horse* (a fifth lecture in the volume is from a talk given to seminarians at Holy Cross College) show a Baxter tending to be increasingly discursive and anecdotal, and climbing too enthusiastically on some of his personal hobby horses, so that much of the material cannot be considered 'academic'. However, in the title lecture, he does offer a most insightful critique of Burns's poem 'Tam o' Shanter', which certainly can be taken as a piece of serious academic writing. Baxter had been acquainted since childhood with the Scottish poet,

17 This Introduction as a whole tends to focus on the moral/religious basis of Baxter's critical writing.

and in his analysis we can see the paths of poet and critic converging, as he aligns his own poetic temperament (or rather the temperament of two decades earlier to which he looks back with nostalgia) with that of Burns.[18] The concepts of the tribal, the drunken and the bawdy, in a context of superstition and witchcraft, feed into the themes of sex/death, the Muse and the *anima*, which figure so prominently in much of his poetry. He can identify with his subject, while at the same time standing outside of it in a process of analysis.

Less successfully, in one of the other lectures, 'The Virgin and the Temptress', Baxter essays a critique of his own poem, 'Henley Pub'. Quite apart from the fact that he tries, rather artificially, to combine so many disparate elements in this particular poem, he cannot be objective at all in discussing it, since he is talking about a work of his own, which he has thought about and revised over a period of time. Moreover, because it had received a degree of criticism, he ends up basically offering a justification of it, and the personal background elements are never far out of sight. It thus has a looser and more anecdotal feel. *Aspects of Poetry in New Zealand*, on the other hand, for the most part shows a tighter approach and is much more satisfactory when being assessed by academic criteria. It is worth noting in general, too, that though when offering a critique of poetry Baxter normally just dealt with a poem as such, he could on occasion also consider 'secondary' literature on the material (albeit limited), one of the hallmarks of academic writing.

In the last four or five years of his life, Baxter's involvement in and writing about academic matters declined markedly. Instead, his written thoughts in prose concentrated increasingly on religion and secularisation and the Roman Catholic Church, together with his Roman Catholic faith,

18 He quotes with approval Burns's warning against 'those who try to court the daimon through scholarship: "A set o' dull conceited hashes/ Confuse their brains in college classes . . ."' *The Man on the Horse* 93 (2. 193).

along with ethical issues such as marriage, sexuality, birth control and homosexuality. He also wrote extensively about drugs and drug addiction, attitudes of the police, war and militarism, the crisis of identity facing the younger generation, the underprivileged, aroha and community, and the injustices done to Māori. He did write a smattering of reviews and related material, but he had in essence left academia well behind.

When looking at what he wrote over his career as a whole, one gets the impression, as has been foreshadowed earlier in this paper, that he never came to terms with his ongoing relationship with academia. While he took apparent delight in mocking it[19] and relegating it to a status of inferiority, there is always some sense that he would have liked to have been able to walk in this world as easily as in the world of creative writing and to have been accepted as an equal there. It looks as though he envied those who could, and disguised this by the broadsides he delivered against them and what they represented. One cannot also totally avoid the suspicion that when he happened to disagree with some critic's assessment of a particular poem or poet's work, his strategy was simply to write it off as 'academic'. He himself could be 'academic' or pedantic when he wanted to and, as a practising poet himself, his critique of other poets' work was not altogether objective, in that he understandably based it on his own experience of the process of poetic composition. Although he could be pompous at times, and sometimes, especially when he became anecdotal, could sound like a preacher, such 'faults' were generally more than compensated for by penetrating criticism and flair, as for many years he was a lively contributor to the ongoing discussion about New Zealand poetry.

19 He has a field day in this regard in his unpublished play, *Spots on the Leopard*. Worth noting too is his cynical 1963 poem 'To Any Young Man who Hears my Verses Read in a Lecture Room' (*CPoems* 265) where he ridicules some 'cheese-headed ladder-climber' reading one of his poems from a rostrum. A putative young man in the audience, he contends, should rather be concentrating his attention on a girl in the second row.

In any case, I am sure that he would have been highly amused to think that over forty years after his death an academic such as myself would be writing this account. I have to admit too that I have some sympathy for his expressed attitude to academia, when one considers that the discourse of at least some academics displays pomposity and pedantry without Baxter's acumen and often entertaining way with words. And so it seems apt to conclude with that pleasant if heavily biased thought from his poem 'Envoi' [to 'University Song'] (*CPoems* 52), the last two lines of which, he later commented, captured the crux of 'that peculiar schizoid calm that characterises university life: the calm of a populous graveyard' (1. 483):

> *Per ardua ad astra*: blind
> Inscription from a catacomb.
> *Lost, one original heart and mind*
> Between the pub and lecture-room.

# *The Incarnational Formalist: The Known Habits of Association in Baxter's Criticism of Poetry*

Nicholas Wright

What does it mean to know how or why one writes and reads as one does? From where might such knowledge come, and how might it bear on the experience of the self as a 'cell' within the social body? These are, one might suggest, among the more pressing questions an early- to mid-twentieth-century literary critic might have pondered; certainly they are implicit in the literary-critical prose of Baxter. His essays collected in *The Fire and the Anvil* (1955) are largely devoted to them:

> To my mind a literary critic has two main tasks: to examine individual texts; and to broaden and enrich in the reader's mind his known habits of association, thus clarifying for his own age the nature and scope of the *formal engagement*. ('The Criticism of Poetry', *Complete Prose* 1. 146)

In this instance Baxter is quoting from Wordsworth's preface to his *Lyrical Ballads* (1801). As Wordsworth puts it: 'by the act of writing in verse an Author makes a formal engagement that he will gratify certain known habits of association' (quoted in 'Criticism' 1. 146). Baxter's italics remind us that the work of the critic – as with the work of the poet and reader, Baxter saw all three positions as 'closely related' (1. 146) – is always a kind of formal work, but what can this term mean for a poet and critic like Baxter who, to judge by popular opinion, was less likely than many New Zealand writers to 'gratify' any of the culture's 'known habits'? Baxter's italics indicate a significance he does not clarify. In lieu of further elaboration one might ask: whose habits are those requiring of gratification? To what degree is the '*formal engagement*' complicit in the conservation of privilege? But what, too, is meant by 'formal'? Can it mean convention – a mode of engagement determined by established, hence formalised, associations? Or does the term more simply represent the need to find textual forms by which to acknowledge, represent and perhaps question the organic complexities of private and social experience? In both cases the term carries an implied preference for ritual, consensus and, indeed, tradition.

To know one's habits of association is, one might say, crucial to the critical project of questioning how and why one reads and writes as one does. And yet Baxter's prescription (above) for a critical practice begins to sound increasingly conservative: the verbs he appends, as if in qualification of Wordsworth's definition, 'broaden', 'enrich' and 'clarify', sound like terms enlisted in the service of consolidation more than dissent. What, then, is the nature of Baxter's 'formal engagement'? Or, to frame this in cultural and literary-historical terms, is it the case that Baxter ought to be seen as a not exceptional member of his own time, as a critic as pervious as anyone to his culture's known habits of association? To read Baxter's critical prose from this perspective is, necessarily, I think, to read him as a formalist critic, which is to say as a critic, reader and poet deeply influenced by the ideological literary-critical paradigm that dominated the analysis of poetry in the twentieth century. Indeed, perhaps it is the depth of this influence that lies behind Frank McKay's assertion that '[Baxter] can hardly be said to have contributed anything new to the theory of criticism' (*Baxter as Critic* xvi). What I'd like to consider, however, is what this brief critical observation has masked for decades: the undiagnosed formalist habits of association that not only determined Baxter's criticism of poetry but also the way we have learned to read according to what John Newton has called the 'Baxter effect' – that blurring together of the textual and the empirical. As I will argue, far from preventing this sort of conflation, Baxter's formalism in fact insists on it. As I will only have space to suggest, the implications of such a formal engagement for those of us in our small literary culture who continue to read *after* Baxter continue to haunt the ways we think about how and why we read and write as we do in the twenty-first century.

What happens, then, if we choose to read Baxter's literary criticism in its own literary critical context? To perform such a reading is to read Baxter in concert with the 'strong ghost' of Matthew Arnold, but also, and more significantly, Baxter's near contemporaries: T. S. Eliot, F. R. Leavis and Cleanth Brooks.[1] As I hope to demonstrate, it is not difficult to see how Baxter is almost always formalist in his writing about poetry. More compellingly, Baxter's formalist tendencies define his response to concerns about society and culture: one has only to reflect on the way Baxter responds to the 'singularly unfertile' 'intellectual climate [of New Zealand]' by addressing the 'idol . . . called prosody' for an example of this ('Criticism' 1. 146). If this approach alerts the reader to Baxter's formalist credentials, it must surely also alert them to the apparent incongruity of claiming him as a formalist; who, many will ask, among his contemporaries or precursors, did as much for culture in New Zealand? Who did so much to challenge the pākehā consciousness of Māori? Who railed as volubly and voluminously against the sterility of a puritanical, institutionalised and conservative mainstream society? And yet such qualities, for all their

1 'Near contemporaries' is, admittedly, a bit of an overstatement, but when one considers the lives of the major formalists (Eliot 1888–1965, Ransom 1888–1974, Richards 1893–1979, Leavis 1895–1978, Tate 1899–1974, Warren 1905–1989, Empson 1906–1984, Brooks 1906–1994, Wimsatt 1907–1979), it is clear to see how Baxter's life (1926–1972) and career fits well with the period of formalism's rise (the 1920s, with Eliot) and its fall (the late 1960s) in America.

attribution to Baxter of positions of disavowal and dissent, are features of the formal engagement I'm describing as formalist. If the great achievement of Baxter's formalism has been to make him appear the antithesis of the sort of text-bound, conventional literary critic who dominated literary study in the twentieth century, this is because of formalism's own zeal for the empirical, for the material and embodied world of feeling and experience.

McKay, who until recently has been the only person to survey the bulk of Baxter's critical prose, certainly can't be enlisted to my cause without equivocation: as is well known, he describes Baxter as an 'intuitive not an analytical critic', and certainly 'not a systematic thinker' (*Baxter as Critic* vi). And yet this unsystematic quality, as we shall see, is in fact the quality that permits the formalist critic the idealistic and mystical reach that so characterises the critical practice a New Critic like Cleanth Brooks neatly encapsulates as 'articles of faith' ('Formalist Critics' 72). If followed through to its unsystematic, unmethodical conclusion, the formalist mode of literary scholarship culminates in a disavowal of both poetry and its critique in preference for tradition-sanctioned universal truths enshrouded in what Brooks refers to as the 'twin concomitants' of paradox: 'irony and wonder' (*Urn* 36). Indeed, the formalist 'method', if pursued as far as Baxter pursued it, reveals itself to be a spiritual method, precisely, in fact, what McKay described as an 'incarnational' mode (vii). Such a mode focuses on and offers to redeem the concrete and contingent objects of the material world – usually conceived as fallen, ruined, or sacrificial – by virtue of the reader's commitment to a regimen of renunciation (of the self, of poetry, of criticism) in the name of an experience (not knowledge) of the ineffable whole, that complex and mystified unity. The incarnational quality of Baxter's formalism becomes the natural bridge between poetry (his criticism) and experience, between, as Baxter himself famously put it, 'writing and example' ('Recent Trends in New Zealand Poetry', 1. 75). For the formalists and New Critics, the great 'verbal icon' (Wimsatt) of the ideal poetry, as well as the ideal reader and persona-like poet, was the well-wrought urn. In this remnant of wonder – that material irony and vessel of the inexpressible – we find an analogue for the embodied textual experience Baxter's criticism introduces as a longed-for, but always deferred, moment of consummation.

*

As Chris Baldick puts it in his analysis of a century of criticism and literary theory, formalism may well be 'the single most influential, and troublesome, intellectual tendency in Anglophone criticism since the 1890s' (10). Certainly, from this side of the twenty-first century, formalist criticism has become a byword for modes of reading that now seem retrograde, non-political and conservative. This was not, however, always the case: the early Anglo-American formalists – Eliot, Leavis, I. A. Richards, William Empson, Brooks, John Crowe Ransom, Robert Penn Warren and Allen Tate, to name a few – all worked under the imprimatur of modernism; all, that is to say, shared in that characteristically modernist requirement of dissent, and all looked askance at the conditions of contemporary culture, disdainful of what we might call the culture's corrupted habits of association. Moreover, to varying degrees, most of them sought to overturn the discipline of English studies and, by so doing, to free it from the institutionalised cult of Victorian belletrism. As Baldick reminds us, English was a discipline still governed by biographical and philological approaches (110). Like Baxter's, many of these new-critical voices defined themselves as anti-establishment and anti-institutional, as critics of culture and, with this, critics of the reading public. The American branch of New Criticism came to be known as the 'Fugitive' school, the 'Southern Agrarians', who, like many of their Anglo counterparts, existed on the fringes of academic and literary culture.[2]

2 It perhaps mattered little to Baxter that Leavis, as with so many of the

Baxter himself provides us with an introduction of sorts to what he appears to have seen as some of the New Criticism's key terms. Baxter's glossary records: '*autotelic, aesthetic distance, rational coherence, concrete universal, designatum, denotatum,* [and the] *fallacy of expressive form*' ('The Creative Mask', 1. 167, italics in original). As we will see, these terms translate readily into Baxter's literary critical practice, but they are also helpful in introducing some of the basic assumptions shared broadly among those trans-Atlantic figures Baxter was influenced by. For 'autotelic' we might read the insistence the formalist scholar places on autonomy – the requirement that the work should sacrifice its relation to the present in order that it might more clearly and objectively permit the passage through its form of tradition, conceived (by Arnold) as 'the best that has been thought and said' in Western (pre-modern) history (preface to *Culture and Anarchy* viii). 'Aesthetic distance' is simply a version of the modernist emphasis – so apparent in Eliot – on the impersonal (*The Sacred Wood*) or, in Arnold, the 'disinterested' ('The Function of Criticism') approach to writing and reading, hence also 'the fallacy of expressive form'. The 'concrete universal', as we will see, encapsulates both ends of the formalist spectrum: devoted on the one hand to the contingent and material (the concrete), and on the other, to the eternal, boundless intangibles of spiritualised experience. Without such categories, as Baxter says elsewhere, 'the appreciation of poetry becomes purely a subjective matter' ('Criticism' 1. 157). Baxter continues: 'That one likes a poem cannot serve as a critical criterion. One may like it for the wrong reason – because it supports

other Formalists and New Critics, shared Baxter's own anti-academic, anti-institutional position. As Chris Baldick points out, the best critics of this period (Eliot, Woolf, Lubbock, Wilson, Murry, Lawrence, Mencken, Mansfield and Burke), worked outside academia, while those who taught (Leavis, Richards, Empson, Tate, Wilson-Knight, Blackmur, Winters and Brooks) did so in 'temporary or insecure positions, usually remote from the centres of academic power, and typically publishing in non-academic little magazines' (110).

a favoured system of ideas' (1. 157). Although Baxter's concern here is with subjectivism, his insistence on a 'critical criterion' – a discipline of reading to set against the distractions of the contemporary moment, whether these be a 'favoured system of [political, ethical, or moral] ideas' – marks him definitively as a formalist.

While it is a mistake to argue for the coherency of something as unsystematic and as loose as 'formalism', certain core assumptions can be identified, as they were by Cleanth Brooks:

> Here are some articles of faith I could subscribe to: . . .
>
> *That the primary concern of criticism is with the problem of unity – the kind of whole which the literary work forms or fails to form, and the relation of the various parts to each other in building up this whole.*
>
> *That the formal relations in a work of literature may include, but certainly exceed, those of logic.*
>
> *That in a successful work, form and content cannot be separated.*
>
> *That form is meaning.*
>
> *That literature is ultimately metaphorical and symbolic.*
>
> *That the general and the universal are not seized upon by abstraction, but got at through the concrete and the particular.*
>
> *That literature is not a surrogate for religion.*
>
> *That, as Allen Tate says, 'specific moral problems' are the subject matter of literature, but that the purpose of literature is not to point to a moral.*
>
> *That the principles of criticism define the area relevant to literary criticism; they do not constitute a method for carrying out that criticism.* ('Formalist Critics' 72)

Brooks provides here an interesting series of negative propositions: formalism offers morality without moralising; the discipline of criticism without method; meaning, but in form rather than in statement; as well as a religiosity felt in the apparition of the whole (that which exceeds 'logic') which in turn must be apparent in the decidedly non-abstract 'concrete' and 'particular', and which, in a poem, always serves the sovereignty of metaphor. The ambiguities only multiply as Brooks continues. It is, perhaps, not difficult to see why Brooks frames these as 'articles of faith', or why such a series of aphorisms might have seemed intuitively appropriate to a mind as receptive to forms of ritual and spirituality as Baxter's. The lauded experience of irony and paradox that the New Critics so commonly espoused, and which was engendered by the interrelation of parts, apparent here in these variously self-denying articles, carries with it the complexity of a theological commitment.

By order of such articles the role of the text is reduced to form itself: it functions as a vessel, its role to enact or embody the lost whole, or, more specifically, 'the universal habits of human thinking' (Brooks and Warren 8) from which, so the argument goes, the contemporary age has alienated itself. The text is thus always that urn in which tradition is remembered. While offering the allure of something 'scientific', or, after I. A. Richards, something 'practical', the formalist close reading, if followed faithfully, resolves itself to the experience of a wholeness which, as Brooks argues in 'The Heresy of Paraphrase' (*Urn*) no sequence of words might adequately explain; such is the nature of real experience, that exalted state to which this mimetic formalism was always devoted. In their zeal for the non-lexical conditions of experience and wonder the formalist's method becomes self-critical, defined, one might say, by its own internalised structures of disavowal and self-sacrifice. To understand why this should be so, if not also to understand the incarnational qualities inherent in Baxter's criticism, is to consider what can be described as the three exigencies of this formalist method: an insistence on the autonomy of the artwork, a conviction in the principle of form as an embodiment or enactment of experience, and a certain faith in irony.[3] As I hope to show in the second half of

3 As Baldick points out, 'The New Criticism ... eventually fell into

this chapter, it is these three emphases that define Baxter's literary-critical formalism.

And yet, to take Baxter at his word, formalism was something he viewed as anathema to the reading and writing of poetry. Where Baxter overtly addresses formalism in his prose his tone is commonly pejorative: formalism is a 'disease' ('Notes Made in Winter' 1. 597), a form of 'blindness' ('Criticism' 1. 149), practised by critics, writers and readers alike. In his review of Curnow's *At Dead Low Water*, he takes a moment to register the 'destructive' influence of William Empson (1. 58), and in 'This Time the Flood', while reviewing the work of two of his favoured poets, Alistair Campbell and Kevin Ireland, he happily impugns Leavis's contribution to literary study: his 'last will and testament, a special dispensation for Romantics, [is] an old pair of suspenders to share between them' (2. 117). Baxter often spoke in tones as humorous and affected as this, but he could, just as quickly, be utterly frank: '[T]wo highly dangerous premises held by members of the academic cult – that there is only one way of writing good poems, and that a metaphor not able to be examined with the kit of tools Leavis left behind him is not true metaphor' ('Flood' 118). Indeed, most recently John Newton, quoting John Weir, could, with confidence, summarise Baxter's relationship to formalism:

> With exceptions, especially late in his life, his prose is more important for what he said rather than how he said it.' Even as a poet, Baxter is the least formalistic of our major writers and, as prose writer, doubly so. He has little ambition to be thought of as a prose stylist. Rather, he has a great deal to say; he's in a hurry to get it said, and typically he wants the attention of an audience that is only incidentally literary. (*New Zealand Books* 8)

But, for all his railing against formalist method – more, one now thinks, a response to its institutionalisation than its

disfavour as it repeatedly discovered the same "universal" literary properties (irony, ambiguity, paradox) in works of widely different kinds from diverse historical periods' (12).

'articles' – Baxter himself was often as willing to acknowledge both his conservatism as well as his commitment to formal analysis, even if in a manner of self-reproach: 'my own work is conservative; and I tend to overvalue the formal aspects of poetry' (1. 74); less diffidently he would later affirm this conservatism: 'I am not in favour of the revolution' ('A Scorpion' 3. 410).

As we have seen, Baxter was certainly aware of the formalist and New Critical traditions, and, as one would expect, positioned himself in relation to them, as he needed to when one sees how very closely his own critical terms, as well as their definitions, correspond to those of his trans-Atlantic contemporaries. In some cases his terms simply overlap – both Baxter and Leavis, for example, acknowledge 'glamour' and 'vitality' as elements of significance in the composition and reception of a poem. More broadly, Baxter and his formalist peers share an emphasis on metaphor and symbol, the concrete and particular, the unity of the whole, truth to experience, and the power of tradition, to determine the worth of a poem. In 'The Criticism of Poetry' Baxter offers '[s]ome possible criteria by which a good poem may be judged' (1. 156). One might simply note here that this very sort of list-making is itself evidence of a formalist approach to literature. Baxter's taxonomy includes: 'Metaphorical exactitude', which Baxter defines as a 'figure of thought rather than a figure of speech, to include all representations in concrete images of an inward event'; 'Clarity', or the way in which 'obscurity' may be discriminated from the all-important 'ambiguity' (1. 156). '[C]larity,' as Baxter suggests in Brooks-like fashion, 'is that quality in a poem by which its parts are related and subordinated to the whole meaning.' Baxter's catalogue continues with entries on 'Formal structure', 'Vigour' ('sheer animal vitality'), 'Glamour or Incandescence' – that combination of 'certain images . . . [which] affect the reader so profoundly that his critical faculty is for the meantime laid asleep' – and, most importantly, 'Significance' – a 'quality ultimately unseizable', the 'umbilical cord which binds a poem to the world of real experience' (1. 156–57). This enthusiasm for universal statement, which is such a feature of formalist criticism, is also shared by Baxter: a good poem is thus one that 'enlarges to a statement about problems and situations common to all men' (1. 153). Indeed, Baxter it seems is always generalising from the private to the public, always universalising experience. We see this in his reading of Karl Shapiro's 'Nostalgia':

> This private elegy and love poem finds a voice for the death which each man has to die, not just a soldiering death: so at its deepest level it ceases to be private and becomes an act of intercession for mankind. ('The World of the Creative Artist' 1. 253)

If Baxter's principles, so expressed, align with the habits of formalist criticism, so too does his use of them. In his commentary on Basil Dowling's 'The Trapped Hare' he approves of the 'application of stone-cold-sober technique to an intense and actual situation. The technique is almost that of prose: what makes the poem valid is the accurate delineation of moral intangibles' ('Trends' 1. 72). Baxter appears to value the poem for its disinterested, prose-like qualities, its sacrifice of the too poetic, but his real appreciation is expressed in that typically paradoxical final formulation: the 'accurate delineation of moral intangibles'. In a later essay, 'The Man on the Horse' (1967), Baxter reads Burns's 'Tam O'Shanter' in terms that are similarly universal, emphasising the poet's 'tribal value on virility, implying an organic attitude towards sex as one of the chief areas of human freedom, associated with fertility' (2. 196). Indeed, throughout his discussion of Burns, the contexts Baxter is most animated by are mythical (Burns's references to Ulysses) and archetypal – 'the tribal womb' (2. 200), 'the earth mother' (2. 202). Further evidence of Baxter's formalist tendencies hides in plain sight: in his review of Alistair Campbell's *Mine Eyes Dazzle, 1947–49* he praises

Campbell for 'metaphor and idea, concrete and abstract, . . . welded together in harmony' (1. 60); less happily, but on a related point, in a review of Eileen Duggan's *More Poems* he discusses the 'three levels in her poetry which rarely combine to make a completely satisfactory unit. . . . Her images . . . do frequently . . . tug against the central argument of a poem' (1. 77–78). Like a dyed-in-the-wool New Critic he is disappointed by the sentimentality he finds in Glover's Arawata Bill poems, but approves of the more successful persona of Harry, from Glover's earlier volume, for he is 'a highly successful unifying focus for oracular statements about human life and destiny' (1. 132).

It is this very concern for the universal (the mythic, the whole) at the expense of a contemporary condition reduced to little more than a vehicle of the past, that now seems, this side of the twenty-first century, so obviously formalist; but, as I mentioned earlier, Baxter's particular formalism is built on three interrelated concerns: autonomy, enactment (or embodiment) and irony. It is these three I turn to now, not only to make more granular this reading of Baxter's formal engagement, but to reveal his debt – his genealogy – to his formalist tribe: Arnold, Eliot and Leavis. As I have already suggested, that critics, poets, and readers working in the middle fifty years of the twentieth century should insist on art's temporal autonomy springs from that typically modern disdain with the present. To a large degree this desire for autonomy stems from Arnold, his reading of the romantics – Wordsworth, Coleridge, if not also Edmund Burke – but also his wariness of the 'public': the 'dilettanti . . . with their narrow, harsh, unintelligent, and unattractive spirit and culture' (*Portable* 464).[4] Arnold's broader concerns, openly acknowledged in terms of class and education, are with his contemporary condition's alienation from tradition; it is this emphasis on culture that also determines his thoughts on autonomy. In passage after passage, and in language that

4 For more on the Romantic distaste for the 'public' see Williams 33–35.

will be reprised by Eliot and Leavis, Arnold evinces a set of anxieties that will become the foundations of Baxter's formalist faith.

Baxter's view of the public is similarly Arnoldian; the public is simplistic and all-too-easily accommodated: 'an audience is delighted to have their suspicion removed that a simple ethical interpretation may not be applicable to every aspect of human knowledge' (1.154). The public lacks the courage of the imagination: theirs is a 'fear of freedom'; 'Literature,' says Baxter, momentarily slumming it in his pronouns, 'would trouble us and lead our feet in perhaps dangerous paths. So instead we pick up the *Reader's Digest*' (1. 146). The poet is, in fact, the besieged citizen of what Leavis called 'minority culture' in 'mass civilisation'. Thus, Baxter half-jokingly muses, 'The actual audience [the poet] gets consists of myopic school-teachers, pimply young men who eat in cafeterias, and fellow-poets. This means, in fact, that he writes for his fellow-poets' (1. 146). As Leavis put it, '[u]pon this minority depends our power of profiting by the finest human experience of the past; they keep alive the subtlest and most perishable parts of tradition' (*Mass Civilisation* 13).

For Baxter, however, it is Arnold's association of autonomy with motifs of renunciation and disavowal – that surrender of the present for the sake of either time past or time future – that is so determining of his own critical views. For Arnold, as for Baxter, the work of the poet and critic is with 'the contemplation of some noble action of a heroic time' (*Portable* 201). Arnold lays out the poet's and the critic's duties thus, and in the process furnishes the formalist critics to come with a Christian and conservative discourse of patience and self-sacrifice:

> If we must be dilettanti: if it is impossible for us, under the circumstances amidst which we live, to think clearly, to feel nobly, and to delineate firmly: if we cannot attain to the mastery of the great artists; – let us, at least, have so much respect

> for our art as to prefer it to ourselves. Let us not bewilder our successors; let us transmit to them the practice of poetry, with its boundaries and wholesome regulative laws, under which excellent works may again, perhaps, at some future time, be produced, not yet fallen into oblivion through our neglect, not yet condemned and cancelled by the influence of their eternal enemy, caprice. (*Portable* 201)

The seeds of Eliot's call for an impersonal poetry ('to prefer it to ourselves'), as well as Baxter's creation of his ego-less persona, can be found here, but what is most significant, I think, is Arnold's demotion of poetry to the role of vessel and to the function of transmission. And, of course, the clearest transmissions might only be obtained by the creation and reading of work construed as autonomous of its own 'capric[ious]' time and culture: the work must be objective, impersonal,

> . . . refusing to lend itself to any of those ulterior, political, practical considerations about ideas which plenty of people will be sure to attach to them. . . . Its business is, as I have said, simply to know the best that is known and thought in the world, and by in its turn making this known, to create a current of true and fresh ideas. (*Portable* 249)

For Arnold, then, the critic prepares the culture for the poetry to come. The critic is thus, to some degree, a sacrificial figure, a martyr, a figure motivated by the larger patterns of culture; their words, if cleansed of the contingency of their own time, their own politics, and thus 'disinterested', might provide a way of establishing a language, free of the corruptions of the immediate past and present. Such a poet-critic is always looking to 'purify the dialect of the tribe' (Eliot, 'Little Gidding'). Such a language, so fit for eternal transmission, can only be a language reduced to ritual and form.

But for all Arnold's influence, it is Eliot who makes the connection between autonomy and tradition that manifests in Baxter's prose and poetry:

> What is to be insisted upon is that the poet must develop or procure the consciousness of the past and that he should continue to develop this consciousness throughout his career.
>
> What happens is a continual surrender of himself as he is at the moment to something which is more valuable. The progress of an artist is a continual self-sacrifice, a continual extinction of personality. (*Sacred Wood* 47)

Eliot's modernist essay seems to have been something Baxter recognised as close to his own project.[5] Eliot's anti-subjectivist position, the strain of anti-egalitarianism we now associate with a modernism wary of mass civilisation, underwrites Baxter's desire to lift the poem out of the obscene ruck of the present. Even where Baxter disagreed with the spiritual wasteland modernists such as Eliot recorded, in his 'refus[al] to allow the scope of poetic form and expression to be limited to what the age demand[ed]' (Dennison 108), he still adhered to a modernist and formalist faith in tradition. In order to give voice to such tradition both poem and poet must be committed to an aesthetic of disavowal or, as Eliot puts it, 'self-sacrifice'. Both poem and poet – a blurring of 'writing and example', as Baxter knew – must become vessels for something greater: the past or, as Eliot's late entry into Anglicanism would suggest, the supernatural. In short, the poem and poet must become urn-like – objects of transmission formally engaged 'not merely [to] the present, but the present moment of the past' and thus, 'surrender[ed] . . . wholly to the work to be done' (*Sacred Wood* 53). Baxter understood this surrender to be one's 'obligation . . . to the language' (1. 155), and in his reviews and criticism of poetry he constantly searches for evidence of the past, the occulted tradition, the 'dead' 'already living' in the present (*Sacred Wood* 53). His landmark 1951 lecture 'Recent Trends in New Zealand Poetry' begins with as clear a formalist and Eliotian statement of tradition as one might imagine: 'The emergence

5 It should be noted that Baxter was seldom unequivocal in his appraisal of Eliot. For an excellent discussion of Baxter's debt to Eliot see Dennison. See also Baxter's 'T. S. Eliot's Background' (1. 739).

of national poetry depends on a mature attitude toward the past' (1. 65). The few lines Baxter quotes from Auden's 'Family Ghosts' help develop his view of the contemporary:

> The strings' excitement, the applauding drum
> Are but the initiating ceremony
> That out of cloud the ancestral face may come. (1. 65)

Those motifs of surrender and sacrifice are to the fore once again; the writing of the present is merely a ceremonial and formal initiation by which we hail the past, and it is this Baxter praises in the poetry of Ursula Bethell: the 'ancestral face . . . was plain to her' (1. 72). Baxter continues: this 'ritual' aspect of art relieves the 'isolation of the individual' by revealing a 'shape in history' (1. 66). Eliot's influence in Baxter's critical prose is apparent elsewhere too: Baxter's well-recorded and intuitive mythologising of experience – 'What happens is either meaningless to me, or else it is mythology' ('Notes on the Education of a New Zealand Poet' 2. 217) – seems entirely in sympathy with the mythic method Eliot outlined in his 1923 review of Joyce's *Ulysses*. Baxter may almost be ventriloquising Eliot in his complaint that the poets of the mid-twentieth century 'possess' only 'the most personal of values', having succumbed to a kind of Eliotian 'dissociation of sensibility' apparent in the division of 'moral and aesthetic factors in art' (1. 75–76). As Baxter elaborates elsewhere, too much of contemporary poetry is merely 'the scratching of a private itch' (1. 151).[6]

By insisting on the autonomy of a work, the formalists implicitly attributed a kind of agency to it; the best poems, although severed from their immediate contexts, were expected to generate meaning on their own terms via 'the

6 Baxter returns to the values of tradition commonly in his prose, as he does here in 'The Creative Mask': 'One cannot ignore the part that tradition plays in generating creative freedom. Tradition is not fathered by that great incubus of the marshes, the master state, but by those men who have realised in part that freedom is a primary human condition, and have written their knowledge into innumerable art forms and even in the customs of the society they inhabit' (1. 177). And here again, for example

relation of the various parts to each other in building up [the] whole' (Brooks, 'Formalist Critics' 72). Indeed, as is apparent in the language of embodiment and enactment favoured by so many of the formalists, the best works existed somewhere between aesthetics and experience. Among Leavis's key terms, for example, we find 'healthy', 'vital', 'plain vulgar living', 'actual', 'life', 'living principle', and 'mature' (among others) littered throughout his many texts. Leavis himself was very clear about this: 'Words in poetry invite us, not to "think about" and judge, but to "feel into" or "become" – to realize a complex experience that is given in the words. They demand, not merely a fuller-bodied response, but a complex responsiveness' (*Common Pursuit* 212). The poem, in so far as it fulfils its service as an autonomous, organically structured vessel of transmission, readily suggests a series of analogues: for Brooks the poem could be thought of as a 'plant' (Brooks and Warren 16), but in Baxter it is the body that comes increasingly to explain his relationship to poetry, especially where that body is conceived as a Christian body devoted to self-sacrifice.

Only such a body, conceived as both a text and a living entity, might transmit the metaphysical truths of the complex whole. Not surprisingly, the critical language of the formalists often reads as a discourse of embodiment. The poem becomes an organ of enactment, a natural medium for the communication of direct, sensuous experience. As Terry Eagleton puts it: 'This whole notion of language rested upon a naive mimeticism: the theory was that words are somehow healthiest when they approach the condition of things, and thus cease to be words at all' (*Literary Theory* 32). The formalist theory of language, in line with the motif of surrender and sacrifice I've been developing is, then, typically paradoxical: it is a theory of language against itself, and with this, a theory of reading

in one of his later essays, 'Conversation with an Ancestor': 'Poetry is not magical but mythical. It presents the crises, violations and reconciliation of the spiritual life in mythical form because this is the only way in which the conscious mind can assimilate them' (2. 140).

and interpretation in which meaning is metamorphosed into experience and feeling. The critic, one might say, is expected to excuse their own critical discourse from the moment of the critical encounter. As I've already suggested, the natural medium by which this act of lexical renunciation might best be performed is, for Baxter, the body. In this respect McKay's description of Baxter's philosophy of poetry as 'incarnational' is most apposite. The same term was vital for Leavis too – a poem's language was often understood to 'incarnate' meaning. Once again Eagleton explains:

> Whereas everyday language simply points to things, poetic language actually embodies them. There is a theology lurking behind this poetics: just as the Word of God is the Father made flesh, so a poem does not simply talk about things, but in some mysterious way 'becomes' them. (*How to Read a Poem* 59)

This metamorphosis (or incarnation) of language as thing, of poetry as experience, is prevalent wherever Baxter ventures into the exposition of a poem. In his defence of a poem by Fleur Adcock he writes:

> The final shape, appropriate for an elegy, is like that of stone from the quarry with some of the chisel marks showing. The reticence and indirectness of the poem seemed to me, after several readings, to give an exact and very moving impression of grief held in check by a difficult resignation. ('Is It Poetry?' 1. 458)

Of a Louis Johnson poem he is drawn to the use of a 'running metre' that 'produces an effect of desolation' (1. 149); in his reading of a Laurie Lee poem he 'senses' its 'immediate physical reference' which 'governs the development of images – a real girl and a November in the mind' (1. 166). As he says: '[t]he statement embodied in a true poem refers to a real occasion of illumination: it is the mirror of a spiritual event', a 'spiritual event in which the reader can participate' (1. 166).

If, perhaps, it is easy to identify formalist tendencies in

Baxter's critical prose, it should be considered that these are merely the symptoms of a spiritual ambition that, in Baxter's strikingly materialist and pragmatic manner, require the conversion of poetic to practice – precisely, of enactment to embodiment. In this respect Baxter mirrors Leavis's method – a method described by Perry Anderson as a kind of metaphysical empiricism:

> The paradox of this great critic is that his [Leavis's] whole oeuvre rested on a metaphysic which he could never expound or defend. Empiricism here found its strangest expression. Leavis, whose work transcended the rut of English philistinism so decisively (and was so hated for it), used its most extreme form to evade open debate of his ideas. His was a metaphysic which refused to justify itself. ('Components of the National Culture')

Metaphysics combined with the ethic of disavowal defines Baxter's critical method too, as is apparent in his conventionally formalist enthusiasm for metaphor and symbol (against paraphrase or exposition):

> But shall we suppose that the poet constructed an elaborate metaphor to say what any paraphrase could say more clearly? No. The metaphor *is* the poem: an inward non-verbal experience expressed in concrete verbal images. (1. 150)

And:

> A symbol reflects the stirring of massive intuitions inaccessible to reason, frequently obscure to the poet himself, and only comprehended by those readers who are similarly moved. (1. 151)

The result of such a critical method is the resolution to silence and, as Anderson suggests, a conservation of the very philistine and positivist attitudes of society the modernists found so repugnant; by this same 'method' art is sequestered among other spiritual events, forgiven its purchase on the real world of facts, class, gender or race. Art becomes beautiful in such a theology, because of its useless autonomy; the artist's job, according to Baxter, is thus 'to be useless and creative – resembling by analogy the apparently useless exercises of the Trappist Monk' (2. 130–31).

As I've suggested, pursued to the ends of its paradoxical or unmethodical method, formalism must surrender itself once again in that ritual of self-refusal or disavowal, which, for the formalist, becomes evidence they have discovered a vessel of the ineffable – that source of reverence to which the critical clerisy were devoted. The great poem, and by extension, the great reading, is one that bears witness to the way 'certain images in combination, especially in the great Romantic poets, can affect the reader so profoundly that his critical faculty is for the meantime laid asleep' (1. 157). A poetry of enactment and embodiment in which language is pitted against itself in preference for 'non-verbal experience' can only result in this suspension of the critical faculties, which is to say, can only leave its reader on the threshold of belief, not knowledge, and only by virtue of the poem's resolution (without resolution) to paradox or what the New Critics conceived of as irony. Nowhere in the corpus of formalist and New Critical prose is this concern so clearly elaborated as in Brooks's essay on Keats's 'Ode on a Grecian Urn'. It is here that Baxter's embodied discourse finds its 'verbal icon'; indeed, Keats's vessel is at the heart of the formalist tradition.

The urn, as I've suggested, is the great image of the ironically silent but eloquent vessel that formalist poetry aspires to, not merely as a model for art, but also for a certain kind of formalist good citizen, a 'cell of good living' (1. 75). Indeed, so much of what I've said about Baxter's formal engagement condenses in this object. The urn is celebrated by the impersonal formalist for its very lack of authorial provenance; it simply is. The urn can exist outside of subjectivity and personality, remaining iconic and mystified because its maker, a figure of sacrifice, has disappeared; only the enchanting remains. Free of its own provenance, the great urn's discovery in the present renders the (capricious) contexts of the contemporary irrelevant. Instead, the urn is supernatural; it exists in some ideal autonomy 'beyond time, outside time'. Indeed, as Brooks says, it 'bewilders our time-ridden minds' with its timeless truth (Sutton and Foster 586). As Brooks points out '[t]he urn itself is a "silent form," and yet it speaks, not by means of statement, but by "teasing us out of thought"' (Sutton and Foster 586). The ironies embodied in this mute form take us beyond thought into reverie, enchantment; its 'unheard music is sweeter than any audible music' (Sutton and Foster 583). In the urn the formalist ideal of a kind of communication without communication is achieved, and a place for art beyond criticism is once again conserved.

Herein lies the curious and animating irony of the formalist (un)method. For the formalist critic, the best poetry is a site of deferral, a negative space whose virtue inheres in its signification of what it cannot, but for some impossible-to-parse moment of irony or ambiguity, transmit. Irony and ambiguity thus consort with wonder and paradox to determine the tenor of mysticism the formalist critic and poet desires. Not surprisingly, perhaps, Baxter's own 'few definitions' for 'examining the process of poetic composition' (1. 167) are all geared to the evocation of this spiritualised and impossible wholeness: 'The world of Thou' is for Baxter what lies 'at the heart of making a poem'; it is that 'common spiritual experience' about which the 'work of the artist is convulsed' whether this be 'God, the natural world, the life of [the poet's] fellow beings' or 'some mystery *other* than themselves' (1. 167). The primal substance of the poem is what Baxter refers to as 'the Matrix' – the poem's 'secret incandescence', not its 'overt meaning', but the 'non-verbal' experience that the 'verbal structure of the poem reflects' and which is that point of contact with the '*world of Thou*' (1. 167). Baxter's formalist tendencies here could hardly be made clearer. 'Form' itself, the third of Baxter's considerations, is simply interchangeable with any number of fellow formalists writing across America and the United Kingdom. For Baxter form is defined as 'the whole complex verbal pattern' but which is 'always felt to be a highly inadequate reflection of the matrix' (1. 167). Such dreams of wholeness and such experiences of inadequacy are, as I've been suggesting, precisely the concomitants of formalist writing and reading. Baxter's remaining criteria follow the well-wrought path of formalist association: he makes mention of 'Texture' ('the use . . . of rhythm and bare and rich vowel and consonant patterns, with their accompanying emotional associations and physical effect'), and 'Time-Life' ('the form of a poem regarded as a complex "living" structure in time') (1. 168). The poem, as Baxter conceives it, possesses the autonomy and agency of any other organic body; it has a life of its own.

As one might expect, then, the 'language of mysticism' – the 'language' of irony – is praised by Baxter in his reading of a poem by St John of the Cross (1. 171); in his reading of Louis MacNeice's 'Brother Fire' Baxter effectively defines irony as 'the central meaning of twentieth-century poetry', though he doubts the 'average reader' is capable of recognising the 'exultation of the prisoner who sees the long-loved-hated cell block go up in smoke' (1. 152). The 'exaltation' Baxter refers to here is the experience the formalists recognised as irony, that 'bringing in of the opposite, the complementary impulse' (Richards 197). 'But such exaltation,' Baxter continues, 'is anathema to the social conscience; hence the average reader cannot make the necessary imaginative act of sympathy with the central meaning of the poem. He replies (through the mouths of educated critics as well as the silence of the multitude) – *this is immoral*; *this is untrue*; or, more devastatingly, *this is meaningless*' (1. 152). If such an experience of exaltation – a response to the formal generation of irony and paradox – exists beyond much of the reading public, it must fall to the formalist elect – the clerisy, as Coleridge once described them – who, in preferring art to themselves (as Arnold urged) must transmit this meaning to society. And yet, what might such a meaning be if the work is treated as autonomous of the specifics of its contemporary contexts? Furthermore, within the negative semiotic space thus cleared, how might this meaning be known, discussed, or tested, if its referent is an experience of irony? For the formalists this implicit insistence on a silencing of critical discussion, as well as those accompanying claims to the temporal and cultural autonomy of the work, means that only those readers and writers sensitive enough to recognise the 'ancestral face' of tradition, which is to say, only those who convene the conventions they themselves define, might bridge the gulf between the present and the past, the poet and the public – that animating antagonism at the root of Baxter's *The Fire and the Anvil*. Formalism, if nothing else, is a deeply conservative philosophy of poetry, reading, and writing.

Even from this brief survey of some of Baxter's thoughts on poetry it should be apparent that he read as a formalist, as did so many of his generation. Those ideas about sacrifice and surrender we have come to associate with the 'bearded mendicant' (Newton, 'Baxter Effect') of the late sonnets, are prepared by Baxter's willingness to surrender art and criticism in his prose. What requires further consideration, however, are the less obvious effects of this formalism, the subtle inducements of what I think has to be described as a formalist ideology – a loose and mystified association of ideas that carries with it a certain spiritual ambition – which anticipated the creation of that spectacle we now all too easily remember as the shambling, humbled Baxter, that persona fashioned by the transubstantiation of text to experience – the conflation of 'writing and example'.

From a formalist's perspective, as unsystematic as this may be, the point at which 'writing and example' find their union is the point at which only form remains – a materiality or body that in being emptied of ego, its bond to the contemporary, becomes purely connotative, a ruined but no less eloquent and evocative figure of paradox or irony. Such a transformation renders the object – no longer simply a poem, but a thing in the world – a site for some impossible and organic expression of relationships otherwise unparsable, indeed, inexpressible but for a feeling we may only register and describe as an experience. It is for this reason that the following, taken from Newton's seminal essay, can be repurposed as an acknowledgement of the success of Baxter's formalist 'method':

> If we wish to speak seriously about Baxter's scope, we need to grapple not just with the text but with what we might call the *paratext* – with the way in which his public persona mediates our reading, and with what that persona means and does in a cloudy arena of lived experience beyond the ambit of textualist criticism. ('Baxter Effect')

What appears to be a riposte to formalism – the naïvete of a 'textualist' reading of Baxter – might actually be its fullest elaboration; the materiality of Newton's verb 'grapple' is so appropriate here as this emphasis on the body, on experience, feeling and 'example' ('life', as Leavis would have put it) is precisely the destination of formalist 'method' if followed, as Baxter did, to its unmethodical and utterly mystified ends – that 'cloudy arena of lived experience'.

For the formalist, the body, life and experience all become the '*paratexts*' (Newton, 'Baxter Effect') of Baxter's work: these are the frames that mortify the work; they are the supplements that crucially defer and displace the poetry, becoming themselves the ideal and impossible poetry, wordless and ineffable. The great temptation for the contemporary reader, and one that Newton importantly undercuts, to read Jerusalem and its community as Baxter's finest poem is thus profoundly formalist, and one that is all too happy to exchange the question of critical appraisal for the mystified and paradoxical inducements of a spiritualised phenomenology 'in which poetry itself has been demoted to an accessory dimension' ('Baxter Effect').[7] To some degree

7 Although writing with a different objective in mind, Murray

Baxter's body politic – evident in the emergence of that figure in whom, as Newton so importantly made clear, 'writing and example' became fully, one might even say, radically, integrated – is deeply informed by his absorption of the formalist ideology, specifically, that aspect of a formalist zeal that urges writing and language towards the realm of the non-lexical – the 'language' of the body that can only be transmitted as experience, wonder, and ambiguity. Such a reading certainly makes the much neglected prose now seem all the more important, and not just as symptomatic of its time, but as evidence of an unsystematic continuity in Baxter's thoughts and beliefs. In reviewing the poetry of others Baxter was constantly reviewing himself as a maker. And in his deep exploration of this formalist ethic of disavowal he was purifying his language and preparing a persona – a body or vessel – of renunciation.[8]

Baxter may well have 'created a problem which our literary culture has not yet remotely assimilated' (Newton, 'Baxter Effect'), but his prose also reminds us of a problem the literary culture has not yet fully identified either: the ideological force of a formalism – broadly a theory of mystification – whose naturalisation via the example of Baxter has helped

Edmond in effect delivers precisely the kind of formalist eulogy Baxter's incarnational criticism calls out for on behalf of the poetry Baxter favoured and wrote. The following passage is quoted by Newton too:

> As I see it, Jerusalem was central in the sense that it moved into the place poetry had occupied for Baxter. Jerusalem was an attempt, concrete, realised, continuous, real, not art, to make a poem which would and could speak to men. In this context the Jerusalem writings and publications exist only as an adjunct to the reality. . . . [The poems] contain a great deal of *literary* dross. In fact they are finally irrelevant to Jerusalem. We could only know the poem Jerusalem had we been there. Writing about Jerusalem contradicts it. Writing about it is an act of distancing and great self-consciousness – a quality often embarrassingly obvious in the Jerusalem sonnets. (Edmond 16)

8 Alex Calder, among others, has noted the importance of the body in Baxter's poetry, which he sees as part of a 're-culturing of nature [that] took a massive design effort, involving not only words on the page and the cultivation of a public persona, but also a pronounced rhetoric of the body (17).

habituate certain strands of New Zealand literary culture to a particular way of thinking about art, literature, and criticism. With what else, one might ask, is a reader left by a method whose goal is to engender ambiguity, irony, and other effects 'too subtle for the intellect'? What remains to be considered is the extent to which this mystification of the work of criticism may even today still sanction conservative suspicions about poetry, intellectuals, and criticism.

## *Works Cited*


Arnold, Mathew. *Culture and Anarchy: An Essay in Political and Social Criticism*. London: Smith, Elder, 1906.

———. *The Portable Mathew Arnold*. Ed. Lionel Trilling. New York: The Viking Press, 1949.

Anderson, Perry. 'Components of the National Culture.' *New Left Review* 50, July–August, 1968: unpaginated.

Baldick, Chris. *Criticism and Literary Theory: 1890 to the Present*. London and New York: Longman, 1996.

Brooks, Cleanth. 'The Formalist Critics.' *Kenyon Review* 13, 1951.

———. *The Well-Wrought Urn: Studies in the Structure of Poetry*. New York: Harcourt, Brace, 1947.

Brooks, Cleanth, and Robert Penn Warren. *Understanding Poetry*. Third Edition. New York: Holt, Rinehart and Winston, 1964.

Calder, Alex. *The Settler's Plot: How Stories Take Place in New Zealand*. Auckland: Auckland University Press, 2011.

Dennison, John. '"Old Masters and Violent Moderns": Baxter, Burns, and T.S. Eliot.' *Journal of New Zealand Literature* 30, 2012.

Eagleton, Terry. *How to Read a Poem*. Malden, MA; Oxford: Blackwell Publishing, 2007.

———. *Literary Theory: An Introduction*. London: Blackwell, 1996.

Edmond, Murray. *Then It Was Now Again: Selected Critical Writing*. Pokeno: Atanui Press, 2014.

Eliot, T. S. *The Sacred Wood: Essays on Poetry and Criticism*. London: Methuen and Co. Ltd., 1920.

———. 'Ulysses, Order, and Myth.' *The Dial*. Chicago. 1923.

Leavis, F. R. Mass *Civilisation and Minority Culture*. Cambridge: Minority Press, 1933.

———. *The Common Pursuit*. Middlesex: Harmondsworth, 1978.

Newton, John. '"By Writing and Example": The Baxter Effect.' *Ka Mate Ka Ora* 1. http://www.nzepc.auckland.ac.nz/kmko/01/ka_mate01_newton.asp

———. 'So wide, can't get round it.' Review of John Weir, ed. *James K. Baxter: Complete Prose*. *NZ Books*, vol 25, #4, Issue 112, Summer 2015.

Richards, I. A. *Principles of Literary Criticism*. London: Routledge and Kegan Paul, 1967.
Sutton, Walter, and Richard Foster, eds. *Modern Criticism: Theory and Practice*. New York: Odyssey Press, 1963.
Williams, Raymond. *Culture and Society, 1780–1950*. London: Chatto & Windus, 1967.
Wimsatt, W. K. *The Verbal Icon: Studies in the Meaning of Poetry*. Kentucky: The University Press of Kentucky, 1954.

# *Invisible Boulder: Baxter Among the Nationalists*

Hugh Roberts

Baxter's relationship to the idea of a 'New Zealand literature' was a fraught and often heavily mediated one. The conventional literary historical account looks back to Baxter's influential talk on *Recent Trends in New Zealand Poetry* at the 1951 Writers' Conference in Christchurch as the moment that marks, in retrospect, Baxter's break with Curnow's 'nationalist' project and the emergence of the 'Wellington Group' of poets 'free from the schizophrenia of the New Zealander who cannot distinguish himself from his grandfather', poets who had 'grown up in entire acceptance of [their] environment, truly inhabiting the country' (1. 69).[1] In addition to Baxter himself, poets associated with the group would include Louis Johnson, Hubert Witheford, Alistair Campbell, Peter Bland, Charles Doyle, Gordon Challis, Keith Sinclair and Fleur Adcock, among others.

The 'Wellington Group' was never truly a 'school' or a tightly knit social group.[2] It would be difficult for anyone coming to their work without preconceptions to distinguish clear unifying characteristics. What united them was negative more than positive: a reaction against what they understood to be the prescriptive nationalist agenda being

1 See Elizabeth Caffin (403–06) for one such account of this.

2 Kendrick Smithyman's somewhat ironic alternative label for the group, 'the School of Johnson', in fact underlined their lack of cohesion. They were a 'School' only insofar as they were all at one time or another published or championed by Louis Johnson. See 'Wellington in the Fifties', 35.

promulgated most notably by Allen Curnow, above all in the introductions to his massively influential anthologies, the Caxton Press *A Book of New Zealand Verse 1923–45* from 1945, and, later, the 1960 *Penguin Book of New Zealand Verse*. Patrick Evans describes the somewhat febrile nature of this reaction in typically trenchant terms:

> Because [Curnow] had seemed to write about landscapes, they wrote about cities; because there seemed to be no people in his poetry, they put people in their own; because he seemed to be a nationalist, they decided that their own poetry would be internationalist . . . The Wellington poets of the Fifties . . . failed because they created an image of Curnow to oppose and had then become like that image. (166–69)

Evans usefully identifies here one of the most perplexing aspects of this controversy: the consistently shallow engagement with the actual content of Curnow's positions. It is tempting to read, say, Erik Schwimmer in Louis Johnson's *Poetry Yearbook*, writing that Hubert Witheford's poems 'are essentially more important than poems merely attempting to find national myths which nobody would think about if somebody had not made them up' (Schwimmer 1951, 67) or Baxter writing in response to the Penguin anthology that 'Curnow makes it abundantly clear in his Introduction that only one kind of substance will pass muster with him: Kiwi stuff, bush broodings, seacoast broodings, mountain broodings, by poets who still think of London as the centre of the cultural universe' (1. 598), and to conclude with Elizabeth Caffin that there is little more at work here than 'personalities and regional antagonisms' fuelled by 'generational conflict' (404).

The oedipal tone of this 'generational conflict' is nowhere more readily apparent than in Baxter's engagement with Curnow. Baxter, of course, had been Curnow's chosen son in the 1945 Caxton Press anthology, a late discovery hailed as 'a new occurrence in New Zealand . . . with qualities of youth in verse which we have lacked; yet with a feeling after tradition and a frankly confessed debt . . . to some older New Zealand poets' (54–55) One can easily see how such a claim, gratifying enough to the young poet, would have come to seem a presumptuous attempt to position Baxter as heir to and flamekeeper for Curnow's generation. Baxter himself recognised the awkward emotional entanglement underlying his feud with Curnow. In a hitherto unpublished draft for what would become his *Aspects of Poetry in New Zealand*, Baxter describes an encounter with Curnow after his talk at the 1951 Christchurch Writers' Conference:

> I remember Curnow congratulating me in a local pub when the talk was over, with a paternal warmth that both pleased and troubled me. I felt like an ungrateful Elisha to whom Elijah was trying to donate his prophet's cloak; I had to dodge the offering, even at the cost of ingratitude, because Curnow's road and mine would always be different (in my case, could only remain real by being different); and the close parallel to the difficulties of a father–son relationship can hardly be ignored. . . . Many of the newer writers, myself included, may have felt too near to Curnow for them to feel safe when treading in his footprints. It was psychologically necessary for them to follow an entirely different track. (2. 75)

It is significant that Baxter could never bring himself to publish anything so generously willing to recognise both Curnow's warm regard for him, even at a time when he was beginning to advocate a break with the concerns of the 'nationalist' generation, and his own suspicions about the oedipal motivations of the younger generation's hostility. In print, Baxter committed himself to the party line; Curnow's own poetic stature is relentlessly diminished ('it was only Curnow who experimented a lot with form, and after all [not being nasty] he did have the least to say,' he writes in 'Notes Made in Winter' in the *New Zealand Poetry Yearbook* of 1962 [1. 597]), and his critical positions reduced to almost parodic simplemindedness.

It is worth taking a moment to remind ourselves just how

distorted Baxter's characterisation of Curnow's position as a generic demand for 'Kiwi stuff' is, not least because one of the pernicious after-effects of the controversy was to distort our understanding of that position; indeed Curnow himself in the very vigour of his engagement with his critics contributed to this, making it seem that he was defending the straw men they were attacking. This distortion is somewhat exacerbated today by the increasing tendency to extend the 'settler society' or 'settler culture' label from the nineteenth century into the 1970s and 1980s (and even beyond). Jennifer Lawn, for example, characterises the Curnow generation as 'settler literary nationalists' who 'sought to develop a local poetic' and 'wallow[ed] in their own magnified sense of alienation and exile' (25) – phrases that would fit right in amid the polemical attacks of the *New Zealand Yearbook*.[3] But it is also important to clarify our understanding of Curnow, I would argue, if we want to go beyond simply dismissing Baxter's engagement with Curnow as oedipal rage and try to move towards a richer understanding of what prompted the intense and lasting passions of the 'Wellington Group' controversy. To do that, we have to understand just where Baxter and Curnow agreed and where they differed.

'Kiwi stuff' – an emphasis on locally distinctive content – was never central to Curnow's project. Indeed, he explicitly deprecates 'harping on what is native, indigenous, insular' in his preface to the 1960 Penguin anthology (Kindle loc. 2938). That had been, for Curnow, the hallmark of the shallow New Zealandism of the *Kowhai Gold* poets and their 'honest striving after indigenous effect, words like kowhai and rata and tui being new toys' ('Introduction' 24). It is remarkable, in fact, how consistent he is on this point. In 'Poets in New Zealand', a decade before his 1945 anthology, he insisted that 'the production of good poetry cannot be assisted by

3 See, for another example, Matthew Bannister, who similarly identifies Curnow as part of New Zealand's 'settler culture', and who suggests that 'local writers and critics such as Allen Curnow saw replacing overseas theory with local "reality" as a central aim of New Zealand art' (np).

the "national literature" sentiment' (*Look Back*, Kindle loc. 509) and in a 1941 essay praising R. A. K. Mason as a model for a 'native poet' he is emphatic that 'one must blot out the notion that New Zealand is a place which it is curiously vital for poets to write about' (loc. 940). Mason's poetry, he says, 'is almost entirely lacking in explicit reference to the New Zealand scene and people' (loc. 865).

'The real question,' Curnow says in his Introduction to the 1945 anthology, 'is not what [New Zealand poets] were to write *about*, but whom they were to write *for*' (17). He is, again, consistent on this point: the same question had animated his 1937 essay on 'Poets in New Zealand': 'For whom are the New Zealand poets writing? That is a question very seldom asked' (loc. 537). The 'alienation and exile' that haunts Curnow's poetry and which he discerns in the writing of his peers is not, *pace* Lawn et al., a condition he sees as that of the New Zealander in general vis-à-vis England or world civilisation, but of the writer in relationship to society. When he writes of Mason and Cresswell adopting the stance of 'solitary mourner[s] and legatee[s] of all that greatness [of the English poetic tradition]' he describes it as a 'braver absurdity', not as a simple acknowledgement of reality. The crucial fact that this 'absurd' position addresses is the poet's isolation from a local 'tradition': 'belonging to a new kind of country where the tradition had no deep root in actual scene and people; to which the tradition could give little because there was yet no life of spirit to receive it' ('Introduction' 28).

One should not overstate this point. It is clear, as the reference to the 'actual scene' in the last quotation indicates, that for Curnow the path towards forging a relationship between the poet and the wider social context would frequently entail some direct engagement with New Zealand's landscape and people. He remarks in the 1945 Introduction, for example, on how frequently the poems in the anthology are devoted to 'sea-coast stuff. The islands are not content within themselves; their coasts are crowded with images of arrival and departure' (45). But it is an important corrective to the prevailing account to recognise that this kind of indigeneity was secondary to Curnow's principal concern: the relationship between 'the New Zealand poet' and 'the common understanding'; the absurdity of believing that a 'splendid talent' could 'burst some day out of emptiness, as if poets required no audience, or as if the kind of audience did not matter. "Nothing will come of nothing"' (44). It is this concern that underlies Curnow's understanding of the New Zealand poet as necessarily a 'prophet to his people', the figure who must occupy the 'absurd' space of a shared cultural framework which has not yet been forged (22). For Curnow, the goal of this 'prophetic' poetry was to bring about a future where New Zealand poets would no longer feel their relationship to their country as a 'problem' that needed to be explored:

> The good poem is something we may in time come to recognise New Zealand by, not something in which we need expect to recognise obvious traces of the New Zealand we know. Local reference ought never to decide our estimate of a poem's worth. (22)

It is on this idea of the poet as 'prophet' that we can usefully begin to think through Baxter's relationship to Curnow's position. Baxter had famously argued that 'every poet should be a prophet according to his lights' in his 1951 *Recent Trends in New Zealand Poetry* lecture, adding, even more famously, in an unacknowledged borrowing from Eric Gill,[4] that the poet 'should remain as a cell of good living in a corrupt society' (1. 75). We should not be surprised, then, by Curnow's positive reaction to the talk, even if it did make gestures toward the emergence of a 'new' post-nationalist poetics. But more than just sharing the idea of the poet as 'prophet' with Curnow, Baxter shared the sense that this 'prophetic' relationship to the poet's community was born of profound alienation. If there is one consistent, recurrent

4 See Gill 282.

theme in Baxter's prose from his earliest writings to his last it is a troubled and anxious meditation on the Curnovian problem of 'audience', of who it is he is writing 'for'. The only occasions on which he insists that this is not a problem are when he is mocking Curnow for the same concern.

This is, for Baxter as for Curnow, a peculiarly New Zealand problem. We can see him wrestling with it as early as 1954, in *The Fire and the Anvil*, where Baxter admiringly quotes from George Barker's 'Channel Crossing' and adds:

> Barker avails himself of a privilege which history has denied as yet to the New Zealand poet. He is able to refer to a Britain which is more than a geographical unit or a social structure built up by historical accident and the demands of commerce – rather a complex spiritual identity of people, time, and place, which his audience in some measure share. . . . Where the texture of community life is sufficiently rich and complex, not only in idea but in fact, the poet can say *We* without surrendering his vision to the dead grip of a constricting stereotype. . . . Why (one may ask) cannot a New Zealand poet say *We* as readily as *I*? . . . Not until a poet, walking up Queen Street or down Lambton Quay, can feel part of a complex spiritual identity as Catullus did in Rome, Baudelaire in Paris, George Barker in London, can [the 'real history of the country, its legend'] . . . live. (1. 178)

The problem remains unresolved in 1965 when, introducing his selection of poems in Charles Doyle's anthology *Poetry in New Zealand*, Baxter laments that 'Our people do not seem . . . to regard local places or events as a focus for legend. . . . One lacks an audience because the audience lacks certain interior facilities that other races have regarded as part of the normal human equipment' (1. 748). And again, at an arts festival in Palmerston North in 1966, he writes:

> There are always moments in history when an artist can reach out towards his country, towards his own people, and feel an answer, a response . . . It is the secret hope of every artist to

> experience a moment of this kind. I cannot think it is likely to happen to any New Zealand artist . . . (2. 21)

The idea took on a particularly powerful resonance for Baxter as he developed as a playwright. Drama is a more self-evidently social and communal form than poetry, and Baxter saw New Zealand drama as consequently uniquely promising but by the same token uniquely challenged in forging a relationship between writer and audience. In a letter to the editor of the *New Zealand Listener* in 1967 he writes:

> I have long been bitterly concerned with the communal and cultural barrenness of the country where I was born, grew up, and where I will be buried. To make New Zealand plays is one way of bringing a moribund community to life. (2. 475)

And still, in his Jerusalem period, in a 1969 interview with Arthur Baysting, also published in the *Listener*, he makes clear his conception of the playwright as the 'prophet' of a not-yet realised cultural world:

> You can't put on a play with much meat in it without the audience finding in it meaningful patches. . . . This is their . . . education. They catch up with the playwright . . . In the kind of country we have, you're dealing with hideously uneducated people – I mean on the emotional level. A sort of frustrated expatriate Englishman who doesn't know who he is and whose fantasies are chiefly of rugby, football or violence. (3. 21)

I have quoted from such a range of works across the broad sweep of Baxter's writing career because it is essential to understand just how central to his conception of the writer's role was this simultaneous desire for community and certainty that he was doomed to be an outsider.

The role of the poet as outsider 'prophet' was not the only point of similarity between Baxter and Curnow, either. It is curious, and must have been deeply frustrating to Curnow, to read Baxter – the champion of the 'internationalist' Wellington Group – describing the New Zealander as a 'frustrated expatriate Englishman who doesn't know who he is'. If Erik Schwimmer could confidently claim that Curnow's nationalist 'myth' was a thing of the past because '[t]he consciousness of the internationalisation of culture is too vivid in New Zealanders who are vulnerable in the extreme to all political and economic developments abroad' (65), Baxter, in fact, remained profoundly troubled by New Zealanders' lack of a clear national identity. It is, again, only when directly attacking Curnow that Baxter will maintain otherwise, that 'the sense of urgency about having been born a New Zealander seems to have gone for good' ('The Kiwi and Mr. Curnow', 1. 441). One of the most striking features of Baxter's critical writing is that within a few paragraphs – sometimes even sentences – of a boldly 'internationalist' sally against Curnow he can turn, as soon as his mind is no longer preoccupied with Curnow himself, to themes that come directly from the Curnovian playbook. Thus in *Aspects of Poetry in New Zealand* (1967), within two pages of declaring triumphantly, à propos a poem of Smithyman's, '[a] poem like this makes me wonder what our exponents of colonial inferiority are talking about' (2. 350), we find him praising the poetry of F. M. McKay for making us 'aware of a permanent substratum of our local experience: the sense that home is never entirely home, that man is an exile from himself' (2. 353).[5]

In this context, Baxter's crudely reductive caricatures of Curnow's critical positions cannot, I would argue, be seen simply as misunderstandings or misreadings. It is not simply that Baxter gets Curnow wrong, it is that he constructs an anti-Curnovian persona whose arguments cannot be reconciled with the positions he adopts when he is not taking up the cudgels against Curnow. When Baxter sums up Curnow's position, as he does again and again, as a series of flimsy straw men – that he's looking for 'Kiwi stuff', that

5 It's worth noting that only a few pages earlier Baxter mentions the fact that New Zealanders visiting Britain still refer to it as going 'back Home' even if they've never been there before (2. 335).

he had developed a 'private mythology in which mountains symbolised many things and some ancestral voyage had been made and New Zealanders were very lonely people on the outskirts of the circus tent of the human family' (1. 441), that Curnow crudely insisted that Mason's poetry '*must* be based on a predicament supposedly peculiar to New Zealanders and universal among them' (2. 72) and so forth – we must ask ourselves what it was in Curnow's actual arguments that Baxter felt either unwilling to engage with or that he needed actively to repress.

To answer this question we must begin by looking more deeply at what Baxter has to say about his relationship to New Zealand when he is not taking up this quarrel with Curnow. We have seen enough already, I think, to recognise that Patrick Evans's claim that 'Baxter had no interest in what Curnow had called "that second unlicked self my country"' (168) is simply unsustainable. But what is most striking is how persistently not only the 'colonial' anxieties of the nationalist poets appear in Baxter's writings, but how often Baxter's response to those anxieties is to appeal to the kind of 'Kiwi stuff' he had falsely claimed to be central to Curnow's project.

There's a story Baxter tells in slightly different forms on several occasions, about his parents travelling in England and being asked in a railway carriage where they're from:

> 'From New Zealand,' they replied.
>
> 'Oh,' said the Englishman. They spent the rest of the journey in silence. This kind of ordeal can be nerve-shattering. I have seen several New Zealand writers come back from overseas, their confidence shrunk to a dried bean, glancing nervously over their shoulders, afraid to set pen to paper in case they betray their colonial rawness. Myself, I think the best answer is a gigantic belly laugh. (*Aspects of Poetry in New Zealand*, 2. 334)

Ostensibly, Baxter offers this story to exemplify a cultural dilemma – specifically Curnow's – which his 'internationalist' generation can treat with the contempt it deserves. But when he goes on to say, defensively, that he 'prefer[s] the dark country [he] was born in' and that the 'literary advantage' of a 'small country' is that '[w]hat one writes can be more readily understood', one feels just how much that 'belly laugh' is whistling past the graveyard. New Zealand is a 'small,' 'dark' country compared to England, and we've seen that he is far from believing that his fellow citizens 'understand' what he writes.

Anxiety about New Zealand's cultural position relative to England goes back to Baxter's childhood. In 'Beginnings', an autobiographical sketch published in *Landfall* in 1965, he writes that:

> The sense of a gap between myself and other people was increased considerably by the fact that I was born in New Zealand, and grew up there till I was nine, and then attended an English boarding school for a couple of years, and came back to New Zealand at thirteen, in the first flush of puberty, quite out of touch with my childhood companions and uncertain whether I was an Englishman or a New Zealander. (1. 726)

That the four-year gap between 'nine' and 'thirteen' becomes a 'couple of years' is perhaps one index that this experience remains foundationally unsettling to Baxter. More direct evidence can be found in an unpublished talk from 1967 titled 'Thoughts of an Old Alligator':

> Twenty years ago or more, I said to myself – 'Well, mate, what are you going to be? Some kind of cosmopolitan? Or a colonial Englishman, haunting the libraries and colleges overseas? Or just a Pig Islander?' (2. 313)

The options here are very revealing. Once again, New Zealand's relative 'darkness' is uppermost in Baxter's mind. To commit to this country is to commit to a certain reduced cultural horizon, to be 'just' a Pig Islander. This is that same 'braver absurdity' that Curnow praised in Mason and Cresswell:

> The English tradition, and the classics that came with it, was all the poetry they knew. English was their language. But from England itself they were separated, belonging to a new kind of country where the tradition had no deep root in actual scene and people; to which the tradition could give little because there was yet no life of spirit to receive it. ('Introduction', 28)

Baxter's 'colonial Englishman' is the figure that Curnow describes as having 'tried to settle the problem by denying . . . the reality of their own living, fancying that thus they were affirming the tradition; as if children should pluck flowers, arrange them on a doorstep, and call it a garden' (29).

Like Curnow, Baxter identifies the 'disadvantage' of this commitment to New Zealand as the artist's isolation from the community: 'At times a New Zealand artist will feel like a penguin exposed (without feathers) on the Antarctic ice-cap . . . very few of his countrymen give a damn whether he produces works of art or not' (2. 313), but unlike Curnow – though like Baxter's caricatured version of him – he posits an intimate spiritual union with the New Zealand landscape and towns – 'Kiwi stuff' – as one of the 'advantages':

> As I get older, the voices of this country within my mind tend to become clearer – the voices of the rivers which flow not only outside me but also inside me – the Clutha, the Rakaia, the Wanganui, the Manawatu – or that small stream in Southland called the Oreti. . . . And then there are the towns, each with their separate voice – the places that have become part of me, because of the people in them whom I have loved . . . the living and also the dead . . . (2. 313)

The movement from the naked penguin to the poet ensconced in and speaking for the towns and rivers of New Zealand leaves the reader a little breathless, but these whiplash turns are characteristic of Baxter's approach to the topic. In *The Fire and the Anvil* (1954) he moves from a trenchant attack on Curnow's 'myth of insular isolation' (1. 181) framed in typical 'internationalist' terms ('[a]t the present time our problems may not differ greatly from those of life and literature in England or America' [1. 182]) to – just a page later – a meditation on the 'settler walking into the fern out of sight of his steading' who 'felt a sudden panic descend, as if the bush were more than so much timber' and in that moment 'felt . . . his European cultural mask torn away' (1. 183). A few pages further on, and Baxter is enumerating the key symbols of New Zealand poetry: 'The Sea . . . The Mountains . . . The Bush . . . The Beach . . . The Island' (2. 190). When he writes that the symbol of the beach is used by 'almost every New Zealand poet . . . at some time or other' and gives as an example Keith Sinclair's 'beach' which 'fends off the wild-tongued sea . . . from our bright crumbling enclosure' (1. 189) he would seem to be hewing closely to Curnow's 1945 Introduction and its reflection upon the dominance of 'sea-coast stuff' in the selected poems and the concomitant significance of New Zealand's 'insular' nature. Finally, we would seem to have returned fully to the Curnovian paradigm when Baxter asserts that the 'dominant symbol' in New Zealand poetry is '*Man Alone* . . . aware of acute isolation from every social aim' (2. 190). When, a little later, Baxter seems to remember his supposedly anti-Curnovian position and asserts '[v]ery likely the symbol of *Man Alone* does not, in fact, reflect a morbid state of isolation from the European cultural tradition' (1. 192) it serves only to underscore how unstable and self-contradictory his position is.

Perhaps nowhere does Baxter embrace the position he elsewhere imputes to Curnow more thoroughly than in the text he wrote in 1961 – in the midst of the bitter back-and-forth over Curnow's 1960 Penguin anthology – for a coffee-table book of New Zealand landscape photographs. Making the 'myth of insular isolation' entirely his own, he tells us that New Zealanders suffer from 'islomania':

> The mere fact of being on a small piece of land surrounded by water fills them with a lasting exhilaration. Any New Zealander, whether one by birth or by adoption, who cuts the

> navel-cord that binds him to England or Europe, and lives his life through on the terms that these islands dictate to him, is probably . . . an 'islomane'. (1. 485)

But, again, the 'exhilaration' is matched by a profound anxiety:

> Alongside the human City, indifferent or even hostile, remains the Wilderness, whose time is still that of the sixth day of creation and whose works belong to the Power that created her. . . . At the fringes of the human domain, where the City encounters the Wilderness, artists are able to discover those forms which become the treasures of their race, and the real knowledge which liberates the intellect . . . (1. 486)

The wilderness – a 'Wilderness of lonely coast or mountains' – as simultaneous threat and challenge to the 'isolated', 'insular' artist who cuts his ties to the rich English or European tradition in order to discover the new, local 'forms which become the treasures of their race': here is everything that Baxter professed to despise in Curnow's 'empty land' myth. And, as we have seen, this is, as we may say, 'more Curnow than Curnow', whose own positions were considerably more complex.

How, then, are we to make sense of this radically self-contradictory set of positions? Is there more at work here than a simple hypocrisy in service of an oedipal resentment against a would-be father figure? I think there is, and I think we can begin to understand what that is by looking at another Curnovian echo in Baxter's writing. In a late piece published in the *New Zealand Listener* titled 'In My View' (1969), Baxter writes that '[t]he Kiwi is indeed a stranger in paradise' (3. 47). He quotes the New Zealand mountaineer Paul Powell reporting the feeling 'that one day these mountains might be my judges' and continues:

> I think the judgment is not to be found in the future. It is always present. Mountaineers and prospectors are in a sense our experiential theologians, solitary Adams . . . relearning

the nature of the Fall by gazing at the beautiful forbidden face of the earthly paradise, which we can indeed enter, but never possess, because we are alienated from it and from ourselves. (3. 47)

A very similar pattern of thought can be found in Curnow's 1945 Introduction. Curnow offers us the following quotation from Matthew Arnold's 'The Function of Criticism at the Present Time' as an epigraph to the section of his argument that makes the crucial pivot from 'what they were to write *about*' to 'whom they were to write *for*':

> That promised land it will not be ours to enter, and we shall die in the wilderness: but to have desired to enter it, to have saluted it from afar, is already, perhaps, the best distinction among contemporaries; it will certainly be the best title to esteem with posterity. (15)

Arnold, of course, is alluding to Moses's so-called 'Pisgah View' of the promised land to which he would successfully lead his followers, but which he himself would never enter. It is significant that Curnow tells us it is a 'refugee' who framed that question of 'for' versus 'about' for Curnow, and that Curnow draws parallels between New Zealand writers and those perennial refugees, the Irish and the Poles.[6] This is the condition being diagnosed in Curnow's most widely anthologised poem, 'The Skeleton of the Great Moa in the Canterbury Museum, Christchurch':

> Not I, some child, born in a marvellous year,
> Will learn the trick of standing upright here. (13–14)

We are struck by the similarity of Baxter's and Curnow's positions here, but it is equally important to register the differences. Curnow references pre-Christian as well as contemporary political models as parallels to the New Zealand writer's state. The 'promised land' is not 'paradise'; it is an earthly territory uniquely – even divinely – suited

6 See, for example, 22–23, 25–26.

to a particular people. 'Paradise', on the other hand, is less a territory than a state of being, one from which we are not merely 'exiled' but 'fallen'. Baxter's passage rests heavily on the Christian concept of Original Sin, an inherent flaw fully remediable only in the afterlife and only by God's grace. Curnow, then, offers us an essentially comic vision of the New Zealand writer's relationship to the land. We may not, like Moses, live to see the happy ending, the future marriage of writer to nation, but it is conceptually, if not actually, available. No drastic epistemic or anagogic rupture stands between us and that 'marvellous' denouement. Baxter's vision, by contrast, at least in its relationship to any imaginable temporal resolution, is tragic. Our fatal flaw is always at work: we have found paradise, but we know we're unworthy of it, 'the earthly paradise, which we can indeed enter, but never possess'.

It is this theological dilemma which, I believe, helps us to understand Baxter's fluctuating and contradictory relationship both to New Zealand and to the New Zealand 'nationalist' poets. It also helps us to understand much that can seem confounding in Baxter's stance as a poet and as a social critic. The problem presented by Curnow – at some level unnameable, explicitly, by Baxter – was his comic premise. If both Baxter and Curnow frame the artist as outsider – 'a tribesman left over from the dissolution of the tribes' (2. 131) as Baxter puts it in *The Man on the Horse* – Curnow's error, from Baxter's perspective, was to imagine that a new tribe might one day be reconstituted. There is a telling moment when Baxter praises Frank Sargeson for 'not, like Shakespeare, hold[ing] up a mirror to fallen nature – but to fallen nature which has forgotten its fall' ('Back to the Desert' [1954], 1. 225). Reminding us of our fallen nature: this, surely, is the leitmotif of Baxter's prose writings. It is central to his attacks on New Zealand's 'puritanism' and priggishness, his constant empathy for the outcast and the downtrodden, his insistence upon humility and his profound suspicion of the smug self-satisfaction of the Harry Fats of this world. But when it comes to situating himself in relationship to New Zealand, it was a mission that could leave him no satisfactory or stable position from which to speak.

The closer Baxter knits himself to New Zealand, whether as the voice of its people or the voice of the land, the more he must remind himself that he is unworthy of that role, that the land 'judges' him and finds him wanting. But to turn his back on New Zealand, to adopt the 'internationalist' stance of the 'tribeless' cosmopolitan, is to alienate himself from the divine. It is not hard to see why Baxter could feel profoundly attracted to entirely opposite positions. The more-Curnow-than-Curnow Baxter who feels the voices of New Zealand's rivers flowing inside him is one who feels the presence of the divine. The 'internationalist' Baxter who can dismiss 'Kiwi stuff' as irrelevant to a universal participation in world literature is one freed of the crushing sense of his unworthiness to occupy the former position. One begins to recognise that Curnow's ironic poetic counterblast to the 'internationalists' was very specifically diagnosing Baxter's dilemma:

> To forget self and all, forget foremost
> This whimpering second unlicked self my country,
> . . .
> Why that'd be freedom heydey, hey
> For freedom that'd be the day
> And as good a dream as any to be damned for. ('To Forget Self and All')

Another way to think about this is that Baxter is fundamentally a satirist, and that his satire is rooted in his tragic perception of New Zealand's fallen state. It is interesting to note that Curnow is largely unsympathetic to the satiric mode, even though the 'prophetic' relationship he sketches between poet and society would seem conducive to it. He notes, for example, Glover's and Fairburn's frequently satiric vein but frames it as a weakness that gives 'what might have been a good poem the air of a nervous joke'

('Introduction' 38–39). From the comic perspective, satire – which, as Friedrich Schiller argues, is rooted in the perception of the gap between the 'ideal' and the 'real' – must be understood as a step toward an ultimate closing of that gap (196), and therefore as merely instrumental. For the tragic satirist, like Baxter, the work of satire is to 'remind us of our fallen condition'; the gap between real and ideal that it seeks to have us understand is not closable – our only hope is that the real will, in the end, yield to and be replaced by the ideal. The more Baxter loves and identifies with New Zealand, the more urgently he must chastise it – and himself as a representative of it – for its irremediable failure to be what it should and cannot be.

It is tempting, and to at least some extent correct, to identify New Zealand's 'fallen' condition as integrally related to its history of colonial usurpation. Certainly for the later Baxter, this was the indelible 'original sin' ('this wholly unjust desecration and seizure of the lands of another race' ['The Capital Graveyard' (1970), 3. 183]) which pākehā New Zealanders could attempt to mitigate, but never wholly expiate:

> The difference between the Maori and pakeha cultures is the difference between a community of neighbours and a society of strangers. . . . The Maori is indeed the elder brother and the pakeha the younger brother. But the teina has refused to learn from the tuakana. He has sat sullenly among his machines and studied his account books, and wondered why his soul was full of bitter dust; or else he has got up and hacked the body of his Mother – the earth we tread on – to pieces for the sake of money. If I write angrily, it is because of grief . . . I think we may already have destroyed what should have been our future. ('In My View' [1968], 3. 13–14)

There is, no doubt, a touch of the Rousseauist 'noble savage' in Baxter's view of the Māori: '[t]he only free people I have ever seen are in the Maori pas,' he tells us in *A Walking Stick for an Old Man* ([1972], 3. 502). It's instructive to compare Curnow's 'Landfall in Unknown Seas' (1943) and its reference to 'The stain of blood that writes an island story'; Curnow is no less aware of the long history of bloody conflict that the colonial era unleashed, but he does not make that conflict into a moral combat between good and evil, innocent and fallen: 'Always to islanders danger / Is what comes over the sea.' But there is also no doubt that Baxter's anger at the depredations of pākehā New Zealanders was real, and powerful: 'Until they shovel the sods over me, my anger will never die, on behalf of those who are having the Maoritanga squeezed out of them drop by drop, as a man squeezes a lemon. . . . So far "integration" has meant a ruthless and inexorable assimilation' (3. 502).

But Baxter's simultaneous love for and rage at New Zealand predates the clear crystallisation of his views on Māori/pākehā relations. The peculiar, unstable mixture of devotion and denunciation is the hallmark of what I called, above, the leitmotif of Baxter's writing, reminding us of our fallen nature:

> When I consider our immediate environment in this place . . . I would like very much to feel a sense of joy and identification – This is my land; these are my people: here I have chosen to live and die . . . But it is not like that at all; or hardly at all. If I appear to stoop even when standing upright, like a man carrying an invisible boulder on his back, it is because I know and ceased to love my country, to curse her and wrestle with her, in the hope that she might wake up a little from a sleep that seems almost to be death (unpublished draft of 'Shots Around the Target' [1966], 2. 14).

New Zealand's colonial history was one ready source of material both for angry denunciation and for the agonised sense of what could have been: 'a chance to become in some measure white Polynesians' (3. 13). But there were other sources, too: New Zealand's 'puritanism', its worship of the almighty dollar, its suburban small-mindedness. What remains, and reveals itself as foundational of Baxter's understanding of his poetic role, simultaneously tragic and satiric, is the desire to be loved by a community who will, in the name of and through that love, both hear and understand him when he tells them exactly how and why they are unworthy of the love which prompts him to speak.

If we began with an apparent paradox – Baxter's profoundly contradictory stances towards Curnow and the 'nationalist' school – we end, I hope, with the recognition that this was a paradox Baxter could not resolve without erasing the very grounds from which his writing, prose and poetry, sprang. In 'Shots Around the Target,' a talk given at an arts festival in Palmerston North in 1966, Baxter gave us perhaps the most revealing statement of this dilemma: 'Metaphorically I tend to think of my own poems as semen deposited by me in the sad barren belly of this society. She is determined to bear no children – that is, she won't allow any living acts or thoughts to survive inside her' (2. 32). The metaphor is one that sits uncomfortably on more than one knife-edge; there is 'love' here, of a sort, but it feels uncomfortably close to rape. There is a procreative desire, but coupled with a recognition of its absolute futility (she is 'barren'). This is Baxter's 'invisible boulder' and it is one he cannot carry comfortably or discard:

> I feel like giving her the go-by. But deep in the marrow of my bones I still have an agonised despairing affection – all the stronger because it hurts so much – for this poor old maltreated bitch, this graveyard among the nations. . . . I want to say – 'You could be beautiful' – or else 'There's still time to learn something from the Maoris' – but she is too busy counting her money to listen and I find myself talking to myself. (2. 32)

## *Works Cited*

Bannister, Matthew. 'Kiwi Blokes: Recontextualising White New Zealand Masculinities.' *Genders* 42 (2005). 10 October 2016. <http://researcharchive.wintec.ac.nz/217/1/kiwi_blokes.pdf>.

Caffin, Elizabeth. 'Poetry 1945–90.' In: *The Oxford History of New Zealand Literature in English*. Ed. Terry Sturm. Auckland: Oxford University Press, 1991. 385–445.

Curnow, Allen. 'Introduction.' In: *A Book of New Zealand Verse 1923–45*. Ed. Allen Curnow. Christchurch: Caxton Press, 1945. 13–55.

– . *Look Back Harder: Critical Writings 1935–1984*. Kindle ed. Ed. Peter Simpson. Auckland: Auckland University Press, 1987.

Evans, Patrick. *The Penguin History of New Zealand Literature*. Auckland: Penguin Books, 1990.

Gill, Eric. *Autobiography*. London: Jonathan Cape, 1940.

Lawn, Jennifer. *Neoliberalism and Cultural Transition in New Zealand Literature, 1984–2008: Market Fictions*. Lanham: Lexington Books, 2016.

Schiller, Friedrich. 'On Naive and Sentimental Poetry.' In: *German Aesthetic and Literary Criticism: Winckelmann, Lessing, Hamann, Herder, Schiller, Goethe*. Ed. H. B. Nisbet. Cambridge: Cambridge University Press, 1985. 177–232.

Schwimmer, Erik. 'Commentary.' In: *New Zealand Poetry Yearbook One*. Ed. Louis Johnson. Wellington: A. H. and A. W Reed, 1951. 65–70.

Smithyman, Kendrick. 'Wellington and the Fifties: The True Voice of Feeling.' In: *Essays on New Zealand Literature*. Ed. Wystan Curnow. Auckland: Heinemann Books, 1973. 29–42.

# *That 'austere anti-aesthetic angel': James K. Baxter and Puritanism*

Kirstine Moffat

It is necessary to begin with an apology to James K. Baxter. In my previous musings on the Puritan legacy in New Zealand I have chastised Baxter, along with other writers and critics of his generation, for using Puritanism as a reductive catchphrase to summarise all that they most despise about New Zealand society (Moffat, 'Destruction'). The phrase that I have repeatedly used to epitomise Baxter's perceived antagonism is his description of Puritanism as an 'austere anti-aesthetic angel' (*Complete Prose* 2. 328). Returning to this phrase as I meditate at much greater length on Baxter's relationship with Puritanism, I realise that I am guilty of flattening and simplifying what is a much more complex engagement with Puritanism in his prose writing. Baxter's phrase contains both condemnation and implied praise. He was vehemently opposed to what he regarded as the Puritan suspicion of imagination and sexuality, and throughout his writing castigated all the social and religious forces that sought to curb and quell aestheticism and the natural, instinctual self. Yet, he also refers to Puritanism as 'austere', a quality that much of his writing and his own life choices suggest he regarded as admirable, particularly as it relates to a paring back and relinquishing of the unnecessary paraphernalia of capitalism and materialism. And what to make of 'angel'? Surely this is more than simply alliterative effect. It too undercuts the antagonism of 'anti-aesthetic' to suggest that in Baxter's eyes there is at least a trace of the divine about Puritanism and its legacy.

Ambiguity and complexity are the hallmarks of Baxter's engagement with Puritanism in his prose writing. My discussion begins with a consideration of 'Puritanism' as a word that has been loaded with ambivalence from its coining in the sixteenth century. I then turn to the more simplistic ways in which New Zealand authors, critics and social historians have used the term. This forms a necessary contextual backdrop for the succeeding analysis of Baxter and Puritanism, which begins with the autobiographical essays in which he reflects on the formative influences that shaped him as a man and as a writer, progresses to his nuanced writings on human duality and his preference for Catholic mercy over Protestant castigation of the sinner, and ends with his rebuke of both church and state, through which he emerges as a prophetic figure reminiscent of a fiery Puritan preacher.

### *'The very plague of the Church and the Commonwealth': The Anti-Puritan Tradition*

'Puritan' and 'Puritanism' are hotly contested terms that have generated much debate between religious scholars and historians. It is not my intention to delve into the minutiae of these disputes, but to point to the key ways in which what Patrick Collinson calls 'the P word' (41) was used in the early modern period and, more particularly, in the New Zealand context.

The first printed use of the term 'Puritan' was in the 1572 *An Admonition to Parliament*, which declared that 'we in England are so far off from having a church rightly reformed according to the prescript of God's Word, that as yet we are not come to the outward face of the same'. The 'outward marks whereby a true Christian church is known' were identified as 'preaching of the Word purely, ministering of the sacraments sincerely, and ecclesiastical discipline which consisteth in admonition and correction of faults severely'. The anonymous authors of what Collinson describes as a 'public polemic in the guise of an address to Parliament' (118) embrace the term 'Puritan', turning what was coined as a derogatory description of Reformed Protestant extremism into a badge of honour.[1]

*An Admonition to Parliament* points to the way in which Puritan became 'the brand name for a certain kind of Protestant religiosity, social conduct and politics', linking the various English and Scottish denominations, influenced by the theology of Martin Luther and John Calvin, who called for the Church to be purified of Catholic hierarchies, ritual and ornamentation (Collinson 27). From its inception, those who identified themselves as Puritan were strongly non-conformist, seeking to reform both church and state into a godly Commonwealth and unafraid to speak out against a range of theological and social issues, from the wearing of liturgical vestments, to the need for parliamentary reform, to the evils of adultery and fornication.

John Coffey and Paul C. H. Lim highlight that from the late sixteenth century 'Puritan' was also used as a 'term of abuse', a 'handy smear word for bishops angered by clerical nonconformity, metropolitan playwrights provoked by censorious moralism, and villagers driven to distraction by assaults on traditional festive culture' (1). John Whitgift, the future Archbishop of Canterbury, derided that

> his name Puritane is very aptely giuen to these men, not because they be pure no more than were the Heretikes called Cathari, but because they think them selues to be *mundiores ceteris*, more pure than others, as Cathari dyd, and separate them selues from all other Churches and congregations as spotted and defiled. (18)

In 1605 Oliver Ormerod promised that his *Picture of a Puritane* would promote a 'full detestation of the Puritan-faction' through its exposé of the Puritans' 'Perseuerance in Schism' and 'disdaine to be ruled' (in Sasek 238–54). Two years later John Sprint railed against Puritanism as

1 For a history of the pejorative use of 'Puritan' see Holden.

promoting 'a schismatically, private, and prepared spirit to any headlesse error or brain-sicke heresie' (*Propositions, Tending to Proove the Necessarie Use of the Christian Sabbaoth or Lords Day*, 1607, quoted in Poole, *Radical Religion* 188). James I went as far as describing the Puritans as 'verie pestes in the Church and Commonwealth' of Scotland in his 1599 *Basilikon Doron* (49), a claim that he returned to in his later critique of the English Puritans whom he regarded as 'the very plague of the Church and the Commonwealth' ('A Puritane Set Forth in his Lively Colours', 1642, quoted in Poole, 'Dissecting Sectarianism' 45). For William Shakespeare 'Puritan' was a fitting epithet for the lugubrious Malvolio in *Twelfth Night* (2. 3. 140).

This revulsion against Puritanism continued well into the twentieth century, with historians and authors from the eighteenth century onwards focusing more on a perceived anti-pleasure Puritan repressiveness than on theological radicalism. Lord Macaulay, the nineteenth-century British historian, claimed that '[t]he Puritan hated bear-baiting, not because it gave pain to the bear, but because it gave pleasure to the spectators' (Macaulay 1. 168). Even more famous is H. L. Mencken's and George Jean Nathan's assessment that 'Puritanism is the haunting fear that someone, somewhere, may be happy' (39). Other often-cited definitions include G. K. Chesterton's definition of 'the essential of the Puritan mood' as 'having righteous indignation about the wrong thing' (564), Oscar Wilde's quip that 'No son of mine should ever take the side of the Puritans: that is always an error' (153), and D. H. Lawrence's claim that 'To the Puritan all things are impure' (10).

New Zealand social historians, literary critics and writers are particularly fond of this glib shorthand. 'Anguished self-flagellation,' scoffs Gordon McLauchlan (*Passionless People* 17). 'Misplaced demands and guilts,' complains Robert Chapman (98). 'A contempt for love, a sour spit, a denial of life itself,' protests Bill Pearson (225). These responses are linked by their perception of Puritanism as the source of all that is damaging to the psyche: guilt; repression; gloom; self-righteousness. The New Zealand critical revulsion against Puritanism mirrors the twentieth century attack on Calvinism by Scottish authors and critics. Poet Edmund Muir captures these sentiments, writing that 'Calvinism was . . . a religion which outraged the imagination' and 'helped to produce that captivity of imagination in Scotland . . . What Knox really did was to rob Scotland of all the benefits of the Renaissance' (308–09).

This vilification is one-dimensional and misleading, signalling a failure to grasp that Puritanism is a complex phenomenon consisting of antithetical elements. The American historian Charles A. Beard acknowledges that at times Puritanism is a synonym for 'harsh restraint . . . sour faced fanaticism . . . tyranny . . . intolerance . . . stinginess'. However, he argues that it also advocates 'equal rights . . . liberty . . . democracy . . . resistance to tyranny . . . self-government . . . industry' (16). This dichotomy is evident in the women's suffrage campaign in New Zealand. Patricia Grimshaw (ix) and Alan Grimes (8) have pointed to the 'Puritan' origins of the movement in New Zealand, America and Australia. Emerging from the prohibition campaign, the New Zealand woman's movement was committed to both moral improvement and a radical overhaul of government policy to give all women, Māori and pākehā the vote (Macdonald; Lovell-Smith). H. R. Trevor-Roper writes that '[e]very age has its own social context, its own climate, and takes it for granted. . . . To neglect it to use terms like "rational", "superstitious", "progressive", "reactionary", as if only that was rational which obeyed our rules of reason, only that progression which pointed us – is worse than wrong: it is vulgar' (15–16). This kind of vulgarity has dogged the history of Puritanism, particularly in New Zealand where, since Jane Mander diagnosed the New Zealand 'disease' as Puritanism in her 1920 novel *The Story of a New Zealand River* (27), historians, literary critics, and creative writers (particularly the cultural nationalists of the

1940s–70s) have seized on the term as a convenient cover-all for everything they detest about New Zealand society and have ignored the positive aspects of its legacy.

Frank Sargeson's declaration in a 1950 broadcast that 'what is pervadingly characteristic of New Zealand is its own particular variety of puritanism' (60) struck a chord with social historians, popular polemical writers and literary critics. Keith Sinclair insists that the 'moral attitudes of [New Zealand] society were moulded, perhaps more decisively than in Australia or the United States, by puritanical forms of Christianity' (278), Gordon McLauchlan comments that 'a strong strain of puritanism runs through the New Zealand character' (*Big Con* 51), and Bill Pearson goes as far as asserting that 'we are the most puritan country in the world' (209). From Sargeson to Pearson, this claim that New Zealand is a Puritan nation is not made with a sense of pride, but with a sense of gloom. Puritanism is viewed as a solely negative social influence, a harsh, repressive, destructive creed.

The most comprehensive catalogue of the Puritan deficiencies comes from H. Winston Rhodes:

> It relies too heavily on a series of prohibitions. 'Thou shalt not' is more often used than 'Thou shalt'. Its morbid consciousness, especially in relation to sexual impulses, fosters feelings of guilt for no valid reason and tends to destroy all reverence for warm physical life. Its heavy emphasis on the importance of work, irrespective of value, and its distrust of all forms of leisure that do not involve energetic muscular activity lead to an almost pathological suspicion of irregularity, of artistic endeavour and of happy-go-lucky non-conformism. Conventional respectability and an ingrained materialism are disguised by outward forms of piety; and prudery becomes synonymous with virtue. (40–41)

These definitions of Puritanism are linked not only by their negativity, but also by their focus on Puritanism as a secular force. Rhodes writes that critics such as Sinclair, commenting on the Puritan presence in New Zealand society, are 'not thinking primarily of the seventeenth-century Puritans in England nor of the dream of the promised land that may have been in the minds of many of the Pilgrim Fathers who reached America in the same century', but of Puritanism as a 'secular' form (40).

Literary critics such as Pearson and Rhodes speak of the need for New Zealand literature to be at the vanguard of the attack on Puritanism. Pearson's call for artists to take part 'in awakening New Zealanders from their fretful sleep' of complacent Puritanism and provincialism (230) is typical of the perception that authors have a duty to reform all that is wrong with society – in other words, rid New Zealand of Puritanism. Robert Chapman celebrates

> [t]he attitude which the New Zealand writer takes to his society, and which informs his work . . . [which is] based on the possibility here of a truly human ease and depth of living and on an attack on the distortion produced by an irrelevant puritanism of misplaced demands and guilts. (98)

For Eric Cook, the only hope of revival for the 'Puritan corpse already smelling' was the 'release of the pent splendid force of sex' (Jones 30; Stenhouse, 'Puritanism' 160). Gordon McLauchlan's influential social commentary *The Passionless People* (1976) reprised the work of Pearson and Chapman, castigating pākehā New Zealanders as 'a racially and culturally homogenous group of people who have nurtured in isolation . . . a Victorian, lower-middle class, Calvinist, village mentality' (1). Many of these commentators blamed women for perpetuating Puritanism, leading to what Lawrence Jones terms 'literary misogyny' (427). Denis Glover lampooned New Zealand's 'lady writers' as a 'bunch of bores in stuffy drawers', A. R. D. Fairburn railed against 'the menstrual school', and Frank Sargeson divided New Zealand literature into a 'major', 'masculine' tradition and a 'minor', 'feminine' tradition (Murray 65, 168; Sargeson 28–33).

For much of the twentieth century, McLauchlan's, Pearson's and Chapman's assessments of Puritanism as the disease from which New Zealand society and New Zealand letters needed to be purged and cured remained unchallenged. Mark Williams has identified the enduring pattern of New Zealand literary representations of religion as 'pervasive, utterly negative, deeply implicated in resented female power, and identified with puritanism' (11–13). My own work (Moffat, 'Destruction'; 'Two Preacher Novelists'; 'Mr Calvin and Mr Knox') has sought to broaden the discussion, pointing to both the seeds of the anti-Puritan tradition in nineteenth-century literature and the presence of literary voices, such as Bannerman Kaye, Guy Thornton and Herman Foston, that engage with Puritanism in positive ways. The most important corrective comes from the scholarship of John Stenhouse. His pivotal 2012 essay on 'Puritanism, Literary Culture, and New Zealand History' seeks to 'rescue puritans and their churches from the condescension of posterity' and highlights that the New Zealand engagement with Puritanism was far more complex than previous assessments have acknowledged ('Puritanism' 154; see also Stenhouse, 'Religion and Society'). Stenhouse begins his exploration of New Zealand Puritanism with Baxter, acknowledging that, as for so many authors of his generation, Puritanism was a 'poison' that had contaminated the self and society, but also pointing to the 'puritan origins' of Baxter's 'anti-puritan self' ('Puritanism' 151, 163). Other scholars, in particular Liam McIlvanney ('Poems Like Hand Grenades'), have drawn attention to the ambivalence of Baxter's relationship with his Calvinist inheritance, and the remainder of this article builds on this foundation, highlighting the complex nature of his engagement with Puritanism in his prose writing.

## *'the bones of a dinosaur': Baxter's Calvinist Inheritance*

Biographers and literary critics have highlighted that Puritanism, in both its theological and secular forms, was a formative influence on Baxter. Vincent O'Sullivan writes that

> Through both parents he drew on a stern Protestant tradition

> which he reacted against strongly, but never outgrew. His later strictures against New Zealand society, and his eventual rejection of almost everything which defines our European social life, spring from his feelings against [the Calvinist ethos]. (3)

Baxter's biographer Frank McKay traces the different strands of this inheritance. On his father's side, the theological legacy was Scottish Presbyterianism, although religion played little part in his grandfather John Baxter's life until he gave up alcohol for thirteen years after hearing the Plymouth Brethren preach in Brighton (McKay 6–7). More significantly, Baxter was the heir to the deeply non-conformist, radical Puritan strain through his father Archibald Baxter who, along with his brothers, was a committed pacifist. Archibald was a humanist with socialist sympathies. He did not go to church, although his outlook was grounded on his 'own understanding of Christ's command to love thy neighbour' (7). Like the radical sixteenth-century Puritans, he was prepared to suffer for his beliefs, refusing to relinquish his pacifism even when subjected to brutal torture by the military during World War I.

In contrast, Baxter's maternal grandparents, particularly his grandfather John Macmillan Brown, 'represented for him a system of education, a puritan devotion to hard work and material advancement, conformity, and respectability' (32). The outlook of his mother, Millicent Baxter, particularly on matters relating to sexuality, is captured by Baxter's description of her reaction to he and his cousin showing each other their bottoms: 'God and all his bulldozers were on the march [and I felt] fear . . . the most extreme I have ever felt' (Oliver 28). McKay writes that much of Baxter's life was 'lived in reaction to the strict regime of his childhood and the strong personality of his mother' (45). Like Sargeson and Hector Bolitho, Baxter thus adds to the myth of the Puritan mother as a negative and repressive influence, curbing the natural instinct for sexuality. However, while Baxter's preference 'was for the attitudes and style of the Baxters', he 'could not disown altogether, much less reconcile, the contrasting side of his inheritance. As he wrote much later, "In contradiction . . . I was born". The result, from childhood, was a divided self and a perennial inner conflict' (45).

In 'The Man on the Horse' and 'Notes on the Education of a New Zealand Poet', two of the autobiographical meditations that form part of *The Man on the Horse* (1966), Baxter identifies Puritanism as a shaping influence and a force against which he started to do battle from a young age. These reflections follow a similar trajectory to famous anti-Puritan narratives such as Samuel Butler's *The Way of All Flesh* (1903) and Edmund Gosse's *Father and Son* (1907), with literature providing a liberating influence and bringing the individual to a place where, to use Gosse's words, he can claim 'a human being's privilege to fashion his inner life for himself' (251). This pattern is also evident in several twentieth-century New Zealand narratives, such as Constance Clyde's *A Pagan's Love* (1905), Hector Bolitho's *Solemn Boy* (1927), Arthur H. Adams *A Man's Life* (1929), and Frank Sargeson's *I Saw in My Dream* (1949). In each of these novels literature, socialist politics and nature propel the protagonist to reject his or her Puritan upbringing (Moffat, 'Destruction'). In the autobiographical essays discussed here, Baxter outlines a similar trajectory, and it is here that he is most like the anti-Puritan authors and commentators of his generation, with Puritanism very definitely positioned as the enemy against which the writer must struggle and overcome.

In a passage that has received astute critical attention from Stenhouse, Baxter writes that the 'society into which I had been born (and, indeed, modern Western society in general) carries like strychnine in its bones a strong unconscious residue of the doctrines and ethics of Calvinism' (2. 192). Stenhouse emphasises the connection Baxter draws between the 'sick society' he inhabits and himself ('Puritanism' 151). The Calvinist inheritance is described as a lurking, potentially deadly presence. Baxter's choice of poison, strychnine, is significant. It is not a gentle poison; when taken in sufficient quantity it violently attacks the body, causing muscular convulsions and eventually death through asphyxia. Calvinism may not yet be fatal, but its poison is an indelible and immovable fixture in the bones of New Zealand society, an ominous, noxious presence. Given the associations of bones with an underlying structure – of the body, of a building, of society – the image speaks to the embedded nature of the contamination.

Another equally vivid image also links Calvinism to bones. Here Baxter compares the 'Calvinist ethos which underlies our determinedly secular culture' to 'the bones of a dinosaur buried in a suburban garden plot' (2. 220). 'Dinosaur' conjures pictures of the prehistoric, a once mighty presence that is now extinct, relegating Calvinism to an outdated, outmoded past. But Baxter's point is that, even if society does not acknowledge its presence, Calvinism is still a shaping force. The bones are buried, but represent the foundation on which the garden, or New Zealand society, is built. While the dinosaur itself may be dead, its essence seeps into the soil of the garden, just as Calvinism permeates the minds and morals of New Zealanders.[2] Geoffrey Miles, John Davidson and Paul Millar link this passage to a dialogue Baxter constructs between Sisyphus and the Boulder, with the Boulder chastising Sisyphus for bad language when the Greek mythological figure explodes: 'You great bloody heap of the fossilized dung of a dinosaur.' Tellingly, Miles, Davidson and Millar write that the Boulder symbolises Calvinism, 'a system of values Baxter loathes but knows he must remain in touch with – shoulder to the rock – if his

2 I have found no evidence to suggest that Baxter was reading H. G. Wells's *The Invisible Man* when he was writing *Man on the Horse*, but I was struck by a passage from this novel that links strychnine to the prehistoric and also contains an implied reference to bones. The protagonist, reflecting nineteenth-century perceptions, regards strychnine as an aid to sleep and performance-enhancing tonic, declaring that 'Strychnine is a grand tonic . . . to take the flabbiness out of a man.' Dr Kemp replies, 'It's the devil. . . . It's the palaeolithic in a bottle' (132).

writing is to remain relevant to the lives of his fellow New Zealanders' (Miles et al. 16).

While the Calvinist legacy may be an 'unconscious residue' in wider society, Baxter himself is highly conscious of this force at work in his own psyche. In the same passage that compares Calvinism to dinosaur bones, he writes that as a child he was under great 'pressure . . . to accept' the core tenants of Calvinism: '*work is good; sex is evil; do what you're told and you'll be all right; don't dig too deep into yourself.*' At this stage, he 'could not fight these chiefly inward pressures', lacking 'the experience to contradict them and forge against them' (2. 220). He was haunted by the image of Prometheus, chained against the rock and enduring the daily devouring of his liver. Jettisoning Puritanism seemed as impossible as Prometheus escaping from the rock, but resisting it was as heroic as Prometheus's defiance of the gods to give humanity the gift of fire or his father's refusal to relinquish his pacifist beliefs.

As a young man, Baxter struggled against the Puritan fixation with sin, particularly the sexual sins of the body. Later in life he used the 'two heavy volumes of Calvin's *Institutes* as paperweights', but the words of this Protestant manifesto continued to haunt him: 'For our nature is not only utterly devoid of goodness, but so prolific in all kinds of evil, that it can never be idle. . . . the whole man is in himself nothing else than concupiscence' (2. 192, quoting Calvin). Reading a ghost story in his formative years about a boy who dabbles in black magic and is pounced on by supernatural hounds before he reaches the safety of the church, he drew parallels between the narrative and his own sexual experiments. 'I think it stirred up in my mind the Calvinist image of reprobation. I had only to substitute auto-erotic practices for black magic, and there I was in the centre of the tale' (2. 220).

Baxter's father was an important influence as he gradually freed himself from the tentacles of Puritanism. While Archibald's 'Pacifist Church' shared many features with organised religion, such as a pantheon of martyrs and its own set of scriptures, it promoted free thought rather than conformity. The key pacifist scriptures were 'Tolstoy and Gandhi and the New Testament suitably interpreted' and from an early age Baxter was made aware of the poetry of 'Burns and Shelley and Byron and Blake and Tom Hood and Henry Lawson'. Baxter writes that these early lessons, including the bullying he encountered because of his father's beliefs, were ultimately 'valuable, for they taught me to distrust mass opinion' (2. 217–19).

As McIlvanney has so insightfully written, Scottish poet Robert Burns was a strong, liberating, formative force. In 'Letter to Robert Burns', which Baxter quotes in 'The Man on the Horse', he applauds Burns for 'crack[ing] the wall of Calvin's jail' for both the Scottish nation and, by implication, himself (2. 194). Baxter describes the first volume of verse he was given, a volume of Burns's poetry, as 'a tribal gift' through which he could 'communicate with the dead and myself understand the language of the daimon'. It was also 'a kind of protective talisman', warding off the lingering effects of Calvinism (2. 192). It is no accident that in 'The Man on the Horse' Baxter's reference to the shielding properties of Burns immediately precedes his discourse on Calvin's *Institutes*. He writes that '[i]n Burns's poems the struggle of the natural man against that inhuman crystalline version of the total depravity of the flesh and the rigid holiness of the elect was carried out with superb energy, precision, and humour' (2. 193). As a man and as a poet, Burns's 'bawdry' formed what McIlvanney terms 'a welcome antidote to the repressive Calvinism of the Kirk' (14).

'Notes on the Education of a Young Poet' highlights four other authors whose influence on the young Baxter was significant. John Lehmann's *New Writing in Europe* linked him to 'a secret tribe of friends and lovers who waited, guns and poems and contraceptives in their hands, to welcome my coming of age' and, even more importantly, gave him a sense of a possible audience for his own verse. The reading experience was so profound that it had 'some of the force of a religious conversion'. Ethel Mannin's anarchist tract *Bread and Roses* had a similar liberating effect, its emphasis on free will helping Baxter 'realise that I could in fact determine in some degree what course my life should take'. He decided that 'Bohemia' was his destination, an important term in Baxter's thinking that I will return to in the next section of this discussion. Carl Jung's *Modern Man in Search of a Soul* gave him cause for hope that as well as the ghosts and demons that haunted him there was the 'possibility that my subconscious mind might contain sources of peace and wisdom' (2. 222).

Above all, A. S. Neill's *A Dominie's Log* suggested that the 'Calvinist engine' could be put 'in reverse' and the mind 'de-educated'. Crucially, this enabled the eighteen-year-old Baxter to realise that the instinctive battle he had been fighting against his Calvinist education emerged from 'a kind of subconscious wisdom, and not from any source of malign perversity' (2. 223–24).

What is remarkable about Baxter's reflections on his formative influences, particularly in the context of the New Zealand engagement with Puritanism outlined at the beginning of this discussion, is his awareness that his deep struggle against the 'strychnine in his bones' helped to mould him into a great writer. He writes:

> The negative aspects of my growth were in the long run the most help to me as a writer. They tempered the axe of intellect, as it were. A writer cannot avoid the task of exploring and understanding the private hell which lies just below the threshold of his own mind. (2. 222)

T. S. Eliot writes of 'the vital importance for a society of friction between its parts', declaring that 'one needs the enemy' (58–59). Writers need something to engage the emotions, to stir convictions, to react against. Puritanism was such a force in Baxter's development.

### *'a permanently split mind': Puritan versus Anti-Puritan*

Baxter's prose reflections on the ongoing Puritan influence on New Zealand letters and New Zealand society establish a powerful dialectic between two opposing forces. At times he terms these the 'Puritan' and the 'anti-Puritan' and at times 'bourgeois' and 'Bohemia'. Throughout, his message is the same: be wary of the comfortable, conformist siren call of Puritanism and the bourgeois. It may represent ease, but it also stifles imagination and individuality. Yet, unlike the one-dimensional critics of Puritanism of his generation, Baxter also continues to acknowledge that there is some good in the Puritan tradition, if only to provide the aspiring poet and social critic with something to react against and a necessary inward tension out of which good art can emerge.

The quotation which began this chapter, Baxter's description of Puritanism as an 'austere anti-aesthetic angel' comes from his essay 'Aspects of Poetry in New Zealand' (1967). To place the fragment within its wider context, Baxter identifies the 'endemic problem of our poets' as a 'struggle' with 'the austere anti-aesthetic angel of Puritanism'. Here he sets up the parameters of a battle, a wrestling with Puritanism as a force that has the capacity to stifle the imagination. Yet the battle can be energising, giving the writer a sense of purpose. Baxter does not dismiss Puritanism entirely, acknowledging that 'a Puritan society can contain a great deal of primitive energy'. However, in order to 'transform this energy into aesthetic forms', he argues that authors have to 'develop non-Puritan modes of thought and feeling'. The Puritan suspicion of the 'natural forces latent in society and the individual', which represent a negative energy, must be transformed into a 'positive' acceptance of appetite (2. 238). In Freudian terms, Baxter is essentially urging an acceptance of the id.

To illustrate his argument of the damaging effects resulting from a failure to win the struggle against Puritanism, he provides two examples which act as warnings. In the first he chastises a 'Puritan community' that 'may severely inhibit its writers and even throttle them', using as his anti-model a female author who gave up writing after her 'vigorous and perceptive' portrayal of a young married couple was castigated by New Zealand critics. The second profiles the case of Percival, whose brothel-visiting, drunken self was kept at a crippling distance from his poetry, resulting in anaemic and 'saccharine' verse (2. 328–29).

Baxter diagnoses Percival as suffering from 'a permanently split mind', an inescapable part of a 'Puritan ethic' that 'promotes neurosis' through its rejection of fallen humanity. Puritanism, for Baxter, is not misguided because of its theology or value, but because it seeks to repress parts of the self that are natural. It is this 'blocking from consciousness of necessary knowledge about oneself' that 'plays havoc with the communications of art' (2. 329).

Perhaps the most fascinating essay to tease out these dichotomous elements in the New Zealand character is 'The Puritan Devil' (1966). Here Baxter begins with the by now familiar evisceration of Puritanism, emphasising that it fosters 'split minds' (2. 124). Several critical analyses of Baxter, in particular Pat Lawlor's *The Two Baxters*, have emphasised the two sides of Baxter's personality. Lawlor's reflections begin with an introduction by Kevin Maher, who writes that

> There are at least two Jim Baxters. . . . One is the patient, resigned, 'teach-me-to-care-and-not-to-care' Ash-Wednesday Baxter, bruised and educated by life, with a sympathy as wide as the world and a gentleness that is Franciscan. The other is the petty, still mixed-up teenager, lashing out indiscriminately at rather old-fashioned stereotypes of Puritans, Catholic teachers, bureaucrats, middle-class conformists, repressed celibates and all the rest . . . (Maher in Lawlor 7–8)

In 'The Puritan Devil' Baxter describes a somewhat different division than the world-weary, empathetic Baxter and the angry, impatient Baxter outlined by Maher. Baxter identifies one aspect of the New Zealand psyche as 'half rational, clinical, polite, more or less humane'. This does battle with 'the other half, negative, unillumined, violent, a wilderness of primitive prejudices and phobias, waiting to be stirred into action by some politician with an axe to grind' (2. 124). This second mind, or aspect of the national psyche – comprised of the 'sexual and aggressive impulses which the individual is unable to cope with' – is at odds with Puritanism, but 'not destroyed' by it. '[S]hoved further back in the mind', this 'Puritan devil' is a lurking presence. Baxter urges that rather than being relegated to the subconscious, this presence needs to be acknowledged and, if possible, accepted. The first stage involves a necessary rebellion against the tenants of Puritanism. This gives birth to the 'anti-Puritan', a 'person who has been singed by the fires of the Puritan "Satan" – and instead of running like mad, has had the courage to pull off the mask from that formidable figure and reveal what was there all the time – a tangle of nursery phobias – a "demonic" not a diabolic entity' (2. 125).

This is the point where most of Baxter's contemporaries stopped. Writers and commentators such as Pearson, Chapman and McLauchlan idealise this anti-Puritan, the author who can castigate provincial society, exposing its flaws, and lambasting its adherents. The role of the author, in this view, is to shock through the vigour of the anti-Puritan message. Baxter goes a step further. He acknowledges that 'A Puritan has to become anti-Puritan before he can become merely normal', recognising that anti-Puritanism is a part of a wider rite of passage. Note that anti-Puritanism is not the destination, it is a step on the journey of being 'merely normal'. Here Baxter uses 'normal' to describe a place of equipoise and harmony in which Puritanism no longer has any power. The anti-Puritan self is just as controlled and shaped by Puritanism as the Puritan self. Baxter's goal is a state beyond this, where '[o]ne would hope to cease to be anti-Puritan; to reach the point where one no longer cared a bugger who objected to the word "bugger" – but this takes time' (2. 125).

Did Baxter ever reach this place beyond the anti-Puritan?

McIlvanney suggests not, arguing that 'Baxter, for all his defiance of "the Puritan devil", remained deeply in thrall to his Calvinist heritage, so that the writing of bawdy verse was never the easy indulgence of a natural impulse but always the anxious infraction of a feared and hated creed' (45–46). Vincent O'Sullivan perhaps allows for the possibility, writing that

> one of the enduring interests in Baxter is that he simply cannot be reduced to any category we try to fit him to. . . . It is the breadth of what probably we regard as his contradictions that will continue to make him so much more worth reading than anything his outright admirers, or detractors, put up on his behalf. (in Lawlor 75)

My encounter with Baxter's prose has certainly been with a man of contradictions, who simultaneously rejects Puritanism and acknowledges that it is a necessary part of a functioning society, who fashions himself as anti-Puritan but longs for a state and place of unity rather than division. An important step on this journey is to acknowledge the Puritan devil within, 'to *eat* him, chew him up, horns and tail and all, and swallow him down, and assimilate him as part of one's own personality' (2. 126). The imagery is grotesque and cannibalistic, but for Baxter only through this kind of vigorous acceptance can the possibility of progression beyond the anti-Puritan be found.

### *'natural man, though wounded, is still the earth lamp who holds the oil of grace': Puritanism and Catholicism*

'Conversation with an Ancestor', one of the essays that comprises *The Man on the Horse*, suggests that if Baxter did succeed in moving beyond the anti-Puritan, the credit for this, in his eyes, lies in his conversion to Catholicism in 1958. Here his dissection of the 'conflict of the bourgeois and Bohemian values' in New Zealand is framed in historical and theological terms. Baxter is particularly balanced in his anatomisation of the 'bourgeois family man' in this essay, acknowledging that he 'will always have the burden of maintaining most of the values of civilised life' and most of the 'necessary virtues – amiability, patience, prudence, punctuality, whimsicality, thrift and caution'. The danger lies not in these 'necessary virtues' but in the forgetting and repressing of the 'natural man' (2. 138). After twenty years 'of doubt and fumbling' Baxter came to believe that the split between the bourgeois and natural selves had its roots in the development of Christianity, particularly in the Reformation and the birth of Calvinism:

> The Calvinist thesis that the Fall is absolute and the natural man totally depraved has led . . . to a kind of idolatry – a deep reliance, torn still by an anguish of uncertainty, on the civilising influence of education, culture, and the power of the State – as if these could eradicate the turbulence of the passions and put in their place an abstract social benevolence.

The Bohemian, or anti-Puritan, refuses to relinquish natural man and this impulse is sanctioned by Catholic theology which teaches that 'the Fall was not complete, and the natural man, though wounded, is still the earth lamp who holds the oil of grace.' Catholicism teaches that 'the only viable solution' to the split psyche that results from the Fall 'is a difficult humanism which works towards an understanding of the passions without being overthrown by them.' This Catholic humanism, unlike Puritanism, does not require an 'abandon[ment]' of art, but creates an environment in which creativity is possible because the natural self can be accepted rather than repulsed (2. 138).

Tellingly, Baxter argues in this essay that neither the Bohemian nor the bourgeois self is 'whole'; each is a 'half-man . . . because each turns away from some essential aspect of life'. Wholeness and 'balance' can only be achieved when 'those aspects of human nature which a neo-Calvinist would ignore or repudiate' are accepted. The 'capable writer' embraces the 'two sides of the life of man – the instinctual and the social, the wild and the domestic, the passionate and the rational –

and their art is the fruit of radical tension' (2. 139).

Catholicism provided a means for Baxter to achieve this 'balance', offering an accommodation between aspects of the self, in particular the man who was conscious of failure and sin and the man who longed for God. His criticism of the Puritan theological tradition is at its strongest in his prose writings praising the gift of mercy that he found in the Catholic Church. Baxter felt alienated by the emphasis that the Protestant churches (particularly those founded on Calvinist theology) placed on godliness, on demonstrating through moral action a state of grace that identified the believer as one of the elect. In contrast Catholicism offered for Baxter both a welcome to all sinners and a way back for those who strayed through the sacraments of confession and penance. Writing of Baxter's conversion to Catholicism in 1958, Elizabeth Isichei argues that what 'attracted him above all was the fact that the Catholic church was not a body of self-selected spiritual athletes, but a place where misfits, alcoholics, and prisoners could feel at home' (236). In 'Literature and Belief' Baxter writes about Séamas, an alcoholic contending with girlfriend trouble, money trouble, and trouble with the law, whose 'moral difficulties in no way disturbed the clear-cut faith which was his birth-right as an Irish Catholic'. Baxter declares that it was Séamas who 'taught me that belief, not virtue, was the entrance ticket at the door of church . . . He made possible for me to become a Catholic' (2. 157).

Baxter elaborates on these views in 'The Sacrament of Mercy' (1967). He writes that the Protestant churches 'require that one should already be a good man before one approaches God. There is an unwritten entrance ticket of at least minimal virtue.' This was all very well for individuals who resisted the sins of the flesh relatively easily, or who were predisposed towards a calm, certain belief. But what of the radicals and questioners, the doubters in search of some sort of comfort, the 'hoboes, poor men, reprobates, no-hopers, habitual criminals'? Baxter, who himself battled against alcoholism and sexual appetite, identified strongly with these figures. Where could he find a pathway to God and a spiritual home? The answer lay in Catholicism, in particular penance, which required a recognition of error and a desire to change, not a demonstration of virtue: 'because of the institution by Our Lord of the Sacrament of Penance, a man does not require any virtue at all to be received into the Catholic Church, apart from the virtue of Faith which is itself a free gift from God' (2. 371–72).

Isichei writes that 'Baxter's spirituality was dominated by Mary . . . rooted in the essentially medieval belief that she was endlessly loving and forgiving' (244). Puritans and Calvinists represented 'the Other, outside the beloved church', but they too could be rescued from Purgatory through Mary's intercession (248). Baxter pleaded with Mary for the 'sheep of Calvin, clipped for Judgement Day' to be hoisted 'from the fire' ('Guy Fawkes Night', *CPoems* 259). This desire to see even those he despised and castigated receiving mercy marks Baxter as distinctly un-Puritan. A division of all humanity into the saved and the damned is a distinctive feature of Puritan theology. The seventeenth-century theologian Richard Sibbes wrote that there are 'two grand sides to the world, to which all belong: there is God's side and those that are his, and there is another that is Satan's, and those that are his' (quoted in Ryken 11). Puritan theologians such as Sibbes relished the thought of reprobates and unbelievers, including Catholics, writhing in the torments of hell fire. The preacher Jonathan Edwards went as far as declaring that 'the sight of hell torments will exalt the happiness of the saints forever' and 'make them more sensible of their own happiness' (234). In his desire for the 'sheep of Calvin' to be 'hoist . . . from the fire' Baxter exhibits a compassion that demonstrates he was able to transcend the anti-Puritan self discussed above, perhaps not always, but certainly in very profound and real ways.

### *'Militancy is to sow the seed of an alternate society': Baxter as Prophet*

In 'The Fortunate Country' Baxter outlines a tongue-in-cheek dream of a New Zealand utopia dominated by a 'Catholic majority'. In this world of large families and minimal state interference, there is plenty of bawdy and a resurgence of the arts, in part due to the abolition of cinemas, television and computers (2. 625). However, the reality of the society he inhabited was very far from this dream. Fired by his devotion to the poor and his embrace of Māori spirituality, Baxter's rage was increasingly directed not just at bourgeois, Puritan society, but also at aspects of the Catholic Church that had nurtured him. Isichei writes that Baxter 'grew increasingly alienated from . . . middle-class Catholicism, in which concern for the poor, if it existed at all, was often inadequate, ethnocentric, insincere, and accompanied by a non-radicalised lifestyle' (245).

In his later writing, particularly his 'Handbook for the Christian Militant' (1972) and 'A Walking Stick for an Old Man' (1972), Baxter's message is increasingly radical. Of course, in this Baxter was following models from within the Catholic Church, from Saint Francis and Ignatius Loyola to Mother Teresa. But, as I draw this discussion of Baxter's complex engagement with Puritanism to a close, it is also tempting to see residues of his Calvinist inheritance in his fiery diatribes. The early Puritans were militants and radicals, and the message of egalitarianism, community, and inward divinity articulated by sects such as the Diggers, Levellers and Ranters is echoed by Baxter. Indeed, aspects of 'Handbook for the Christian Militant' and 'A Walking Stick for an Old Man' bear a resemblance to Puritan pamphlets such as Abiezer Coppe's *A Fiery Flying Roll* (1649), which railed against hypocrisy and inequality and revelled in a vision of God as the great Leveller. Like Coppe, Baxter divides his message into short, sequentially numbered heads, each one self-contained but also contributing to the core message of radical societal and theological reform.

Meditating on whether Baxter can be described as a prophet, Ishichei comments that 'if he is a prophet, he was one with a remarkably simplistic social vision. Everything is black and white. He idealises the Catholic meths drinker, condemns the businessman and politician' (240). This simplicity and certainty of vision likewise bears a resemblance to Puritan prophetic writing such as *A Fiery Flying Roll*, as do Baxter's oratorical flourishes, metaphoric language, and combination of Old Testament allusions and New Testament teachings.

'A Handbook for the Christian Militant' rails against the 'practice' of the Catholic Church whose 'truth is . . . narrowed and structuralised' (3. 489). Baxter is particularly critical of the church's preoccupation with wealth, writing that the 'church has married herself to Dives our capitalist Pharaoh' (3. 490). This 'castrated church' is also so 'obsess[ed] with sexual purity' that it has lost its humanity and compassion (3. 492). It is as if the Catholic Church has been infected by what Baxter and other writers of his generation regarded as the key components of the Puritan 'disease': conformity, repressive morality and materialism. The Church worships a 'false Christ' who is

> fashioned in the image of the middle class liberal who wants people to improve their personal morals but who does not challenge Pharaoh. His lost militancy is a ghost without a final resting place, directed now against pornography, now against change in the abortion laws, but never against the power structures of the pyramids. (3. 497)

Baxter calls for a rejection of this provincial mindset and a return to a church characterised by a social conscience and social justice. Christ is the prototype of this church militant: 'To feed the starving was militant. To ride into Jerusalem on a donkey's back was to be the leader of a political demonstration' (3. 497). Gandhi and Te Whiti provide powerful models of individuals who have inspired a radical rejection of worldly aspirations and values in favour of a life of simplicity dedicated to improving the lot of others. For

Baxter, the kind of uncompromising but peaceful militancy exhibited by Te Whiti is necessary 'to sow the seed of an alternate society' (3. 499).

The reference to Te Whiti points to Baxter's engagement with Māori spirituality and his call for the nurturing of a radical and liberating 'Maori Christianity', particularly evident in 'A Walking Stick for an Old Man' (3. 507). Russell Phillips writes that for Baxter God is found in 'the human community of all races and persons' (278). Baxter seeks to articulate and foster his vision of a church which 'exists for others beyond the confinement of any one dogma or belief. The identity of God is found in the community as opposed to the Church as a rigid and confined institution' (279).

One image from 'A Handbook for the Christian Militant' draws together the threads of my argument and is a fitting way to close. In section twenty-five of this guide to a reformed church Baxter retells the parable of the Good Samaritan. The victim in need of rescue is a drunk, 'lying in a Wellington street, with blood and vomit coming from his mouth'. Puritan society, Catholic society 'step over him and round him'. But one man 'takes him home and washes him and gives him his own bed to sleep in'. The Good Samaritan in Baxter's parable is 'a young man of homosexual temperament', and through this figure Baxter recasts the sins of the 'Sodomites' as a 'lack of the virtue of manuhiritanga, that is, the practice of mercy and respect to the guest and the stranger' (3. 493–94).

Here Baxter the prophet is very much in evidence, haranguing New Zealand society for its complacency and injustice and using his Samaritan to articulate his belief that salvation is to be found on the margins, with the misfits and troublemakers and radicals excluded from bourgeois society but embodying God's love. The narrative also highlights Baxter's eventual answer to the divisions and hypocrisies of Puritanism: kindness, compassion and love. The traces of both Puritan and anti-Puritan linger in his castigation of society, the rhetoric bearing a resemblance to Puritan indignation against a world that fails to measure up, and the target of his diatribe being the hollow morality of a bigoted, racist, materialistic Puritan nation. But his late works suggest that, at least to some degree, he was able to transcend both the Puritan and anti-Puritan selves that lurked within to refashion himself as a prophet of freedom, mercy and justice.

## *Works Cited*


Anonymous. *An Admonition to Parliament.* London: John Fielde, 1572.

Beard, Charles A. 'On Puritans.' *The New Republic*, 1 December 1920. 15–17.

Chapman, Robert. 'Fiction and the Social Pattern.' In: *Essays on New Zealand Literature*. Ed. Wystan Curnow. Auckland: Heineman, 1973.

Chesterton, G. K. 'What I Saw in America.' In: *Collected Works of G. K. Chesterton.* Vol. 21. San Francisco: Ignatius Press, 1990. 35–264.

Coffey, John, and Paul C. H. Lim, eds. *The Cambridge Companion to Puritanism*. Cambridge: Cambridge University Press, 2008.

Collinson, Patrick. *The Elizabethan Puritan Movement*. London: Methuen, 1967.

Coppe, Abiezer. *A Fiery Flying Roll: a word from the Lord to all the great ones of the Earth*. London: 1649.

Edwards, Jonathan. 'The Eternity of Hell's Torments.' 1739. In: *Knowing the Heart: Jonathan Edwards on True and False Conversion*. Ed. William C. Nichols. Ames, Iowa: International Outreach, 2003.

Eliot, T. S. *Notes Towards the Definition of Culture*. London: Faber and Faber, 1948.

Gosse, Edmund. *Father and Son: A Study of Two Temperaments*. London: Penguin, 1989.

Grimes, Alan P. *The Puritan Ethic and Woman Suffrage*. New York: Oxford University Press, 1967.

Grimshaw, Patricia. *Women's Suffrage in New Zealand*. Auckland: Auckland University Press, 1987.

Holden, William P. *Anti-Puritan Satire* 1572–1642. New Haven: Yale University Press, 1954.

Isichei, Elizabeth. 'James K. Baxter: Religious Sensibility and a Changing Church.' *Journal of New Zealand Literature* 13 (1995): 235–256.

James I. *Basilikon Doron, or His Majestys Instructions to his Dearest Sonne, Henry the Prince*. London: Wetheimer, Lea & Co, 1887.

Jones, Lawrence. *Picking Up the Traces: The Making of a New Zealand Literary Culture 1932–1945*. Wellington: Victoria University Press, 2003.

Lawlor, Pat. *The Two Baxters*. With an essay by Vincent O'Sullivan. Introduction by Kevin Maher. Wellington: Millwood Press, 1979.

Lawrence, D. H. 'Sketches of Etruscan Places.' In: *Sketches of Etruscan Places and Other Italian Essays*. Ed. Simonetta di Filippis. Cambridge Edition of the Works of D. H. Lawrence.

Lovell-Smith, Margaret, ed. *Writing By the Women Who Won the Vote*. Auckland: New Woman's Press, 1991.

Macaulay, Lord. *The History of England from the Accession of James II.* 1848. 8 volumes. London, 1882.

Macdonald, Charlotte, ed. *The Vote, the Pill and the Demon Drink: A History of Feminist Writing in New Zealand 1869–1993*. Wellington: Bridget Williams Books, 1993.

McIlvanney, Liam. 'Poems Like Hand Grenades: Baxter, Burns, and Bawdry.' *Journal of New Zealand Literature* 30 (2012): 29–51.

McLauchlan, Gordon. *The Big Con: The Death of the Kiwi Dream*. Wellington: G. P. Publications, 1987.

———. *The Passionless People*. Auckland: Cassell, 1976.

Mander, Jane. *The Story of a New Zealand River*. Auckland: Godwit, 1994.

Mencken, H. L., and George Jean Nathan. 'Clinical Notes.' *The American Mercury*, July 1925: 352–55.

Moffat, Kirstine. 'Destruction, Transformation, Rebellion, Alienation: The Critique of Puritanism in Pre-1930 New Zealand Novels.' *Journal of New Zealand Literature* 16 (1998): 86–96.

———. '"The manliest and noblest of all pursuits and professions": Two Preacher Novelists.' In: *Sacred Histories in Secular New Zealand*. Ed. Geoffrey Troughton and Stuart Lange. Wellington: University of Victoria Press, 2016. 123–38.

———. '"Mr Calvin and Mr Knox": The Calvinist Legacy in the Fiction and Poetry of New Zealand Scots.' In: *Calvin, The Man and The Legacy*. Ed. Murray Rae, Peter Matheson and Brett Knowles. Adelaide: ATF, 2014. 213–234.

Muir, Edwin. *John Knox: A Portrait of a Calvinist*. London: Jonathan Cape, 1930.

Murray, Stuart. *Never a Soul at Home: New Zealand Literary Nationalism and the 1930s*. Wellington: Victoria University Press, 1998.

Pearson, Bill. 'Fretful Sleepers.' *Landfall* 6 (1952).

Phillips, Russell. 'James K. Baxter: A Dialogue with His Later Theological and Philosophical Thought in the Context of Aotearoa/New Zealand.' *Journal of New Zealand Literature* 13 (1995): 267–284.

Poole, Kristen. 'Dissecting Sectarianism: Liberty of Conscience, the Swarm, and Thomas Edwards's Gangraena.' In: *Form and Reform in Renaissance England: Essays in Honor of Barbara Kiefer Lewalski*. Ed. Barbara Kiefer Lewalski, Amy Boesky and Mary Thomas Crane. Newark: University of Delaware Press, 2000. 45–69.

———, *Radical Religion from Shakespeare to Milton*. Cambridge: Cambridge University Press, 2006.

Rhodes, H. Winston. *New Zealand Novels: A Thematic Approach*. Wellington: New Zealand University Press, Price Milburn, 1968.

Ryken, Leland, ed. *Worldly Saints: The Puritans as They Really Were*.

Grand Rapids, Michigan: Zondervan, 1990.
Sargeson, Frank. *Conversation in a Train and Other Critical Writing*. Ed. Kevin Cunningham. Auckland: Auckland University Press, 1983.
Sasek, Lawrence A. *Images of English Puritanism: A Collection of Contemporary Sources, 1589–1646*. Baton Rouge: Louisiana State University Press, 1989.
Shakespeare, William. *Twelfth Night*. Ed. David Carnegie and Mark Houlahan. Calgary: Broadview Press, 2014.
Sinclair, Keith. *A History of New Zealand*. Harmondsworth: Penguin, 1958.
Stenhouse, John. '"Like Strychnine in its Bones": Puritanism, Literary Culture, and New Zealand History.' *Journal of New Zealand Literature* 30 (2012): 150–176.
———. 'Religion and Society.' *The New Oxford History of New Zealand*. Ed. Giselle Byrnes. Melbourne and Auckland: Oxford University Press, 2009. 323–356.
Trevor-Roper, Hugh. 'The Past and the Present. History and Sociology.' *Past and Present* 42 (February 1969): 3–17.
Wells, H. G. *The Invisible Man, The War of the Worlds, A Dream of Armageddon*. London: Unwin, 1924.
Whitgift, John. *An Answere to a Certen Libel Intituled, An Admonition to the Parliament*. London: Imprinted by Henrie Bynneman, 1572.
Wilde, Oscar. *A Woman of No Importance*. Oxford: Oxford University Press, 1998.
Williams, Mark. Introduction. *The Source of the Song: New Zealand Writers on Catholicism*. Wellington: Victoria University Press, 1995.

# *Baxter and God: Reflections*

Paul Morris

Sitting at my desk behind a substantial blockade of collections of his poetry and now of his prose, I have a sense of James K. Baxter, the long dead and self-proclaimed Kiwi everyman,[1] as heavy and substantial, collected, cogent, coherent.[2] It is strange, as I have mostly thought of him until now as oracular, momentary, his often challenging and piercing thought fragmentary, unfinished and conflicted. John Weir's prize-winning, magnificent four-volume *James K. Baxter: Complete Prose* is impressive, tectonic and, most of all, monumental.[3] And it really is a monumental achievement: Baxter's prodigious prose, ordered with provenance detailed and contextualised, together with high order scholarly apparatus. But something generates in me a sense of unease. It resonates with my feelings in response to the wonderful 'collected' *Colin McCahon: A Question of Faith*, which took the insightful, multifaceted and unsystematic painter and framed and rendered him themed and accessibly messaged.[4]

1 For Baxter, this seemed mostly to be an aspirational identification with an undefinable collective 'them' ('I was born among them / And will lie some day with their dead ['Pig Island Letters' 2, *CPoems* 278]), with continual and considerable alienation between these two poles.

2 I have in mind Weir's edition of the *Collected Poems* and Millar's *Selected Poems*.

3 *James K. Baxter: Complete Prose* won the PANZ 2016 Gerard Reid Award for Best Book design, and the Upstart Press Award for Best Non-Illustrated Book, awarded to Fergus Barrowman for the books and Spencer Levine for the set slip-cover.

4 See Marja Bloem and Martin Browne; on the question of McCahon's faith, see Gordon Brown. At the McCahon retrospective exhibition in Wellington, Auckland and then Sydney, the same seventy plus works were presented in the different spaces giving rise to different priorities

It is not that religion did not play a significant role in McCahon's life, of course it did, but in complex, nuanced and ramified ways. In that assemblage, however, attention is selectively and almost exclusively focused on what is portrayed as his religious quest, ignoring other arguably equally significant ways of framing the motivations and dimensions of his life and work.

It is, however, a very different matter with editions of complete works where the intention is to be as comprehensive as possible but the materials are still arranged and presented – in this case as the story of a life – and this narrative is given form by the editor's priorities and concerns.[5] John Weir has divided Baxter's prose into three volumes in chronological order and of roughly equal girth: Volume One – Dunedin and Christchurch: the Early Years 1943–48 and the Wellington Years 1949–65; Volume Two – Return to Dunedin 1966–68; Volume Three – The Jerusalem Years 1969–72; with Volume Four providing the Introduction, references, notes and an excellent index. Each volume's cover has an evocative image of Baxter from the period and inside an invocatory quotation from Baxter's prose. So, the cover of Volume One is a photograph of the young Baxter in 1948 wearing his coat reversed, signifying his becoming a believing Christian, a 'turncoat', and the invocation is about the poet as necessary prophetic voice and moral figure (1. 75). Volume Two begins with his confession of faith, an untimely belief in the 'strange caresses of an all knowing and all loving father' (2. 105). The cover of the third volume is adorned with a marvellous photograph (by Ans Westra) of Baxter reading the lesson at St Joseph's Church in Jerusalem. The invocatory passage is about all of us as God's guests needing to extend his hospitality universally (3. 251). The final volume has a colour photograph of Baxter praying with rosary in hand and the invocation is his confessionary prayer (3. 566–67).

and linkages and thus diverse understandings of the exhibition.

5 Collected editions often begin with the most notable or well-known works followed by lesser writing, published and unpublished.

Each volume could just as easily have had a different cover photograph, perhaps the landscape that so inspired his writing, and the invocations could have been just such prose topographies, but Weir has framed the whole life and each of the phases of that life with a religious motif as guideposts to his dominant narrative of Baxter's life of faith. The introductory essay at the beginning of Volume Four is centred on the religious transitions of Baxter's life, told as a progressive and transformative narrative of the ever more complete evolution of faith, in the manner of a modernised life of a medieval saint. It is the story of man who, after many deviations and backtrackings, finally found his way home to the Roman Catholic faith where he remained. There are many other stories about the poet that can be and have been told, that contextualise these faith dimensions within other and perhaps fuller and more subtle accounts of his life.

What is wrong with emphasising Baxter's evident and lifelong religious concerns? In itself, nothing. This new colossal collection, however, raises two significant issues for those pondering a new assessment of Baxter's life and writings. First, religion, for many, including some creative artists, is the historical and still principal contemporary resource for discourse on the big questions: of good and evil; of life's purpose; and of giving expression to the tensions and conflicts that define our frangible human condition. Our larger-than-life figures, our rare aesthetic and artistic cultural heroes, who so well articulate our deepest concerns and frame our identities and cultural identifications, stray way beyond artist, playwright and writer towards the saintly; those who embarked for us on the journeys of self-discovery, or faith, that somehow include us and that we privately and publicly share. Their special and significant lives require signs and a message that can be accessed by us, and hopefully later generations, as their individual, creative, human lives come to inform the collective life of the nation. Even if McCahon and Baxter fail to satisfy the stringent qualifications for the sanctification of historical or contemporary figures, they are significant future resources for the values and orientations of our culture, or at the very least, stages on the way, and their lives of faith, now rendered exemplary, are an integral part of our continuing contemporary culture-making.[6]

Secondly, and of more importance analytically, is that the authoritative narrative of faith, having defined one pole of the saint's dichotomised heart, assumes the counter-prevailing force or pull. For Baxter, a version of the two Baxters: mean, materialist, uptight, aggressively conformist, Presbyterian, or more generally Protestant, pākehā New Zealand; versus liberation, generosity, inclusion, social justice, spirituality and embracing love. This overly schematic bifurcation is hardly true to the mature complexities and insights of Baxter's understanding of his own life, or, for that matter, any reflective life. It falls into the very 'romantic' trap that he spent a lifetime trying – consciously, and sometimes successfully – to avoid. Baxter's self-understanding of the certainty of his own impending defeat and his abject failure to take control of his life are matched by his unceasing struggles to do so. Baxter was a dreamer repeatedly committed to extravagant and impossible enterprises, all of which were in time ultimately abandoned. He was a spiritual and intellectual wanderer who always had yet another destination in sight. Baxter was not a man split in two but splintered into many parts, now inevitably further obscured under this new collected format.

So, to write about Baxter and God in the aftermath of his literary and cultural sanctification, one has to begin by deconstructing the received portrayals, retrieving his scattered and unsystematic theological ruminations on God, and recontextualising these anew. The collected works render accessible the full range of these engagements and allow us

6 On the processes of sanctification in general, see Woodward and Higgins; for the politics of saint-making, see the collection by James Hopgood, especially the editor's essay on contemporary celebrity and saints (124–142).

to ask again about the poet as believer and religious thinker. Hopefully we will be able to see more clearly his obsessions, repetitions, tropes, and the patterns and development of his religious thinking. Baxter was not a theologian nor a philosopher of religion and his readings of theologians and philosophers were always partial, often most idiosyncratic and inadequately contextualised, and sometimes just factually and interpretively wrong. The significance of the contributions of his prose to his 'theology', in the sense of his experience and ruminations on God, is simply that while his poetry captures emotions and religious sentiments and conveys them in metaphors and experiential imagery, his theological and religious prose allows for extended and more complex and potentially satisfying engagements and reflections.

This essay traces his religious thinking and the role that it plays in his life, with a particular focus on the flurry of theological creativity during the Jerusalem years. The argument is that his use of theological language and concepts provided him with a ballast and certain foundation from which he proceeded to think, write and live. Theology generated the lexicon and semantic register that gave meaning to his activities and provided both the measure of the failures of his own life and the blueprint for his vision of a resurrected New Zealand restored spiritually to God. While his religious language is only sometimes explicitly theological, his particular matrix of myth and metaphor offers something potentially much more interesting and significant: the framework for a uniquely religious *Weltanschauung* or worldview, rooted in the experience of New Zealand's nature and culture.

Baxter's religious biography is manifold, a tale of a seemingly perpetual outsider. Unbaptised as an infant in the land of the baptised, he later came to understand himself to have been shaped by Scottish, paternalistic, Presbyterian family traditions which he experienced as vengeful, watchful and morally punitive and which largely served to thwart natural happiness and pleasure. Although bordering on caricature, this morally upright, dissenting portrayal created both an unfulfillable aspiration and the ethical foil for his lifetime of transgressions. His father's stand as a conscientious objector created pressures on the whole family and led to Jim and his brother becoming boarders for a number of years in Quaker (the Religious Society of Friends) schools in Whanganui and Sibford in the English Cotswolds. This left a lifelong attachment to a Quaker spirituality focused on what the dissenter, George Fox, called the light of Christ, 'that of God in everyone', an inner, immanent experience of the sacred that is potentially present in us all. This 'Quaker conscience', the foundation of the spirituality of social justice manifest in its opposition to slavery, war and all forms of exploitation and its explicit encouragement to stand firm in one's convictions, remained with Baxter for life, manifest both as integral to his own spirituality and his recognition of Christ in others.

When he was a young child, his mother read the King James Bible to him. At Sibford School he had come top in scripture, and later as a student he continued reading the Bible. His interest in Christianity is evident through these years, both as poetic resource for cadence and narrative themes and as the paradigmatic redemptive model for his sinner's life. His ideal of the religious life evolved to become the antidote to the seductive classical, heroic, 'romantic' life. In 1948 he was baptised as an Anglican and later that year married Jacquie Sturm in an Anglican ceremony. He was much drawn to St. Paul's notion of the moral struggle created by inherent human perversity (Romans 7:19, 'For the good that I would I do not; but the evil which I would not, that I do') and thus to the theological teachings concerning original sin. Baxter explained his conversion to Christianity in terms of a necessary transition from Pelagian to Augustinian; from a modern to a lost man mired in sin and in dire need of God's saving grace, a saving grace he came to experience and treasure. He became an active Anglican, albeit with a theology that he considered was particularly forgiving of 'sensual failings' and with an ongoing non-conformist's objection to the Church's close relationship with the state. In an era of growing religious de-institutionalisation, particularly evident in literary cloisters, Baxter's move can be seen as that of a serial outsider.

In the early 1950s Baxter increasingly emphasised the prophetic role of the poet as the vital articulator and communicator of society's injustices. However, his writings about religion during this period are sermonic and at times haranguing, with Christianity offered as the true alternative to a range of modern viewpoints and positions. His formulations of theological doctrine are clumsy, overly tight and consistent, as if the truths of Christianity were the winning and logical outcome of debate. His 'orthodox Christianity' was the logical counter to his perception of a dominant pessimistic New Zealand society that failed to adequately and ultimately generate life's purpose and meaning. Baxter's complicated theology was paralleled by a *sancta simplicitas* evident in his devotions of the mass. During this period his life and marriage were under considerable stress as he oscillated between uncontrollable religious and alcoholic binges, leading to him joining Alcoholics Anonymous. Acknowledging a power greater than himself and surrendering himself to it and the required confessions enhanced this simple faith, giving him the religious and psychological strength to eschew alcohol.

The promise of further strengthening his new religious toughness led to him receiving instruction and being rebaptised as a Roman Catholic in 1958, although at the expense of a marital separation. He described New Zealand as the 'land of authorities' (1. 16) where people craved external and certain direction, and he felt at home under the authority of the Roman Catholic Church. He became a regular and devout communicant, although he continued to lurch between bouts of unbridled religious enthusiasm and deep despair.

A UNESCO fellowship in 1958 was particularly significant for Baxter's religiosity and family life. Jacquie and their two children joined him overseas. His travels to Japan, Thailand and India reaffirmed his identity with, and commitment to, the marginalised and poor, while highlighting the positive values of village and community. India, in particular, with its unkempt sadhus and their ashrams, created a model of an intentional spiritual community led by a mendicant renouncer of all worldly pleasures and goods. He would later become the Catholic sadhu of Jerusalem and beyond.

Back in New Zealand he returned to settled family life in Wellington and a number of seemingly more stable years. His boredom and restlessness necessitated him changing his employment, and within his religious life he entertained a growing desire and need for deserved and redemptive suffering, and came to understand regular confession as an alternative form of moral management to alcohol. His non-conformist parents embraced Catholicism in 1965, attracted by both the faith and model of their son and Pope John. The Burns Fellowship took Baxter back to Dunedin in 1966–67, and he remained a further year at the Catholic Education Office there. He wrote for Catholic publications and taught at both schools and seminary. His essays on religious and theological matters, later collected and published, are framed by the Church's teachings and as such are conservative while being edifying and accessible.

At the end of this period, and at a time when he reported doubts about the Church's doctrine of the Holy Spirit, he had a transforming religious vision; he was called by God, summoned by the word 'Jerusalem'. This revelation and his move to Jerusalem was a religious turning point for Baxter which he hoped would effectively reunite his family and renew his relationships with his children and wife. He became a kind of 'secular monk' or Catholic lay-sadhu, taking vows of poverty and restraint. This period generated new theological concerns. He rejected almost all of his earlier theological reflections as middle-class comfort and became radicalised, focusing not on himself and his own spiritual condition but on that of the community that is God, the community of those at the margins, particularly the young and homeless. He became the New Zealand sadhu-hippie, a transition beyond his own concerns and those of the Church, which generated his most original and interesting theology. His life was as chaotic as ever, seemingly centred in Jerusalem, with unsustainable community houses in Wellington and Auckland, rural projects planned, and increasing doubts about the meaning and value of it all. He stressed the need for these communities to be bicultural, and oscillated between the communal projects themselves and his family as the model for this communal future. He also expressed his doubts about both.

During the Jerusalem years his relationships with God, Christ and Mary continued to intensify, but theologically he searched for a model of *ecclesia*, elect community or 'church' in the broadest sense, beyond the institution of the Roman Catholic Church yet still rooted in it. His community was inclusive of the lost, the drugged, the destitute and the dangerous alongside the idealistic young, and to extend potentially to all New Zealand. In *A Walking Stick for an Old Man* (3. 502–07), *Thoughts about the Holy Spirit* (3. 512–36), and especially in *The Six Faces of Love* (3. 235–54), Baxter developed the nascent framework for a unique New Zealand contextual and relational theology: bicultural, drawing on and yet resisting Presbyterian, Anglican, Catholic and Māori spiritual resources, and focused on relationships between people and God, on and in this land. This relational theology echoed the developing Catholic liberation theology in Latin America but reset in Aotearoa New Zealand. Alas, it remains but a framework, as Baxter's deteriorating health, growing dispiritedness and fears, and almost constant travelling proved unconducive to the systematic production of theology. In fact, he remained as conflicted as ever, devoutly faithful to God and Mary but desperately bound up in his own sinfulness alongside his heroic and inclusive visions for us all.

His new theology drew not on theological sophistication or tradition but on love and direct relationships – love and relationships that he understood as immediately certified by God. While still convinced of the absolute centrality of a Jesus who participates in the life of humanity and a humanity that can also participate in the life of Christ and the rituals that embody these truths, his new theological concern was with experiencing God in our response to the needs of others, all others, in our families, bicultural society and humanity, of creating an ever-growing community of care and concern across time and space; one not limited to the institutional Church.

*A Walking Stick for an Old Man* addressed our country's bicultural realities and historical injustices, and issued a rallying call for a just militancy (3. 489–502) to create a new community beyond pākehā complacency, conformity and exclusivity. Baxter understood 'religion [to be] the single deepest factor' (3. 507) in the bicultural crisis and considered the model of the Māori prophets to be essential in the transition that would enable us all to see God in the Māori community too. This idea of militancy is developed in 'A Handbook for the Christian Militant', focusing on the Biblical Exodus narrative as a typology for the liberation of New Zealand from its pharaohs, integral to the building of the new embracing *ecclesia*/community. The principal source for his new theological model was Martin Buber's *I and Thou.*[7] Baxter read this both as a guide to relationships (he uses it as a model for his feelings for his granddaughter) and for a theology of the new community beyond the Church. Baxter clarified his intuitive experience of the emptiness of urban modernity in terms of Buber's 'It-world' contrasted with the 'Thou-world' of relationship beyond the calculations of 'use and experience'. From Buber he learned that community was not a sociological abstraction, a metaphorical and

7 For Baxter's use of Buber, see *Six Faces of Love* in *Complete Prose* 3. 235–54.

potentially universal communion, but something concrete, a real community of real people in relation, in the messiness of their real lives, in a real place, in Jerusalem. This encounter with Buber gave Baxter a new way of understanding that relationships create community and that community is none other than the 'Eternal Thou', or God, the community of love. Baxter grasped Buber through a Catholic lens and identified the 'Eternal Thou' as the Holy Spirit or Ecclesia, the third person of the Holy Trinity. This understanding features directly, or is assumed, in all his later writings although it is often presented alongside seemingly incompatible mystical and kenotic theologies.

Baxter's experience of God was central to his experienced universe, albeit in dynamic and changing ways. The vengeful Father gave way to Quaker non-conformist inner conscience, which in turn became the Anglican Christ. He did indeed come home to the Roman Catholic salvific community and Church via his Marian devotion and love of Christ. His Jerusalem revelation led him to become a Catholic sadhu committed to the socially marginalised, and his discovery of Buber widened his God to include the communities of relationship. Reading Baxter's collected prose allows us to see these developments both more clearly as outline and more muddily as continually punctured by self-doubt and indecision, by fear and self-loathing, by bravery and bravado, and by a listlessness that served his poetic muse. Religiously, Baxter was in need of repeated acts of *metanoia*, of *teshuva*, of turning and returning to God for renewal and transformation towards the light only to return again to the darkness. The collected prose permits his repeated tropes to be more evident and to expose his obsessions to reveal a most conflicted man, a New Zealander, a Christian, and one who struggled on our behalf to make some sense of life in this colonial settler state. His writings about God, Christianity, theological issues and morality were prodigious and allow us to share his lifetime of deep and changing religious concerns. His lifelong quest for acceptance and forgiveness is a provocation to all New Zealanders and his theological vision of an inclusive, moral, community, divine in content and sanction, is worthy of consideration as a challenge to our existing injustices and prejudices. We still await the workings out of his contextual and relational New Zealand theology.

## *Works Cited*

Bloem, Marja and Martin Browne, Eds. *Colin McCahon: A Question of Faith*. Amsterdam and Nelson: Stedelijk Museum and Craig Potton, 2003.

Brown, Gordon. *Towards a Promised Land: On the Life and Art of Colin McCahon*. Auckland: Auckland University Press, c. 2010.

Buber, Martin. *I and Thou*. Trans. Ronald Gregor Smith, Edinburgh: T & T Clark, 1937.

Butler, Alban. *Butler's Lives of the Saints*. Collegeville, MN: Liturgical Press, 2000.

Higgins, Michael. *Stalking the Holy: The Pursuit of Saint Making*. Toronto: House of Anansi, 2006.

Hopgood, James, Ed. *The Making of Saints: Contesting Sacred Ground*. Alabama: Alabama University Press, 2005.

Woodward, Kenneth. *How the Catholic Church Determines Who Becomes a Saint, Who Doesn't, and Why*. New York: Simon and Schuster Touchstone, 1996.

# *Kenosis: The Difficult Spirituality of James K. Baxter*

Doreen D'Cruz

In considering the spirituality of James K. Baxter, all roads ultimately lead to Jerusalem as the place for the visible working-out of a vocation answered through radical self-renunciation. John Newton, in *The Double Rainbow*, sums up the convergence of factors that led Baxter to the establishment of his Jerusalem commune. There was, to start with, the compelling vision that Baxter had in late March 1968, about which he had confided in a letter to Roderick Finlayson. This event occurred at a turning point in his career, following on from the conclusion of his Robert Burns Fellowship, and with the approaching end of his employment with the Catholic Education Office, under the patronage of Bishop Kavanagh of Dunedin. In addition, the visionary pull towards Jerusalem correlated with the activist strand in Baxter's public persona, while Jerusalem's history as a mission station provided the apt location for unifying his Catholicism with his growing commitment to his 'taha Māori' (Newton 29–33). On top of all these, Jerusalem, as Jacquie Baxter believed, was the culmination of a journey that began with his searing encounter with poverty in India during his UNESCO Fellowship in the late fifties (Newton 31). All of these drivers carry some conviction, but are insufficient to explain the extreme practice of voluntary poverty, the persistent denial of all material comforts, the painful tribulations inflicted upon his body, the surrender of the solace of books, and the forfeiture of identity, which are features of Baxter's persona during his Jerusalem years. To understand all these as well as his momentous self-conversion in which he sought to bury his poetic persona and pass into lowliness and nothingness as Hēmi te tūtūā, one has to turn to the notion and practice of kenosis, or self-emptying, which had a simultaneous life for Baxter along with all else that transpired at the Jerusalem commune.

As a practising Catholic, Baxter's kenotic practice may have found its inspiration in the Christian doctrine of kenosis as contained in St Paul's Letter to the Philippians (2: 1–11), a connection also suggested by Mike Riddell (23). Described by John Lounibos as 'an early Christian liturgical hymn that summarizes the incarnation, life, death, resurrection, and exaltation of Jesus Christ' (52), these Pauline verses collocate the incarnation of Christ as man with a self-emptying of his own Godhead. St Paul writes: 'Have this mind among yourselves, which is yours in Christ Jesus, who, though he was in the form of God, did not count equality with God a thing to be grasped, but emptied himself, taking the form of a servant, being born in the likeness of men' (Phil. 2: 5–7). Through the void created by Christ's self-limitation in the renunciation of the 'form', though not, as Alva McClain maintains, the 'nature', of his Godhead, he takes on 'the form of a servant, being made in the likeness of man'. As the hymn proceeds, this humbling leads to Christ's obedient death on the cross. It is this Christian model of kenosis that St Paul holds up to the faithful at Philippi, 'pleading that men shall have in them "the mind" which was in Christ Jesus, and which impelled Him so to act as the passage describes, in the interests of others' (McClain 89). McClain goes on to argue that 'the great ethical end of the kenosis [expressed in the hymn] was servanthood', which was the first of the two steps in Christ's 'humiliation': 'In the first step, as God, He had emptied Himself, taking the form of a servant. Then, as man, he humbled Himself, becoming obedient unto death' (94). This elaboration of the Christian doctrine of kenosis is important for understanding the theological contexts that almost certainly would have influenced Baxter's kenotic practices.

The direct invocations of the term 'kenosis' are few and far between in Baxter's writings collected in the *Complete Prose, Volume 3 – The Jerusalem Years 1969–1972*. The first of these references is in the opening essay, 'The Rosary; a Meditation', originally published in *The Tablet* in January 1969. The other references are mostly scattered through *Jerusalem Daybook*. However, the implied references to 'kenosis' and the immersion in its practice consume many of the prose works of this period and feature strongly in *Jerusalem Sonnets*, *Autumn Testament*, and 'He Waiata mo taku Tangi'. In 'The Rosary', he provides a meditative commentary on the Joyful and Sorrowful Mysteries that are remembered in the first ten of the fifteen decades of this prayer; he refrains from offering a commentary on the final five Glorious Mysteries that correspond with the final five decades, pleading 'lack of space' and doubting he had 'the spiritual knowledge' (3. 6). It is in his commentary on the third Joyful Mystery, the Nativity, that he invokes the term 'kenosis': 'This was His kenosis, His self-emptying. Yet kenosis does not mean degradation. . . . He was born from a sinless Mother'. But through the Passion of Christ, His descent amongst humanity reaches the abyss of 'identification with man the moral leper' (3. 4). Baxter will return to this theme of Christ's voluntary surrender to the abjection issuing from the sadism and cruelty of the Crucifixion in 'Notions from the Passion' (3. 225–27): 'Yes; atrocity. Jesus went to the heart, the black terrible centre, of human atrocity, and died there' (3. 225). He thus gives imaginative force to what Christian kenosis means – Christ had 'set aside Godhead and even the safeguards of humanity'. Hence, he says, 'we should – I trust I do – love him with a burning love, a love as unprotected as his own, without reservation' (3. 225).

The passages on kenosis in *Jerusalem Daybook* (3. 294–341) offer insight into the shaping of Baxter's spirituality through a self-emptying that sought to practise love without the boundaries of self-protection. In perhaps one of the better-known passages, he notes how the doctrine of kenosis constructs a shared ground between Buddhists and Christians but hastens to add that one end of the sought-for void is 'to make more room for God and one's neighbour' (3. 325). Here, in the final proviso, he also finds the difference between the two kenotic traditions, as Gavin Drew's recollection of a personal homily from Baxter demonstrates: the purpose of 'Christ's self-emptying – and consequently Christian self-emptying – is a pouring out of oneself for others'. In contrast, the Buddha's advocacy of the void had as its goal 'the cessation of . . . feeling' (Drew 32). But Baxter also knew the exactions and costs of an abandonment to love – the 'broken heart', the 'dark night' of the soul, and the inevitable Crucifixion of Love on the Cross of the Law (3. 323, 315). Hence, the imitation of Christ involves a violent stripping of one's security and even of the configurations that bind one's identity, as Baxter testifies: 'Who is harsher than this God of ours? . . . the terrible One who grips our living entrails, who drives both good and evil from our souls, as if both were enemies, and fills us with anguish and darkness' (3. 303). In words reminiscent of W. B. Yeats, he declares that God has turned 'this man into an old coat and a broken stick' (3. 303). And in this 'dark night', Christ (indistinguishable from 'God') oscillates for him between the extremes of 'peace' and 'terror', 'joy' and 'sorrow', 'life' and 'death'.

Rocked violently between these polarities, Baxter may well say, 'Christ is . . . not my security' (3. 303). It may well be that the very process of kenosis demands a dying of the self, the loss of the self's ordinary coordinates for negotiating existence, an unmooring from its habits and habitats, all under the invitation of Christ, on a journey in which 'security' stands as its redundant antithesis. Perhaps Baxter's first line from Sonnet 38 of *Jerusalem Sonnets*, the song of the dying thief at the side of Christ, may convey the cleft in the 'I' that sunders self and security: 'I am dying now because I do not die.'[1] Daniel Stollenwerk has identified this line as taken from St John of the Cross (24). It comes as a coda to the immediately preceding final two lines of Sonnet 37: 'As the cross is lifted and the day goes dark / Rule over myself He has taken away from me.' The entire sonnet had been a testimony to each thing that had been taken away from the self, leading up to the final loss of executive authority over the surviving remnants of the self. Hence, there arises the agony of a dying that comes from being transfixed to a self whose emptying is only partial.

Baxter's idea that radical Christianity entails a renunciation of security for the self makes an early appearance in a review that had originally appeared in *The Tablet* in 1969. Entitled 'Golden Age of Devotional Writings' (3. 30–33), Baxter surveys three separate works published in 1969, by Theo Westow (*The Agony of the Church*), Karl Rahner (*Servants of the Lord*), and Anita Roper (*The Fifteenth Station*). Although he calls Westow 'a flawed prophet', Baxter seems to take on board his suggestion that the acronym 'R. C.' should mean 'Radical Christian' rather than 'Roman Catholic' (3. 31). He quotes at some length Westow's observation about the Church during the Second Vatican Council as turning away from its 'too unrealistic security, its overblown prestige, its worldly pomposity' and taking on 'gradually the true likeness of the suffering servant of Yahweh'. But it is the final sentence of the quotation from Westow that Baxter reads as the 'sting . . . in its tail' (3. 31). Westow aims it at 'those who, mistakenly, belong to the Church because they wanted that security which their faith in fact requires them to surrender' (cited in 3. 31). Notably, as if Baxter had found in Westow's work a theme that chimes with his own spiritual quest,[2] he reproduces from it a passage on the surrender of security that was intrinsic to Christ's Passion and must characterise the spiritual journey of anyone

1 All citations of Baxter's poems, except '[The Ikons]', are from *CPoems*.

2 In 'Property and Poverty', a series of anecdotes and thoughts, Baxter

who seeks to follow him (cited in 3. 31). Expatiating on this theme, Baxter declares, '"God is our spiritual security," says the soporific devotional writer absorbed by a million hearts avid for the certainty of salvation'. On the contrary, the 'true lover of God' throws away security for a love that is without calculation and which seeks neither merit nor salvation (3. 32). Baxter's commentary on Westow's book is significant because it anticipates so thoroughly the surrender of security that reaches its agonising climax in *Jerusalem Daybook* and *Autumn Testament*.

The prayer of kenosis that Baxter reproduces in *Jerusalem Daybook*, first in Māori and then in its English translation, registers the trusting surrender to Christ that leads the way towards emptying himself of his worldly attachments. His entire reliance has to be upon Christ, as Baxter's translation of the prayer of kenosis shows: 'Jesus is my water; Jesus is my food; Jesus is my prestige; Jesus is my money; Jesus is my love; Jesus is my sickness and my death.' It is a prayer he composed himself and which he regards as 'chop[ping] through a great deal of the stupidity inside me'. He calls the prayer a 'blood transfusion', as presumably the metaphor evokes the sense of a dying self being bled dry of its vanities and desires, and reaching in brokenness to Christ, who is both the provider of sustenance and the cause of his sickness and his death. This prayer of kenosis is ultimately a prayer of acceptance – 'one accepts whatever happens as the gift of Jesus' (3. 338).

Baxter's prose writings of the Jerusalem period embody three phases of the kenotic experience, which sometimes interlock with each other. There is first the call from Te Atua and the reception of a charism, which involves submission to the bidding of Te Atua. Hence, when he finds himself 'walking on hot coals' and tempted to give up, he 'remember[s] that, as far as I know, God wants me to be here. So I have to stay put. When I am no longer needed, God will make it pretty plain' (3. 293–94). Although Baxter declares that he has no

had already allied his spirituality with the loss of security. (See 2. 614.)

'telephone line connected to the throne of God' (3. 289), his kenotic journey is in obedience to what he perceives as the call of Te Atua. Secondly, in a journey whose renunciations are also physical, not just intellectual or aesthetic, the bodily tribulations endured are in sympathetic identification with the Passion of Christ and the Way of the Cross. Finally, kenosis involves a surrender of those intellectual and spiritual fences that keep the self in its fictional comforts and the idea of God secure. This last aspect of kenosis takes Baxter to an encounter with a darkness in which 'God' is no longer discernible. This is, arguably, the most painful part of his self-emptying.

### *The Divine Call and the Reception of a Charism*

Besides what is contained in the excerpts from the letters that he wrote to Roderick Finlayson and John Weir, reproduced in *The Double Rainbow* (23–24), Baxter has also left what is perhaps his most detailed account of his visionary experience as an irresistible visceral urging from God in 'Extracts from "Jerusalem Journal" 22' (3. 289–92). He describes the physical pain and the invasiveness of the divine visitation in terms that approximate the roasting of his body and the plucking of his entrails. He intuits that Te Atua was with him 'in a new mode', when for 'six nights' he lay awake' and was 'like a potato roasting on hot coals' while, 'like a hawk' upon 'a dead possum', Te Atua tore at his 'guts'. The compelling message from this experience was the 'unfamiliar notion' that 'it was necessary for me to go to Hiruharama'. To Baxter who declares himself as 'not a man who sees visions', this idea was either preposterous or 'a thing I was meant to do' (3. 289). With the knowledge of what has come after, it is evident that he came to the latter conclusion.

Baxter writes of the divine invasion in explicitly allegorical terms at the beginning of *Jerusalem Daybook*. He tells the anecdote of a man who, despairing over his life, chose not to commit suicide, but rather to barricade himself in 'a large corrugated iron tank', which he 'furnished . . . simply with the necessities of life' such as a bed, food, 'electric light and heating, and even a large crucifix hung on the wall to remind him of God and help him pray'. But the man was assailed morning and evening by 'volleys of bullets', by which he was sometimes wounded. The 'iron walls' of his home 'were pierced' with bullet holes, which he desperately 'plugged up' (3. 295). In due course, he used the holes for a different purpose, to look out upon the world, and eventually when the iron rusted he walked out, expecting to be shot by the unknown assailant. Instead the 'other man' holds his 'gun down' and explains that he is not his enemy. And there were 'scars upon the other man's hands and feet, and these scars were shining like the sun' (3. 296). The allegory not only alludes to the unhoming that must occur in order to follow the path of the crucified Christ, but also shows that such following occurs through divine insistence.

The call to Jerusalem and the role Baxter perceived for himself there are understood by him also through metaphors and symbolic figures that are both Christian and Māori. He is 'the seed in the ground from which a tree could grow'. To become that seed, 'te purapura iti', he had to become poor and strip himself of all the coverings of self that would inhibit growth. Baxter is drawing upon Christ's parable of the mustard seed, 'the smallest of all seeds', which becomes a tree upon which birds nest (Matt. 13. 31–32). In shrinking to a seed, there is harboured the notion of kenosis, achieved principally through poverty. However, a parallel image to this has an indigenous source. Baxter envisages himself as the 'old kumara, the one who has to rot so that the new ones can grow from him'. As he himself acknowledges, this is a 'terrifying' image as it foresees painfully his own 'disintegration'. These organic images of dying in order to facilitate new growth, through which ngā mōkai can flourish, lead to the splitting of the Baxter persona into the 'dead body', presumably that of James K. Baxter, which 'stinks in the ground', and the 'poor man, Hemi', who is the live one (3. 290). Thus Baxter gives personal meaning to Christ's injunction, 'he who finds his life will lose it, and he who loses his life for my sake will find it' (Matt. 10. 39). He empties himself of one identity and passes into another.

As Hemi in Jerusalem,[3] he is a 'ghost', 'the blank card in the pack, the one whom children call the ghost' (3. 290). Baxter explains this vitiated condition as pertaining to the status of a pākehā 'in the pa, unless he has a Maori friend, an elder brother, to throw his coat over him' (3. 290). He repeats the words of Hana Jackson that 'pākehā' and 'kehua' are similar words. But the ghosting of the pākehā, and his accompanying relegation to the position of younger brother or 'te teina' in the pā, are not matters rooted in racial essentialism, but rather they have their sources in pākehā deficiencies in the virtues earned through poverty, suffering, communal love, and from 'the theology of immanence' (3. 290). Although unexplained in the context of its immediate articulation, Baxter elaborates upon this theology in *Jerusalem Daybook*: 'God lives among us. When we share our kai, it is often like the meal of fish and bread Te Ariki prepared on the lakeshore for his friends. God also dies among us' (3. 315). Baxter's longing for a Māori tuakana with whom he can share kai does not reach culmination in the way he had hoped. He learns from the Māori prophet that 'the Tuakana was Te Ariki in his Maori aspect' (3. 290). And the Māori face of Jesus, he saw, was 'smashed and bleeding', and it was his personal calling to cleanse that face. Conversely, the pākehā face of Christ was locked in a rigor mortis, a death bred out of complacency, and 'the desire for money and prestige' (3. 291). It was not his calling, Baxter thought, to minister to this aspect of Christ. The 'two faces of Christ' are of Him in His crucified and suffering aspects in New Zealand, with the agony of one face being continuous with the agony of the other. In surrendering himself to being a 'ghost in the pa',

3 John Weir notes that 'Extracts from "Jerusalem Journal"' 'seems to have been the third draft of *Jerusalem Daybook*' and 'JKB entitled this draft *The Book of Hemi*' (see 4. 398, no. 645).

Baxter undergoes a stripping of his pākehā self, an implicit dying, so that he can minister to his suffering tuākana, in his Māori aspect. However, as Baxter acknowledges, many of ngā mōkai are 'in fact pakeha', who 'are capable of acquiring a Maori heart' and 'dread the slaughterhouse in which they see their relatives expiring' (3. 291).

Yet another 'persona' through which Baxter articulates his kenotic calling is that of the donkey upon which Christ rides to Jerusalem. This figure captures the surrender of direction and sovereignty over personal will that accompanies the disintegration of self and the relinquishing of his pākehā identity. The donkey 'did not know the meaning of his journey, but the Rider knew well enough' (3. 290). The theme of 'unknowing', in which God moves him according to His will, surfaces in a later passage in 'Extracts from "Jerusalem Journal"', when he accepts God's 'boot[ing] him on the backside' and making him into 'a fool': 'If He makes me a fool He must look after the fool He has made' (3. 292). The image of God pushing him unceremoniously into doing the unexpected has a parallel with what the Rider might conceivably do to the donkey to urge it along certain directions. But for the very human Baxter, this goading from the Almighty makes him look like a fool, such as when he goes 'barefooted', prays 'in bus shelters', puts 'his arms around strangers', or walks 'through Auckland with a woman's dress on in the company of camp friends' (3. 292). The donkey and God's fool thus conflate into each other, and are possibly aspects of the surrender of will to God's urging.

Confronted with the mystery of God's will, Baxter resigns himself to 'Te Atua's protection', and declares that 'the most valuable thing I do may well be to say the fifteen decades of the Rosary daily, recite the Canticle of the Sun, and go to Mass when I can' (3. 292). Yet doubt and unknowing are companions, as demonstrated by *Jerusalem Sonnets* 21 and 36, where the 'donkey' shifts between uncertainty about his capacity to 'carry' the Rider and wanting to shrug off his burden in a journey whose path is far from clear. By 'Autumn

Testament' 1, the self seems to have transmogrified into a boulder (14) at the edge of nothingness, in the place of absence signified by 'Wahi Ngaro, the void from which all life comes' ('Autumn Testament' 2, 1).

Baxter writes in *Jerusalem Daybook* that the way to that void is through poverty. Still, he cautions us against the fallacy of equating poverty with goodness. Rather 'poverty is availability' (3. 304), and is born from the spirit of detachment through which self-love is snuffed out so that one becomes as the void 'on which Te Wairua Tapu moved at the beginning of the world' (3. 304). However, there is anguish of spirit in the knowledge that 'one cannot yet be entirely poor' (3. 310). In 'Song for Sakyamuni', stanza 2, he recognises the near inescapability of self-love, except in the moment 'without premeditation', when the spirit of God acts through one:

> My loves, I grant, are all self-love,
> Except for the love I cannot call my own,
>
> The wind that moves in the branches of the tree
> Without premeditation – (3–6)

The meaning of the poverty of self is given vivid anecdotal significance through his account of, and imaginary conversations with, Charles de Foucauld, his brother in spirit, who had also succumbed to the absurdity of being God's fool in endeavours that seemed ridiculous, quixotic and even fruitless. Baxter finds in him a model of one whose self-emptying had involved a surrender to the inexplicability of God's will, even when it seemed to be in contradiction of all worldly wisdom. De Foucauld had lived among Algerian tribesmen, 'doing nothing, unaccepted by them, in poverty, weaving a few baskets'. 'He wanted to convert them', but he made no converts and was eventually killed by some of the tribesmen. But, now, after his death, 'they are pouring into the Church' (3. 309). Poverty, in Baxter's terms, is more than material poverty. It is an abandonment to God's will with a 'holy indifference' to all circumstances and vicissitudes (3. 310). This is an indifference in which the self dies to itself.

One of the more telling Biblical images that Baxter uses for such self-voiding, in the same passage in *Jerusalem Daybook* in which he contemplates the case of Charles de Foucauld, is to become like the 'eye of the needle': 'when I know I am nothing, then through the eye of the needle God can do what He wants to do' (3. 304). Baxter's image is, of course, derived from Christ's words spoken after the wealthy young man, who wanted to know what he 'must . . . do, to have eternal life', had left in sorrow for being unable to respond to the call to poverty: 'It is easier for a camel to go through the eye of a needle than for a rich man to enter the kingdom of God' (Matt. 19. 17–25). As Baxter reads this saying of Christ, he seems to suggest that in order to pass through the eye of the needle, the self must reduce to the nothingness required by it. Yet the way to this void cannot occur through any self-engendered heroism. For therein lies the defeat of the project. For example, after a twenty-seven day fast, Baxter expected 'a spiritual breakthrough', but instead 'found [himself] standing like a blind child in front of God'. There was no illumination, no arrival at an earthly paradise. For these to happen, '[t]o become Adam in paradise, one has to go the long way home, back through the eye of the needle' (3. 339). The 'eye of the needle' is one of the many metaphors through which the spirit of kenosis is given verbal recognition.

Baxter declares that 'the journey [towards kenosis is made] bearable' by the fact 'that one travels always in company'. He follows this statement of communal consolation with the single-line cryptic assertion, 'Because God is, we are able to be' (3. 339). Baxter finds the continuity between the divine and the human most particularly in the incarnation. In 'Thoughts about the Holy Spirit: from a Reading of the Prison Letters of Paul' (3. 512–36), he describes Christ's incarnation as the 'root' from which 'the new creation, the wholly human society and the perfecting of non-human creatures grows like a tree' (3. 516). The incarnation is, however, not just a discrete event in time. In a letter to Colin Durning, Baxter, like Durning, recognises it as an ever-continuing happening. He writes to Durning, '[Y]ou obey the God who is always being born' ('Extract 5 from Draft of *Autumn Testament*' 3. 418). Hence, the 'God [Who] is' exists not merely in the eternal; nor is he merely contained in a segment of history, but is continually reborn, suffers, and dies in the unfolding of the temporality humans occupy, and also lives in their communality.

Baxter intuits that the special charism he is entrusted with by Te Atua, on behalf of the Māori Christ, rests with the cultivation of a community in His spirit for ngā mōkai, and that this comes with a terrible moral burden:

> To mishandle one's private potato patch is one thing. To mishandle a farm of many paddocks is a grave matter. . . . And if the hair of the head of the soul of one of nga mokai is harmed by me, I desire to burn in Hell for ever. (3. 291)

Notwithstanding, he accepts the charism from Te Atua, responding to its irresistible force, and submitting himself in the process to the wounding of the body and mind that is asked for, while keeping before him the sacred nature of his responsibility.

### *The Way of the Cross and the Wounded Body*

Some may argue that Baxter's passage into the identity of 'Hemi' is a stage in his self-mythologisation. Conversely, it may be maintained that 'Hemi' marks the journey towards his death along the Way of the Cross. In Catholic liturgy, the Way of the Cross is counted through the fourteen stations that commemorate Christ's Passion from the point of his condemnation by Pilate to his being laid in the tomb after his death on the Cross. The indignities, pain and sense of abandonment suffered here take us to the final and most difficult meaning of kenosis – the detachment from one's ultimate home, the body. Hence, it is entirely congruent with the idea of Christian kenosis that the wounds of the body may yield their own special grace. In *Jerusalem Daybook*, although Baxter gives priority to the wounded soul, he notes also the wounding of the body as necessary for making one's self available: 'The soul has to be wounded as well as the body. Wounds are like fountains in the soul. Through our wounds we achieve availability' (3. 325). 'Availability' signifies, among other things, the breaking 'out of fictitious worlds' and the collapse of the 'frame of reference' that inhibits and dulls our souls (3. 329). Baxter's tramping 'forty miles with sore feet in the rain' may involve more than a symbolic departure from fictitious confines, through the undeniable visceral experience of cold, discomfort, and pain that brings one to the rough performatives of experience. He says, 'It is a different man who takes his coat off at the end of the journey' (3. 325). Indeed, the 'coat' that is shed may be emblematic of a layer of self-attachment that is also surrendered.

For Baxter, it is through anguish, not through spurious comforts, that the longing for God achieves a palpable presence. Comforts inhibit one's direction towards God. In the imagined charism received from God by Baxter, the 'sense of comfort' is what he is enjoined to surrender 'above all': 'A comfortable servant might begin to serve comfort instead of serving me' (3. 304). Accordingly, Baxter's question to God in Sonnet 1 of the *Jerusalem Sonnets*, despite its wry humour, carries a more serious spiritual implication in the attempt to discern the divine will:

> 'Lord,' I ask Him,
>
> 'Do You or don't You expect me to put up with lice?'
> His silent laugh still shakes the hills at dawn. (12–14)

The body, tormented in its quest for God, and in apparent obedience to the perception of God's will, also encounters the rebuke of God for the hidden pride that may reside in a self-mortification that aims to emulate Christ. In Sonnet 14, the poet steals into the church at night by 'the side door . . .

/ Like a timid thief', where in violation 'Of God's decorum', he lies down on the floor 'cruciform' and hears the necessary words that let the world fall into perspective for him:

> 'More stupid than a stone, what do you know
>
> 'Of love? Can you carry the weight of my Passion,
> You old crab farmer?' I go home in peace. (12–14)

It is perhaps the peace that comes from having dissociated, at least for then, the commemorative walk with Christ along the Way of the Cross from the insidious grip of the ego.

Hence, by 'Autumn Testament' 26, it is a more resigned, perhaps less spiritually ambitious man who weaves his praying the Sorrowful Mysteries with the ebb and flow of ordinary life. He disentangles a cicada from his hair just as he begins the third Sorrowful Mystery, 'the Crowning with Thorns'. Between that and the fourth Mystery, 'the Carrying of the Cross', he comes across Rex, who complains about the 'new overseer . . . a little Hitler'. Thoughts of Rex and of his bones that 'pull / Out of their socket' are woven into the praying of this Mystery. By the 'black plastic tank,' he kneels for the fifth Mystery, the Crucifixion, 'God's Death'. Through this interweaving of Christ's Passion with the cicada's loss of freedom, the assertions of petty power, the corporeal pain of another, the summer drought, and the 'cool' shade under 'the pungas', Baxter makes apparent the sense of the suffering God's immanent presence in the painful, and perhaps even joyful, vagaries of the world for which he died.

Facing the God whose wounded body and whose death are the sources of forgiveness and communion, Baxter sees human wounds as themselves the channels of penitence and grace. In '*Autumn Testament*: Letter to Colin [Durning]' (3. 474–80), he writes,

> Te Ariki tells us – 'What sorrow is like my sorrow?' . . . His sorrow is both ours and not ours. It is beyond us, yet spears slide out of it to pierce our little hearts. I say to him, 'Let me

> have your sorrow,' but probably I am insincere. I love him, yet his sorrow terrifies me. To go into it, out of the arms of the tribe, is too like dying before death. (3. 479)

Through the body surrendered to pain, Baxter walks with and keeps vigil with Christ's sorrow and agony. In '[I walked south . . . ]' (3. 467–68, square brackets are as in text), his account carries some resemblance to a personal Way of the Cross. Having got a ride from National Park to Raetihi, he refuses the hospitality offered by the truck driver who had brought him there and also by a Māori boy, who runs out to offer him a bed just as he is passing out of town. It is fifty miles from Raetihi to Wanganui, the time is 8pm, and Baxter is walking with bare feet. He is entirely dependent on God for transport, a 'bludger' upon divine mercy: 'If God 'doesn't want me to have a ride, then I don't get one' (3. 467). Thus he 'learn[s his] religion' through the piercing pain of his feet on the tarseal. The numbness produced by the cold offers a temporary reprieve before feeling returns as if 'you are walking on embers' (3. 467–68). It is through such self-abandonment to pain that he comes close to death, a letting go of 'the visible earth' in the passage to 'the invisible Father' (3. 467). In the short description of this walk, Baxter gives the most direct and explicit account of the kenosis that is acquired through the wounded body to which he had made reference in *Jerusalem Daybook* (3. 325).

In Baxter's theology, the discomforts of the wounded body, as well as of the wounded soul, in a journey of mortification, mark the path to God. Hence, he advises his reluctant twin, his 'Brother thief', in 'Autumn Testament' 22, not to 'rail at / The only gate we have to paradise' (13–14). That 'gate' involves the prayer in which the body hanging by Christ on the Cross also experiences the soul-shaking pangs of divine abandonment as Christ did:

> This body that shivers
>
> In the foggy cold, tasting the sour fat,

Was made to hang like a sack on its thief's cross,

Counting it better than bread to say the words of Christ,
*'Eli! Eli!'* (6–10)

The passive voice, coupled with the infinitive, is noteworthy here, indicative of an envisaged end, perhaps yet to be reached, which gives weight to the first line of the sonnet, 'To pray for an easy heart is no prayer at all'. For that is to seek immunity from the very insecurities that bring one to the place beside the suffering Christ to receive the grace that flows therefrom. The performatives that move between spiritual and corporeal pain shake the soul out of its complacency, just as a flea is shaken from a blanket, and falls to the ground to be buried there (11–12). Baxter's spirituality here bears resemblance to that of Charles Péguy, for whom the 'wounds', the 'chinks in [one's] armour', provide the 'way in for grace' (cited in Valente).

By way of a spirituality that embraces the agonies of human corporeality 'in the shadow of sorrow and death' (3. 254), Baxter gives significance to the enormity of the incarnation in which God entered the human condition and limited himself from his own Godhead. It is a route that carries him to the 'desert' where 'anguish' stands for the place where he cannot find God; yet he remains mindful that God 'has been obviously present in every venture of my life' (3. 413). In his declaration that he does not 'find Him in any created thing', Baxter seems to have moved out of the state in which he gloried in the immanence of Christ, and thus perhaps comes to actually utter his own version of 'Eli! Eli!' The 'thief' imitates his God on the cross, through the sojourn in the 'deserts' of the soul in which God seems to have forsaken him (3. 413).

## *The Paradox of Unhoming*

'Unhoming' leads to the paradoxical route home along the 'long way' that takes one through the paths of detachment signified by the 'eye of the needle', the void. Paul Millar has noted, with particular reference to 'Autumn Testament' 2, 'Gradually the void in Baxter's last poems becomes synonymous with a God' (8). More accurately, the 'void' marks for Baxter the place upon which God moves as well as the unknowing with which he is approached. Baxter's proximity to this God is through the empty spaces in himself. In 'Extract 6 from Draft of *Autumn Testament*', he writes of the 'abyss' that 'open[s] in the rock of my ossification', from where there

> comes . . . anguish, a constant flow of pain on account of our . . . [separation] from the transcendent One whom we can't know by any trick or concept of the active intellect. I trust this anguish. It tells me that God exists and that he is our Father. (3. 470, square brackets are as in the text)

The anguish from the void displaces the fictitious projection through which one tries to possess God. This is yet another stage in Baxter's self-emptying journey to the unknowable God, beyond the constructions of civilisations – 'these woven spider cages/ That tie together the high heads of grass, / A civilisation in each' (Autumn Testament 2, 2–4). The poet acknowledges the fragility of these 'cages' of 'white silk', but 'having learnt / With manhood mercy', he will not 'rip' them apart. Rather the poem concludes with a vision of 'One great white flower' that 'Shakes in the wind'. The wind shaking the flower, like the wind in the trees in the 'Song for Sakyamuni', conveys the sense of Te Wairua Tapu moving upon the void. And Baxter conceives himself too as a channel for the wind, a 'hole in the Maori-pakeha fence that the wind blows through' (3. 447). In the void where attachments collapse, there the spirit of God moves.

It is perhaps from this perspective that one may approach the fall of the icons in the poem '[The Ikons]' (*Jerusalem Daybook*, 3. 310–11). During the simple act of gathering mushrooms, the poet meditates on the dark vacancy left 'Since the great ikons fell down, / God, Mary, home, sex, poetry' and even self reduced to '"The gap inside a coat"'

(11–12, 16). The images and ideas that are the projections of civilisations, or of individual minds, are as attachments that must pass in order for one to stand blindly before the God who exists beyond any human imagining. In this poverty that comes from renouncing the securities that cocoon the self, all that is left is the doing of the task at hand and the longing that will not be assuaged:

> I go on looking
>
> For mushrooms in the field, and the fist of longing
> Punches my heart, until it is too dark to see. (20–22)

William Broughton considers these lines and the rhetorical question that precedes them as containing 'the assertion of grief and despair . . . that mocks the human aspirations of the devotional poet' (155). Yes, there is grief, but not despair. Rather, the lines reflect the insatiable yearning in the darkness of an earthly unknowing for the soul's true home in God that seems all but unreachable, since the river he must cross 'only has one beach' (14). The poet's language fails in the rhetorical question that Broughton has identified; it recognises the impossibility of translating the natural world into something imbued with the divine, since both 'God' and 'Te Whaea' appear synonymous with darkness: 'the darkness I call God, / The darkness I call Te Whaea, how can they translate / The blue calm evening sky' (16–18). This is not a self-mockery by 'the devotional poet' but rather the sign of an unhoming and self-emptying involved in the kenotic journey to God, in which even the idea harboured of 'God' must be renounced. There 'at the centre of the darkness we wait for the light of the spiritus to shine' ('Letter to Colin [Durning]' 3. 476).

And self, formed to an 'ethical code', must be surrendered as well so that love alone consumes the self (3. 447), as he intimates in 'Talk to Training-College Students,' signed off by Hēmi and dated 1972 (3. 442–48), Here, Baxter speaks of himself as 'the religious man' who 'could no longer distinguish good from evil – only love from non-love' (3. 447). This is a further station on the road of poverty that opens the self to the other and God: 'Poverty. Poverty. Poverty is the door broken in the wall between man and man and man and God. To be virtuous is to fall short of poverty' (3. 447). Virtue may well be the sealed door that keeps the self intact and rations its love according to the measure of the law. But in Baxter's self-emptying journey, the 'self' necessarily dies as it is consumed by a profligate love whose very essence is a companionate suffering with the beloved that overrides any calculation: 'Why do I go barefoot and go without sleep and hurt this old body? Because love has to share, directly or indirectly, the pain of the beloved'. The 'beloved' is '[t]he man I love – the One who became us and lived and died with us' (3. 447). In *Jerusalem Daybook*, Baxter reads in the crucifixion the crushing tension between the 'necessary' law, which is the cross, and the boundless love that is crucified upon it: 'Love is crucified on the Law until the end of time' (3. 315). It may be that the call to walk with the 'beloved' along the path of such a love prompts from the Baxter persona in *Jerusalem Daybook* the heart-piercing sense of one whose securities are utterly shattered: 'You think God might take away your health or your happiness or your sanity, but God will always leave you your morality. Don't count on it' (3. 303). There is a price to be paid for loving beyond the limits, and that is to bear the cross of the law and its condemnation upon one's shoulders.

For Baxter, such loving includes a surrender of his sexual body to the demands of others in need. In 'He Waiata mo taku Tangi', he describes 'chastity' as 'a great luxury' for himself, who is 'like a man who rakes / for the live ones in a plague pit' (41–46). However, the loss of virtue hits him hard. In 'Three Kinds of Christian' (3. 546–54), after putting himself down as a sinner – one of the 'anawim', the sort that 'St Paul advised his flock not to sit down at the table with' – Baxter utters the prayer that seeks to avoid the surrender of his sexual body:

> But Lord, Holy One, You who hide Yourself from me, I can't stand losing my virtues. . . . Don't let the girls who have been driven mad by lack of love regard me as their sexual saviour. (3. 549)

This prayer leads up to an account of how he shared his bed, food and clothes on a 'cold night' with a Māori woman who was 'in a state of semi-coma and also had her period and a dose of gonorrhoea'. He thought 'the danger to chastity would not be great', but 'was mistaken' in this, as 'at 2 a.m.' the woman began to make physical advances in order to show her affection. Baxter's receptive response sprang from an understanding that she needed 'a reassurance that she was still a woman' (3. 551). This sexual event was an isolated one in a friendship that was subsequently 'celibate' (3. 552). The woman was adrift, and Baxter shows how the various institutions had in one way or another failed her; she was possibly misunderstood as insane, and was vulnerable to abuse by the police, one of whom had threatened to charge her unless 'she agreed to sleep with him' (3. 551). In this context Baxter's giving his body to her, instead of wrapping himself in his virtue, was a sign of his acceptance of her and his recognition of her dignity as a person. The self-emptying demanded by love thus leads to a paradoxical relationship with virtue.

It is possible that this experience serves as the source of a fictitious account that Baxter weaves around Father Damien of Molokai in 'Aspects of Christian Action' (3. 424–30). Baxter uses as the pretext for his story the rumour circulated in Australia, after Father Damien had contracted leprosy and died, that he had 'slept with leper women' (3. 425). This was vigorously challenged by Robert Louis Stevenson. Baxter had no reason, as he acknowledges, to doubt the chastity of Father Damien, but the false story gives him the occasion for imagining how a fictitious Father Damien may have slept with a leper woman. The Polynesian woman in the story is newly arrived at the leper settlement, dying although not far gone in the disease, because the spirit of life in her has been rendered inert by her isolation and the injury to her womanhood inflicted by the disease. Although she inspires fear in him and the impulse to put himself out of her presence, Damien slowly experiences the continuity between his pain and her pain, and comforts her in the way she desires, through a commingling and communion of bodies. By virtue of the distance that the fictitious narrative allows him, Baxter is able to give this sexual encounter emotional depth, psychological conviction, and moral complexity that perhaps his own personal account lacks. In the story, Father Damien recognises that he had betrayed his God, like a Judas, and in the agony that follows he flagellates himself with a whip (3. 428). Love had overrun the boundaries of the moral law enjoined upon Damien, and he pays the dues exacted by the law in a self-scourging.

So it had been also with Baxter: the sexual body given to a woman who is not his wife must be scourged. Love may not be foreclosed by the law, and virtue may have to be abandoned for the sake of love, but the law still claims its exactions for such a profligate expenditure of self. As we know from Mike Minehan's account of her love affair with Baxter, who was the father of her son, the woman to whom he gave his sexual body is also made a witness to the flagellation of that body (50). This is perhaps inevitable in the context of kenosis. 'Kenosis' involves 'leaving a space or deserting it'; it suggests 'to pour out, make away with, waste away, make void' (Lounibos 52). The 'things' or 'spaces' that are relinquished in the process become the markers through which the self-emptying or self-expenditure is designated. Hence, 'God', 'virtue', and the law persist as the known homes, which the soul must leave in a journey of self-abandonment towards a love that speaks the language of darkness, anguish, poverty and self-inflicted pain. This place of loss and suffering is where the cross of kenosis is erected.

## *Conclusion*

Kenosis is 'self-emptying', but there is a terrible abyss to be plumbed in this concept as it becomes incarnate in Baxter's practice. It signifies nothing less than the surrender to one's death for the love of God and of one's fellow beings. It is to this that Baxter gave himself, as these words of his in *Jerusalem Daybook* suggest: 'If we claim to love God we have to love our own death' (3. 305). The dying means a letting go, for God and neighbour, of all the securities and comforts that hold the self in place. This sometimes means that to love greatly, one may also sin greatly, if only in the eyes of others or according to the moral law. Baxter carried no illusions about his sinfulness, identifying himself with 'Judas' in 'A Prayer of Failure' and in *Jerusalem Daybook* (3. 159, 304). In his talk 'Three Kinds of Christian', he identifies himself as a transgressor of all the commandments: 'it seems to me that there is not one of the Commandments that I have not at some time broken. If there are, I would be very glad to hear about it' (3. 549). However, insofar as these things can be known, he seems to have kept the two greatest commandments – love of God and love of one's neighbour (Matt. 22. 37–40) – to an extraordinary degree. The way towards that love had not been without its failures and moral contradictions for Baxter. But at the same time such great love, combined with a profound sense of his own sinfulness, led Baxter down the dolorous route of a self-dying that forms the heart of his encounter with Christ.[4]

4 I am grateful to my colleague and husband John C. Ross for conversations on Baxter, his loan of books by and about Baxter, and for reading this essay.

## *Works Cited*

Broughton, William. '"Troubled by His Own Absurdity": An Examination of Some of the Sonnets of Baxter.' *Journal of New Zealand Literature* 13 (1995): 143–56.

Drew, Gavin. 'Hard Work.' *Stimulus: The New Zealand Journal of Christian Thought and Practice* 11.1 (February 2003): 31–32.

*Holy Bible.* Revised Standard Version. Cleveland: William Collins, 1971.

Lounibos, John. 'Self-Emptying in Christian and Buddhist Spirituality.' *The Journal of Pastoral Counseling* 35 (2000): 49–66.

McClain, Alva J. 'The Doctrine of the Kenosis in Philippians 2: 5-8.' *The Master's Seminary Journal* 9.1 (Spring 1998): 85–96. (This article appeared originally in *The Biblical Review* 13.4 [October 1928]: 506–27.)

Millar, Paul. 'Hemi te Tutua / Jim the Nobody: The "Gap" and the "Void" in the Poetry of James K. Baxter.' *Stimulus: The New Zealand Journal of Christian Thought and Practice* 11.1 (February 2003): 5–8.

Minehan, Mike. *O Jerusalem: James K. Baxter: An Intimate Memoir.* Christchurch: Hazard Press, 2002.

Riddell, Mike. 'Baxter the Mystic.' *Tui Motu Interislands* (December 2001): 20–23.

Stollenwerk, Daniel. 'Void, Gap, Nada: St John of the Cross' "Dark Night of the Soul" in James K. Baxter's Jerusalem Works.' *Stimulus: The New Zealand Journal of Christian Thought and Practice* 14.2 (May 2006): 24–32.

Valente, Gianni. 'The Return of Charles Péguy.' *Vatican Insider La Stampa* 5 September 2014. Web. 9 November 2015.

# *Becoming the Sore Thumb of the Tribe: The Development of James K. Baxter's Social Voice*

Peter Whiteford

In 1952, the Pegasus Press (Christchurch) published a volume of poetry bearing the decidedly Shavian title of *Poems Unpleasant*. It contained thirty-six poems – a dozen each by the three collaborators, Anton Vogt, Louis Johnson and James K. Baxter, who had all met the previous year at Wellington Teachers' Training College. Frank McKay notes that 'it was Vogt's idea to bring out the joint volume, but his own offering reveals no more than a minor poet' (McKay 131). With one or two exceptions, the same might reasonably be said of the offerings of Johnson and of Baxter. The best known of Baxter's poems is his last in the volume, 'The Homecoming', but it is the first of them, 'Letter to Piers Plowman', that I wish to begin with in this essay. The poem is of interest for a number of reasons: it displays Baxter's early mastery of the sestina, and the fluent handling of formal features that is characteristic of much of his verse; it occupies a significant and early place among the epistolary verse for which he evidently had considerable fondness and which would later develop into the important sequence *Pig Island Letters*; and it reveals Baxter's awareness of the difficult medieval dream poem, *The Vision of Piers Plowman*, and his responsiveness both to Langland's allegorising technique and to some of the principal themes of that poem.

Baxter's poem has been commented on by Lawrence

Warner in *The Cambridge Companion to Piers Plowman*, where it is located as part of a twentieth-century re-emergence of the figure of Piers as 'the missing object of desire or pilgrimage rather than spokesman for righteousness' (211); for Warner, the 'crisis that prompts the letter . . . [is] the subjugation of the spirit to the forces of post-war capitalism and conformity'. Apart from this, 'Letter to Piers Plowman' has received little critical attention. That lack of attention derives, one imagines, from the poem's weaknesses. Although it may not be the 'comedy of bad manners' that David Eggleton suggests some of the verse letters are – indeed, it handles the intricacy of the sestina competently enough – there is some gratuitousness in the drawing in of Shakespeare, Donne and Dante, and some confusion in the progression of ideas in the latter part of the poem. On the other hand, Baxter's response to William Langland's long, unfinished poem is noteworthy. There is little in the formal features of Baxter's 'Letter' that recalls Langland – the decorative use of alliteration, for example, bears no similarity to the patterns of fourteenth-century alliterative verse – but the personification of abstract ideas such as Famine and Justice, the extended metaphor of the ploughing, the setting within a world of monotonous labour, and the fixation with 'pay' (or in Langland, Lady Mede) all recall the earlier allegorical work.[1]

Langland's allegory is theological in its basis, but his exploration of religious matter is mixed with a significant measure of political and social satire. At the heart of the poem is the search of the central figure – the dreamer, Will – for perfection, a search that is conducted within the intellectual and cultural framework of medieval Christianity. Like Baxter almost six hundred years later, Langland is

1 Warner also notes the rather surprising use Baxter makes of figures drawn not from Langland's poem but from a related though little known part of the Piers Plowman tradition, namely the Letter to John Ball. It is from that Letter that John Trueman, John Nameless and Hob the Robber are taken. For Baxter's probable source, see Whiteford 2016.

essentially searching for the Just City, conscious as he does so that he is surrounded by a world that is manifestly unjust, a world of personal sin and corruption at almost every level of society. In Langland's terminology, the world may have been redeemed, but it has yet to be perfected. Initially, his effort is concentrated on seeking to achieve a social solution to the problems he perceives, but ultimately that is abandoned in favour of a personal quest to know how to live well. Langland's position is one that Baxter seems also to have adopted by the time of the Jerusalem period: 'If that Jerusalem which is unbreakable friendship with God has not been established first in the heart, how can the objective Jerusalem of communal charity be built so as not to fall?'[2] But that focus on the personal only really emerges for Baxter after he receives the 'minor revelation' that encourages him to establish 'a community where the people, both Maori and pakeha, would try to live without money or books, worship God and work on the land' (McKay 237). Before that revelation, however, before his partial withdrawal from society, Baxter is unambiguously focussed on social ills and on the compelling need to address and redress them.

Warner's identification of 'the crisis that prompts the letter' as 'the subjugation of the spirit to the forces of post-war capitalism and conformity' is right in a general sense, but most New Zealand readers will recognise within the poem a more immediate and topical allusion, and so a more direct focus for the poem's satire. The fifth stanza includes the lines:

> Here in New Zealand, the middle of the century
> Sees Holland clowning to a castrate island;
> Sees Justice warped to please the roar of custom;
> Sees knave and fool together yoked in the furrow.

The figure of Holland referred to here is Sidney George (Sid) Holland, Prime Minister from 1949–1957, whose government had been elected, in part, on a promise to

2 The epigraph to *Jerusalem Sonnets*, [n.p.].

confront militant unionism. The year in which Baxter's poem was written, 1951, was the year in which Holland did just that, taking a hard line against the New Zealand Waterside Workers' Union. As Gustafson describes it:

> This resulted in a waterfront dispute which started in February 1951 and lasted for 151 days of industrial disruption, social hardship, economic loss, political division and hatred almost unparalleled in New Zealand history. The National government enacted harsh emergency regulations, including strict censorship, and used the courts, police and armed forces to break the unions.

Holland's rhetoric was extreme, declaring the country 'at war', and the draconian emergency regulations he passed made it an offence for any person to assist the strikers or their families: giving bread to their children was outlawed. Whatever the rights and wrongs of that bitter dispute, the ideological confrontation between government and 'wharfies', and the physical manifestation of that confrontation in the violent clashes between police and workers, dominated the country's political scene. Baxter would not have been alone in concluding that proscribing charitable support to women and children amounted to a conspicuous warping of justice.

The background here is significant as it demonstrates that the 'Letter to Piers Plowman' is an early example of the vigorous and very political satire that Baxter wrote from the mid 1960s. It foreshadows, for example, the fierce denunciatory verse aimed at Holland's successor in the National party, Keith Holyoake. Although Holyoake was admired as a liberal thinker when he worked to end the race-based selection of New Zealand rugby teams to tour South Africa, his support for the American war in Vietnam made him a target for Baxter's scorn, and he and his government colleagues became the subject of a number of vituperative poems.

In 1951 and 1952, however, the social criticism was much

more muted, and few of the poems from this period confront any of the social ills that later concerned Baxter. Equally, there is little in the prose that announces or contains a strong commitment to social protest. The entire first volume of John Weir's comprehensive edition, covering the years from 1943 until 1965 when Baxter left Wellington to take up the Burns Fellowship, is remarkably light on any extended social commentary. In the earliest of those years, indeed, it is almost negligible: there is a short parable on worldliness and poverty (1. 14–15); occasional remarks on racism (1. 124); and more frequent comments on the sterility of New Zealand's puritan society and culture (1. 51, 86, 651, 750). Prominent among Baxter's comments about New Zealand society are remarks which reflect his negative thoughts about the education system. John Davidson, in his essay in this volume, discusses Baxter's highly conflicted view of academia and tertiary education, but Baxter is equally forthright in his criticisms of an entire education system that he believed to be stultifying. Perhaps not unexpectedly given his family's pacifist convictions, there are several places in which Baxter writes against war – in general terms in earlier years (1. 89, 318), and then with a particular and consistent focus on the Vietnam war (1. 712, 718, 735, 752). These references are not intended to cover every comment that Baxter makes, but what is clear, I suggest, is that such social criticism as is found in the early prose is a matter of occasional observation. Nowhere does Baxter develop any extended discussion or carefully considered argument about any of the matters that he confronts. Even the two lengthy pieces from Asia, 'Journal of Trip to Asia' (1. 354–371) and 'Notes from India' (1. 371–375), contain little direct comment on the social ills that he observed, despite the widely acknowledged significance of this trip. There are stray observations about children begging (1. 370) or about people with sores in the streets (1. 364), but otherwise the writing has a strong focus on recording his own experiences rather than engaging with or reflecting on what he has seen.

The only extended passage – made more prominent because it occurs in both entries – is the well-known encounter with the leper at Howrah Bridge (367, 374). The long-term effect of this trip to Asia is undisputed: as Paul Millar observes, Baxter 'was overwhelmed by the poverty and affected by the experience of being part of an ethnic minority. His sense of displacement and disorientation is evident in his next collection, *Howrah Bridge and other poems*' (46). But it is striking that the sense of dislocation seems to have so little immediate visible impact on his prose writing.

The introduction to Volume Four draws some attention to the absence of any extended social criticism in the years up to 1965, acknowledging that there was a marked change from the time Baxter took up the Burns Fellowship at the University of Otago. John Weir suggests a reason why this may have been so: 'while he was a family man living in a Wellington suburb, employed as a Government bureaucrat and a practising member of his local parish he did not become outspoken on these issues' (4. 142). The observation may well be right (and few knew Baxter as well as Weir did), but it does suggest a timidity and desire to conform that is at odds with much of the rest of his behaviour. Whatever the reason, the relocation to Dunedin seems to have been a catalyst for a more direct and vigorous engagement as a social critic.

What is much more to the fore in these early years, however, is the gradual development and articulation of Baxter's understanding that social commentary and social protest form an integral part of the role of the artist. While that role is broadly conceived of as something that pertains to all art, it is particularly the writer, or the poet, who for Baxter bears that responsibility. Reading the first volume of his prose in sequence, as Weir's scholarship permits us to do, reinforces just how frequently Baxter articulates this position, and how thoroughly he embraces it.

It is interesting, in this context, to look again at Frank McKay's 'Introduction' to his 1978 selection of Baxter's literary criticism. McKay writes:

> In 'The World of the Creative Artist' [Baxter] wrote: 'In the long run all art centres upon man – not just social man, but the incarnate mystery who lives in squalor and anxiety, suffers death, and is capable of love.' The aspect of the incarnate mystery that fascinated his imagination was 'the natural man', a term he took from Christian theology to describe 'the fallen Adam who remembers, as if in a dream, his first state.' It was a way of looking at the myth of the Fall of Man congenial to Baxter's incarnational mode of thinking. (vi)

McKay's analysis then continues with its focus on the theological dimension, seeing that – not unreasonably – as a major element of Baxter's thinking and of his critical practice. But I am intrigued by the momentary elision that occurs. Baxter's affirmation that art centres on 'social man' receives no attention. The structure of Baxter's sentence might seem to downplay the focus on the social, but it does so only by presuming its existence, and even its priority. It is, perhaps, the benefit of hindsight and a fuller knowledge of Baxter's subsequent career that encourages and validates the greater emphasis on the theological, but it does not do to overlook his clear assertion here that art has at its core 'social man'.

Just as John Weir's scholarship allows us to appreciate how frequently Baxter addresses the social role of poetry, it also allows us to recognise at what an early stage this notion formed part of his thinking. Certainly, the idea that a poet is a figure seemingly at odds with or standing apart from his or her society and his or her age seems to have been there from the outset. An essay he contributed to *Critic* (the University of Otago student magazine) in 1944, for example, describes Wilfred Owen as a 'true prophet . . . because he saw the world in a crystal of doom' and continues that 'a sense of doom must enter into all great poetry' (1. 9). Baxter was a rather gloomy eighteen-year-old at the time he wrote. The connection between that 'sense of doom' and social criticism becomes clear in his later essay (1952) on 'Social Delinquency in Modern Literature', in which he explicitly describes Owen and Sassoon as social critics (1. 89).

One way in which Baxter's position can be traced, almost *en passant*, is through a number of the essays and reviews that he wrote in the Wellington years. If those pieces are taken singly, Baxter appears simply to be responding to and approving of a particular feature that he discerns in an individual; taken together, though, it becomes apparent that social criticism, especially exhibited through satire, comes to be identified as an important aspect of successful writing.

A selection of pieces from the mid 1950s demonstrates this point. In a 1954 essay on Sargeson, for example, Baxter describes him unambiguously as 'a social moralist' (1. 217) – a view he had in fact anticipated some years earlier in a review of *When the Wind Blows* (1. 33). Though critical of the way in which, like many propagandists, Sargeson is guilty of loading the dice in his moralising 'sermons', Baxter clearly accepts social criticism as legitimate, even necessary – 'artists are of necessity disloyal to their community' (1. 223), or as he put it in a more light-hearted vein when defending the lyrics of Tom Lehrer, 'every party needs an uninhibited, satirical entertainer' (1. 419). The following year, in a perceptive essay on Oscar Wilde, Baxter acknowledges in that writer 'a war on society', a delight in 'irritating the bourgeoisie' and even an identification with 'the English proletariat, who were acquainted with suffering and privation' (1. 236). Those might not be the features of Wilde's life and art that are most commonly detected by other critics, but they do reveal again Baxter's emerging sense of a necessary tension between artist and society.

Baxter's 1953 review of John Pick's *A Hopkins Reader* is telling in what it takes as its focus. From the 300 pages of poetry and prose included in Pick's selection, Baxter chooses to quote exclusively from a letter from Hopkins to Coventry Patmore in which Hopkins criticises Patmore for his lack of 'tykishness'. Hopkins had written:

> There is an old Adam of barbarism, boyishness, wildness, rawness, rankness, the disreputable, the unrefined in the refined and educated. It is that I meant by tykishness . . . and said you have none of. (1. 142)

The review does praise Hopkins as an acute and intelligent critic, but it must be said that this is an unusual choice and is scarcely representative of Hopkins's correspondence or of his criticism. The privileging in Hopkins of the raw, the rank and the disreputable clearly appealed to Baxter because it confirmed attitudes he himself held.

A review from 1956 is in some ways even more interesting. In it, Baxter undertakes a comparison of Pope and Swift as satirists. His remarks are worth quoting more fully:

> Swift, an Irishman and political pamphleteer for both Whig and Tory, stood always a little outside the maze of English social and literary hierarchies; to Pope, despite his disabilities, these were the breath of life. Hence Pope speaks to a modern reader at a remove; for all his talent, he is dated. (1. 266)

Baxter undoubtedly admires Pope: 'he is great in anger, and directs the point of a burning-glass upon the vices and follies of *persons*' (1. 267). But his preference is for Swift:

> Swift is the satirist par excellence: he satirises everything, even himself. Yet his public satire bore fruit. While Pope gave benefactions in private, Swift defended the Irish poor with volcanic indignation; perhaps because, like himself, they were outsiders. (1. 268)

It would be possible to continue at greater length to isolate comments in which Baxter confirms his belief that literature has a social voice and a social responsibility – see the aside on Mulgan's *Man Alone* (1. 57) or that on M. K. Joseph (1. 64) as further examples – but the point is clear that among the many things he admires and even demands in a writer is precisely a social voice – a voice whose social criticism may adopt prophetic tones, or may espouse a strong moral basis for its position, but which must engage directly with the world.

At the same time as this role can be teased out from Baxter's occasional reviews and essays, it can also be seen in more developed and closely argued fashion in the several extended pieces that discuss writing and the role of the writer, in particular *Recent Trends in New Zealand Poetry* and *The Fire and the Anvil*. These extended reflections on the nature and function of poetry are sufficiently well known to need no introduction here, and they have received a significant body of analysis and commentary. While no single essay is wholly devoted to the question of social criticism, or takes that idea as its springboard, nevertheless the belief that art has a social dimension and a social responsibility and that artists must adopt a social voice continues to pervade his thinking.

Thus, in *The Fire and the Anvil* – much of which is devoted to matters of craft and form, to prosody, to an examination of metaphor and symbol – we find an insistence on the importance of significance or meaning in the writing and criticism of poetry. Baxter is far from suggesting that poetry should contain 'an earnest moral statement' (1. 154), nor does he accept that it can be 'a sugared pill' (1. 155) – that kind of sermonising or educative role is not what he has in mind – but he does insist that poets provide a 'truth which grows, however imperfectly, from their own unrestricted sight, knowledge and expression . . . [and that a real poem] speaks with the difficult, many-voiced, sometimes serene, often violent language of our real selves. If we understand it, we are bound to find it disturbing' (1. 162). The argument here recalls his earlier assertion that the 'successful poet will be anarchic in his thinking and feeling . . . likely to seem a rebel' (1. 16), as does this assertion in the second lecture:

> The rebellion of artists against the social patterns of their time and place is often cried down as childish and gratuitous; but it is the inevitable accompaniment of their growth towards maturity. (1. 176)

It is that rebelliousness (Hopkins's tykishness), that willingness to embrace anarchy, that gives art its life: 'One can, of course, make one's art a kind of perpetual retreat from every real problem; but in such a situation the art itself gradually withers away' (1. 179–80).

And it might equally be said that it is anarchic, rebellious satirical art that, Baxter argues, gives the kingdom its life. Thus, in the 1957 'Parable', the dying king pleads that his dutiful older son care for the scapegrace younger brother, whose only talent is an extraordinary gift for verse-making 'all with a note of insolent rebellion . . . for while he lives your kingdom is secure' (1. 317).

Similar ideas can be found throughout these essays and reflections, but the *locus classicus* for Baxter's articulation of this position is towards the end of his 1951 talk, *Recent Trends in New Zealand Poetry*. Having spoken at some length on the matter announced in the title, Baxter goes on to address 'the basic problem of the poet in New Zealand, and no doubt elsewhere – that of social criticism' (1. 74). It is a section that includes some of the most frequently cited pieces relating to social criticism, beginning with the rather acerbic assertion that 'It is possible without obvious absurdity for our politicians to call our country a Happy Island, in some degree a just one. But poets are different from politicians'. The difference, Baxter asserts, is that poets tell the truth, and he advances his own belief that 'our island is in fact an unjust, unhappy one, where human activity is becoming progressively more meaningless' (1. 74). What is here advanced as a belief becomes in time a firm conviction, and all of his social criticism springs from it.

Throughout the passage, Baxter plays somewhat erratically with capitals: thus, he writes of a Happy Island, a Just City, an Unjust City, of City and Wilderness, in a process that seems to drive him inexorably to the Langland-like personification of Justice, and so to the second of the much-quoted passages: 'What Justice demands is something more difficult – that he [that is, the modern poet] should remain as a cell of good living in a corrupt society, and in this situation by writing and example attempt to change it' (1. 75).

Hugh Roberts, in another essay in this collection, has drawn attention to Eric Gill's use of the same idea of the 'cell of good living', suggesting that Baxter has borrowed the phrase itself from Gill.[3] Weir's Index contains no entry for Gill, so there is no clear evidence that Baxter knew his work, but it does seem a strong possibility. Baxter is likely to have been attracted by Gill's work, and perhaps by some aspects of his life (including the more controversial), and he might well have been struck by the powerful image. But it is worth returning to Gill's original and examining it more closely. The passage occurs very near the end of Gill's autobiography and represents his effort to 'state in one paragraph the work which I have chiefly tried to do in my life' (282). It is a reflection on his life as he finds himself 'facing death' (278).

His chief work, as he describes it, has been 'to make a cell of good living in the chaos of our world' (282). While it should not be thought of as exclusively physical – Gill is certainly alert to the figurative possibilities of the idea – nevertheless the 'cell' is a real place, a haven of order and integration. It has connotations of a monastic cell, informed by his lifestyle at Ditchling and later in Wales. Moreover, it is a place apart – precisely the kind of retreat that Baxter, at this stage, would not permit. It involves some withdrawal from a chaotic world to create an alternative ruled by harmony and integration. By contrast Baxter's 'cell' is a metaphorical concept: not a place but a person, the Just person, the one who is or should be a cell of good living, standing apart from and in condemnation of the world, but not having withdrawn from it. On the contrary, the express desire is 'by writing and example [to] attempt to change it'. Where Gill looks back over his life and what he has built, Baxter looks forward to what he wishes to achieve – at least part of which involves not a building up but a tearing down.

The other change is just as crucial: where Gill looks to establish his cell against a chaotic world, Baxter sets

3 I am very grateful to Hugh Roberts, whose essay, arriving as I was working on my own, alerted me to this connection.

his against a corrupt one. One cell is ruled by order and harmony, the other by justice and morality. That Baxter should elect not to retain Gill's chaos might be surprising, given how frequently that idea permeates his poetry; that he should replace it with corruption is of equal interest, for however much he rails against sermonising or moralising (what he calls propaganda in *The Fire and the Anvil*), at heart his affirmation of the artist's social voice has a strong moral dimension to it.

But the 'cell of good living' represents just one aspect of Baxter's thinking on this subject. As Bill Manhire has remarked, 'Baxter was given to phrase-making . . . and this made memorable a large proportion of anything he wrote, in verse or in prose' (209). Off-setting the exemplary goodness expected of the poet in *Recent Trends* is the rather more down to earth characterisation set out in a short (and otherwise unmemorable) poem, 'The Dragon Mask': his equally famous assertion that 'A poet is / The sore thumb of the tribe' (*CPoems* 268). There are no doubt a number of ways in which a thumb may become sore, but Baxter does not seem especially interested in causation or even in healing. Rather, it is the constant throbbing that is important for him, the ache that cannot be ignored; the poet, writer or artist exists, in this formulation, as a social irritant, a nagging reminder that something is amiss in the body politic. While the 'cell of good living' seems the more considered of the two statements, the product of a more consciously argued position, one cannot help but think that Baxter was in many ways more readily drawn to the role of the 'sore thumb'. Again, John Weir's presentation of the great expanse of Baxter's prose makes clear how regularly he describes the writer as outsider, as rebel, as irritant, as anarchist, and equally how frequently he performs that role himself.

In the years covered by the first volume, as has been noted above, Baxter wrote relatively little social criticism. The intellectual effort appears to have gone into establishing and affirming such a role for the writer rather than performing that role. One might suggest that Baxter was more interested in theory than in practice. But as John Weir has noted, in 1965 'he entered the public forum in an unforgettable manner when the Vietnam War stirred him to express his opinions with great energy and conviction. "Mr Shand and the Rain of Fire" is a vitriolic attack upon a particular man and warmongers in general' (4. 141). With savage irony, Baxter fastens on the efforts by Tom Shand, then Minister of Immigration, to prevent the entry into New Zealand of Mandy Rice-Davies, who had come to international prominence in the British Profumo affair. Congratulating Shand on his adoption of 'the sterner, higher road' and his 'sensitive awareness of the enormous value of moral purity', Baxter compares that to his own horror at '[t]he rain of unquenchable phosphorus which our New Zealand artillery is at present unloading on Vietnamese villagers'. He then turns Shand's notion of moral purity back upon itself, challenging the minister to withdraw New Zealand troops from Vietnam lest 'young heroic New Zealanders serving in Vietnam may be tempted from the path of virtue'. The conclusion of the passage deserves to be quoted in full:

> The man who decided to exclude an English entertainer from New Zealand, because her past was not what it should have been, cannot condone the establishing of Army brothels or allow our young men to run the danger of disease and moral ruin. We know that if it came to the bitter test you would rather take a gun and fight on the side of the Viet Cong – whose old-fashioned philosophy includes the intention to eliminate all prostitution – than to permit a danger you consider more terrible than gas, napalm, phosphorus or the poisoning of crops. We wait eagerly, Mr Shand, for a public statement from you that our troops must be withdrawn from Vietnam. What else can you do? After all, you are not a hypocrite? (1. 735–36)

This mock encomium, published as an open letter in the *New Zealand Monthly Review*, was followed later in the same year by a letter to the editor published in the *New Zealand Listener* also on the Vietnam War. Together, these pieces mark a significant change for Baxter, and Weir's second volume, covering the years in Dunedin (1966–68), reveals just how readily he maintained his newly found voice within the public forum. He had become the tribe's sore thumb.

His move to Dunedin allowed him to expand significantly on his social criticism. While this may partly be explained by the reasons noted by Weir (4. 142), other factors may also be significant. The congenial atmosphere of the Burns Fellowship provided him with the time and space to write (and write at length) that he had rarely had before. More significantly, it also provided him with numerous invitations to give public speeches and addresses, and in so doing to refine and expand his sense of audience. For as John Weir has further noted, Baxter's prose 'is strongest when he is emotionally involved with his topic and when his language sounds most like his speaking voice. He always needed an audience' (4. 124). The deep emotional involvement is already apparent in the excoriating attack on Tom Shand; the speaking voice comes more and more to the fore in the numerous public engagements he accepted in these years.

Prior to his return to Otago, Baxter more naturally associated the function of social criticism with the figure of the poet. It is 'the modern poet' who is to be the 'cell of good living' just as it is 'a poet' who is 'the sore thumb of the tribe'. To some extent through those early years 'the poet' functioned as metonym for any writer or any artist, but even allowing for that it did appear that Baxter was anointing the poet with a distinctive function within society. The years in Dunedin, by contrast, are marked by a conspicuous body of such criticism in prose and Baxter now just as readily chooses prose for his social criticism as he does verse. The concept of 'voice', to which he was always so attentive in his poetry, now seems to be equally important in his prose, not just in those pieces that were originally written for oral delivery but equally for the increasingly frequent letters to editors that mark these years and that become one of the important vehicles for his social criticism. In both address and especially letter, he is able to derive from the immediacy of his subject matter a corresponding immediacy and urgency of voice that is essential to his critical purpose.

John Weir's extended commentary in Volume Four provides a very perceptive account of Baxter's social comment, describing it as 'always well-considered, principled, and well-written. Sometimes, especially late in his life, it was impassioned and powerful' (140). Over the following pages, Weir goes on to detail the subjects that particularly caught Baxter's attention, chief among them the Vietnam War, the underlying racism in New Zealand, poverty and unemployment, and the materialism of the dominant culture. The Vietnam War and the unacknowledged racism Baxter found in mainstream New Zealand society are specific as to time and place, and each of them is strongly influenced by his own personal family history. The recurrent concern with poverty and unemployment, with the treatment of the marginalised, with a determinedly secular society that too readily abandons those it deems failures – these are all more general, although they obviously have local habitations and names. But whether the subjects Baxter addresses are specific or general, his concern throughout is rooted in a fundamental and abiding concern for justice and a fierce intolerance of injustice. Any wonder, then, that his earliest foray into social criticism in verse castigates a New Zealand that 'Sees Justice warped to please the roar of custom'.

Although Baxter was in Dunedin for only three years, the vigorous activism of those years served to establish him as a controversial, even polemical figure, and that public image remained throughout the rest of his life, overlaid in time by the even more radicalised 'barefooted and bearded eccentric'. Eventually, that activism led him to precisely the withdrawal from society that he had argued against in

*Recent Trends*. And with the withdrawal to Jerusalem comes another of his memorable phrases.

In 'A Scorpion Circled by Fire', Baxter describes himself as 'a Christian guru, a barefooted and bearded eccentric, a bad smell in the noses of many good citizens'. The description is frequently quoted, not always in a way that acknowledges that for Baxter the 'bad smell' is a chosen role, taken on in the awareness that 'the smashed myths have somehow to be replaced or reconstructed' (3. 413).[4] Nor, indeed, is it always recognised that the phrase makes an earlier appearance in *Jerusalem Daybook*, in which Baxter writes:

> God turns this man into an old coat and a broken stick. God makes him the nuns' Devil and a bad smell in the noses of good churchgoing people. It is not a pleasant vocation. (3. 303)

It is not immediately apparent from these two entries that the role of 'bad smell' is something connected to poet or writer, and Baxter certainly does not enforce the connection as explicitly as he does with the 'good cell' or the 'sore thumb'. But such a connection does seem to be implied by the slightly later description of '[t]he man called James K. Baxter, who is like a dead body in the ground, [who] swells up and gives off a stink of words' (3. 304). The 'bad smell' is much more than that of the unwashed figure who roamed around Jerusalem; rather the image is of death and putrefaction. But the smell is the poet's words.

Baxter has clearly moved a long way from the description of the 'cell of good living' he had written some twenty years earlier, and his later career makes that exemplary ambition seem almost touchingly naïve. This latest articulation of his role as a maker of words strikingly reverses (as it perhaps recalls through rhyme) the first description: in the earliest of the memorable phrases, the goodness required of the poets is to be found amid the external corruption; in the latest, it is the poet's words that smell, the poet in whom the corruption

4 The description occurs, for example, in Robert Atwan's anthology, *Divine Inspiration* (99).

is to be found, and the citizenry that is now good. Baxter has travelled a considerable distance in the metaphors by which he links poet and society. He may well be indulging in further irony when he describes both the 'citizens' and the 'churchgoing people' as good, but even if that is the case, it is noteworthy that he has made himself a target for his criticism.

It is not possible to conclude that Baxter genuinely believed New Zealand society was, in the early 1970s, 'a Happy Island . . . a just one', to revert to the language of *Recent Trends*. The social issues that had faced the country ten and twenty years earlier were as pressing when he wrote from Jerusalem as when he had written in Wellington, as is made apparent by the late essay 'The Rich and the Poor', which is published here for the first time. But for Baxter, the quarrel has shifted. He had written in 'Beginnings' of the 'sense of grief' that helped him write his poetry: 'In a way the poems sprang out of a quarrel with the status quo' (1. 724). That quarrel never left him: there is still, in the ugliness of the 'bad smell' image, an undeniable conflict between the poet and 'the status quo'. But his personal effort had shifted to the spiritual as necessary precursor to the social: 'If that Jerusalem which is unbreakable friendship with God has not been established first in the heart, how can the objective Jerusalem of communal charity be built so as not to fall?' The desire to build a Just City, a city of communal charity, remains. But the essential foundations of that city, on which it must stand, have been reimagined.

## *Works Cited*

Atwan, Robert, George Dardess and Peggy Rosenthal, eds. *Divine Inspiration. The Life of Jesus in World Poetry*. New York and Oxford: Oxford University Press, 1998.

Eggleton, David. 'Striding Towards God: The Long Afterlife of James K. Baxter.' *Landfall Review Online*, May 1, 2011. http://www.landfallreview.com/home/ Accessed 30 August 2016.

Gill, Eric. *Autobiography*. London: Jonathan Cape, 1940.

Gustafson, Barry. 'Holland, Sidney George.' In: *Dictionary of New Zealand Biography. Te Ara-the Encyclopedia of New Zealand*, http://www.TeAra.govt.nz/en/biographies/5h30/holland-sidney-george. Accessed 30 September 2016.

Manhire, Bill. *Doubtful Sounds: Essays and Interviews*. Wellington: Victoria University Press, 2000.

Millar, Paul. 'James K. Baxter.' In: Robinson, Roger and Nelson Wattie, eds. *The Oxford Companion to New Zealand Literature*. Auckland: Oxford University Press, 1998.

Warner, Lawrence. 'Plowman traditions in late medieval and early modern writing.' In: Andrew Cole and Andrew Galloway, eds. *The Cambridge Companion to Piers Plowman*. Cambridge: Cambridge University Press, 2014.

Whiteford, Peter. 'James K. Baxter and John Ball: a note on the source of "Letter to Piers Plowman".' *Kotare: New Zealand Notes and Queries*, December 2016.

# *A Green Baxter: James K. Baxter and Environmentalism*

## Twenty-nine notes and speculations laid as markers along the River Road, Parikino to Hiruhārama

Gregory O'Brien

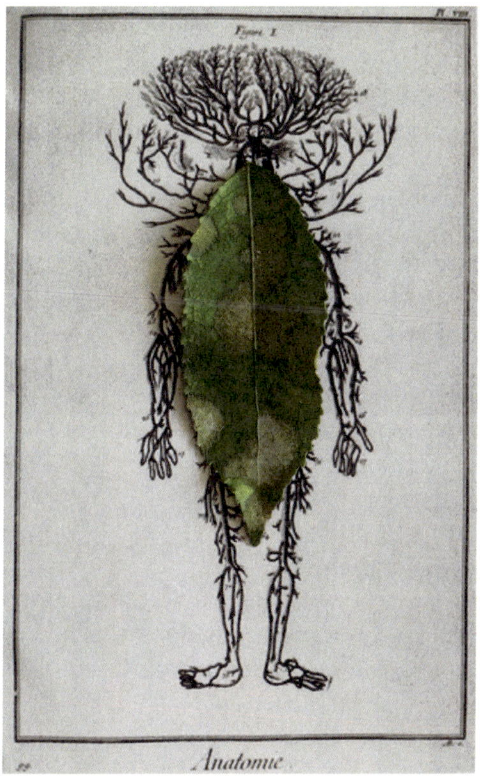


Deborah Smith, *Green Man*, 2011

I

Where to start? Where might you go looking for the Green Baxter – what evidence is there of the poet as trail-blazing environmentalist, holistic thinker, eco-warrior or world-saver? You could look at the prose and verse for evidence of ecological awareness – this, in an era (pre-1972) when such things were not as clearly signposted and surveyed as they are today. Next, you might consider the poet as nature-man/nature-boy. Or, at a deeper, subconscious level, as an antipodean reincarnation of the Green Man of Anglo-Saxon legend – a leaf-faced symbol of rebirth – or an interloper into the affairs of men, the late-comer who livens things up in *Sir Gawain and the Green Knight*. Or you could consider, more generally, Baxter as a student/disciple of the colour green, whose work finds one of its richest sources in the pastoral hues that colour so much Western poetry – Shakespeare, Wordsworth, Hardy, Yeats and onwards.

II

Nature is something New Zealanders can't get too far away from. Our cities aren't big or dense enough to become seriously lost in; our towns are generously spaced. We invariably find ourselves out in the air, land- and sea-scapes. As David McKee Wright wrote in 1900: 'Our cities face the sea, and the winds are blowing free' (Bornholdt, *Anthology* 491). Growing up just outside Dunedin, Baxter didn't have to go looking too hard for nature, and therein found a singular catalyst – overpowering at times, yet fundamentally sustaining, nurturing and inspiring. His prose and poetry reiterate countless times, and with Blakean insistence, that 'the heart of man' resides in nature, not in the city. But the quarrel with the city remained, also, very much a part of proceedings.

III

Early in his writing career, Baxter was already renouncing metropolitan life, with its pyramidal power-structures, encircling suburbia, swarming police-force and its multi-layered injustices. By the late 1960s, he was also distancing himself from the romanticised, idealised landscape of his youth, finding his warmest, deepest accommodation as a person, and hence as a writer, in the communal space of Māori society – marae and wharenui (or in self-styled versions thereof). For him, the marae embodied a fulcrum upon which human affairs and the natural world – in Aotearoa/New Zealand, specifically – found their truest equilibrium: a suitable habitat also for the socially minded poet and the poetically inclined social critic.[1]

IV

The tone of W. H. Oliver's *James K. Baxter: A Portrait* (1983) is established at the outset by a suite of Gary Blackman's photographs of influential places from the poet's early life – monochromatic summations of southern New Zealand coastline, trees and architecture. Most prominent among these photographs is a panorama of Brighton Beach – twenty kilometres from Dunedin – the place to which the poet returned throughout his life and to which he was drawn, he said, whenever he reached a creative or personal impasse.

V

What exact purpose might Brighton Beach have served in the poet's imagination? Did he engage with it as an organic entity – an ecosystem, in present day parlance – or was it simply a Proustian trigger, a talismanic presence or a projection screen for remembered realities? 'A lot of my poems are beach poems,' Baxter professed in a 1960 film

1 A newspaper article included in *Complete Prose* (3. 170) is even more explicit: 'Baxter believes that a viable solution to the oppressive depersonalisation of our society with its economic and power mania lies in small regional communities respecting the land and learning from ancient anarchistic tribes [sic] such as the Maori pa.'

script. 'That is, I will imagine I am walking along a beach – usually the beach at Brighton . . . and this helps the pictures and the words that make a poem to rise up in my mind and take shape' (*Complete Prose* 1. 433). His relationship to this location is further spelt out in a 1966 *Otago Daily Times* article:

> More than half of the images that recur in my poems are connected with early memories of the Brighton township, river, hills and sea-coast – especially the sea-coast. Sitting down to write in a room in Wellington, again and again my mind would make an imaginary journey over the neck of the Big Rock, across the mouth of the Brighton River, and wander round the domain, or up to the boat-house, or along the sandhills, or out to the fishing rocks where the swells come straight in without interruption all the way from Peru. (2. 97)

The poems reiterate the same subjective approach, the beach functioning as a repository of memory and autobiographic detail, rather than as an ecological entity in its own right. In that regard, it remains a 'landscape' and has yet to become an 'environment', in the twenty-first century usage of the latter word.

## VI

Throughout his writing career, James K. Baxter's contemplation and interpretation of nature remained bound to a single (albeit many-facetted) viewpoint. A concept of decentred nature – in which humanity was no longer necessarily the hub – was outside the parameters of his thinking. It would be left to the work of later poets to renegotiate those terms of engagement – notably, Kendrick Smithyman's 'Reading the Maps' (which introduced the mapping grid as another perspectival approach), C. K. Stead's Poundian excavation of volcanic Auckland, 'Scoria' (1979), Cilla McQueen's littoral bricolage, 'Aramoana poem' (1979) and Ian Wedde's multi-voiced 'off/of' (1984). In these poems, a less circumscribed biosphere/environment is manifest; the poets' grasp of their material has become consciously provisional and inconclusive; certainties are lost as the aperture widens. It is as if Wordsworth's 'Prelude' has been elbowed aside by Charles Olson's 'Maximus'.

Continuing in said direction, we might eventually arrive at an 'environmental art' capable of conjuring 'multiple realms including the celestial, human, microscopic, animal, plant, mineral, as well as underlying processes and rhythms of nature', to borrow a description from the liner notes of American performance artist Meredith Monk (3). If Baxter had lived into the twenty-first century, how far his thinking might have evolved in this direction is worth considering.

## VII

James K. Baxter was never one to locate himself too far from the centre of proceedings. His poems of the natural world are records of sensory immersion rather than scenic observation or detached contemplation. In 'At Fox Glacier Hotel', he dismisses a cauterised version of nature observed on the dining room wall:

> One kind of love, a tourist Bureau print
> Of the Alps reflected in Lake Matheson
> (Turned upside down it would look the same)
> Smiles in the dining room, a lovely mirror
> For any middle-aged narcissus to drown in (*CPoems* 368)

Departing from that demure postcard-image, Baxter's mind then turns to the untamed dynamic of the adjacent mountain-scape: 'the huge ice torrent moving / Over bluffs and bowls of rock . . . at the top of the valley – / How it might crack our public looking-glass.' The poem concludes with an image of accelerated glacier consuming all – 'Black pinnacles and fangs of toppling ice'. An end-frame which begs the question whether Baxter's version of nature was too quintessentially Gothic to ever be Green?

## VIII

'The Kiwi is indeed a stranger in paradise. Many reams of paper have flowed off the presses since the day when Ursula Bethell looked up from spadework in her Christchurch garden and noticed that the hills were paradisal judges . . . Mountaineers and prospectors are in a sense our experiential theologians, solitary Adams (as Ursula Bethell was a solitary Eve) relearning the nature of the Fall by gazing at the beautiful forbidden face of the earthly paradise, which we can indeed enter, but never possess, because we are alienated from it and from ourselves.' (3. 47)

## IX

Long before the fanged mountaintops of Romantic tradition had been replaced by the pā-site as prime real estate in his imagination, Baxter was questioning how nature was understood, processed and reiterated in the poetic imagination. Having doffed his hat, in his youth, to the pastoral/bucolic tradition, he soon enough had (sub)urban life to contend with – a subject which gave rise to the great, albeit crushing conclusion to 'Poem in the Matukituki Valley', in which the reader is dropped from the 'sky's purity; the altar cloth of snow / On deathly summits laid', down, down, down, into

> the gentle
> Dark of the human daydream, child and wife,
> Patience of stone and soil, the lawful city
> Where man may live, and no wild trespass
> Of what's eternal shake his grave of time. (*CPoems* 87)

## X

As in the poetry, the tension between a euphoric, quasi-mystical state and the encroachments of banal, quotidian existence is everywhere in Baxter's prose – even in his boosterist account of local scenery commissioned for the 1961 photo-compendium *New Zealand in Colour 1.* The images therein, as Baxter wrote, direct our attention to 'this world in which we live but to which we so rarely belong'. Not content to leave it there, he takes pains to point out that 'alongside the human City, indifferent or even hostile, remains the Wilderness, whose time is still that of the sixth day of creation and whose works belong to the Power that created her' (1. 486). Stirring, unexpected commentary to find in a Tourism Board-sanctioned picture book. In the late poetry – *Autumn Testament* specifically – he traces a similar trajectory, from Green to Grey, from the natural world to the spiritually bereft modern-day society:

> That grove of pines I prayed so long among
> For the first six months, have been cut down for firewood
>
> Or to make the floorboards of houses in the suburbs
> Where children get square eyes (*CPoems* 547)

Perhaps Baxter belongs most comfortably to a tradition of English rural writing which Robert MacFarlane describes, in *Landmarks*, as 'that of dissent tending to civil disobedience' (95), citing writer-radicals such as William Cobbett and the 'gentle anarchist', Colin Ward. Baxter is most naturally the figure on the mound or soapbox, broadcasting, with Whitmanesque aplomb, the contradictions of the world. Bearing in mind that Baxter lived in urban environments for virtually all his adult life up until the itinerant 'Jerusalem' years, 1969–72, he was very much a creation of the built-up city as he was of the natural world. In his writing, he could rarely see one without seeing the other. The Green/Grey Baxter.

## XI

In a 1973 essay, C. K. Stead attributed the power of Baxter's poems to

> their creation of a personality in balance against its surroundings – people, places, scenes, events – in which

> everything quivered with a symbolic resonance, a heightened sense of life. They were poems of the twentieth century in the Romantic tradition as it passes through late Yeats to early Auden; but they were distinctly our own experience (217).

The 'local' was an element in Baxter's poetry which Stead clearly valued – a sense of the poet's specific ground. Far from offering a version of literary nationalism, however, Baxter was offering an alternative to it. 'To avoid nationalism is finally part of a principle of love,' he noted (3. 162), proposing in its stead a healthy, imaginatively charged sense of the regional.

## XII

A cursory glance through the contents of Baxter's *Collected Poems* leaves no doubt as to how married to specific locales his poetry was – in particular to outlying rural and coastal places. In naming these places, Baxter was very consciously honouring them, 'putting them on the map'. In itself, this can be read as a 'Green' gesture – a conservationist act – bearing in mind environmental writer Robert MacFarlane's insistence that, if we value a place, we need to cherish the language that accumulates there: 'Once a landscape goes undescribed and therefore unregarded, it becomes more vulnerable to unwise use or improper action' (27).

## XIII

With characteristic zeal, the youthful Baxter went so far as to make a 'simple, though by no means exhaustive' index of New Zealand poetry's defining nature symbols. These he incorporated into a Victoria University College lecture which was subsequently published in *The Fire and the Anvil* (1955). It's a wilful, partial and marvellously succinct guide (1. 190):

> The Sea: as a symbol of death and oblivion;
> as a symbol of regeneration.
> The Mountains: as protective maternal symbols;
> as symbols of ideal purity;

as menacing and hostile powers.
The Bush: as a symbol of the energy and fruitfulness of the natural world;
as a menacing and entangling wilderness.
The Beach: as an arena of historical change, the arrival and departure of races;
as a place where revelations may occur;
as a no-man's land between conscious and unconscious;
as an arena for sexual adventure.
The Island: as a symbol of isolation from European tradition, both in place and time.

Here we have the poet in school teacher mode (or a conscious parody thereof?) – a role frequently taken up in the *Complete Prose*. In his prose, as in his poetry, Baxter is wilfully provocative, occasionally hot-headed, constantly putting ideas out there (often without a second thought), and generally making as much noise as possible.

## XIV

Anticipating by forty years the face-off, or heavyweight showdown, between Baxter's *Collected Poems* and his *Complete Prose*, C. K. Stead, in the 1973 essay cited earlier, highlights the two competing authorial presences in Baxter's work: the Authentic Poet fighting it out with the Prose Baxter. Stead favours the former on the grounds that the best verse offered 'hard-gained evocations of particular places, events, people', and arrived at a kind of wisdom which, in his mind, was 'richer than any available to [Baxter] in conversation or in prose where, for all his colour and horse sense, he was also rambling and partial'. In the best poetry, the 'prose Baxter,' Stead continues, 'yields precedent to the deep implacable will of the artist to discover the real and the true' (220–21). Another way of putting this: the poet gains access, through his art, to the subconscious, whereas the Prose Baxter is speaking his conscious mind, usually immoderately.

## XV

Interrogating this evasive, Green-inclined figure, we could look further back in time to such verdant, antipodean antecedents as Mary Ursula Bethell and Eileen Duggan – both ardent gardeners, with spiritual ambitions to match their floricultural inclinations. A prolific poet of Green-ness, Duggan was author of what might be the 'greenest' line in all of New Zealand poetry, the opening of her ecstatic nature-reverie, 'The Country': 'All that green calm crept in and flowed around me' (63).

Continuing in this vein, Duggan not only talks directly to a tree (in her poem 'Evergreen') but offers it advice before drawing the poem to its wistful close: 'My heart and you broke off together / In the leafy Spring' (57). One obvious difference in attitude between Duggan and Baxter stems from the fact that the earlier poet remained beholden to an idea of Arcadian New Zealand – a lyrical Eden – and a notion of poetry as its ordained conduit. Duggan's utopian world/island/garden is equal parts Wordsworth and the Palmers Gardenworld spring catalogue, with an overlay of Catholic theology, applied rather too conventionally for twenty-first century tastes. You could say that Duggan suffered from an almost crippling sense of propriety whereas, in dramatic contrast, Baxter elevated impropriety to an almost hallowed status.

Just as the animism and anthropomorphism in Duggan's poetry were bedded down in a compost of religious conviction and literary precedent, Baxter's nature-mysticism was widely sourced. Like her, he indulged in some interspecies conversation. Witness the following lines from *Autumn Testament*, which owe as much to Findhorn-era tree-hugging – that highpoint in 1960s-era Green-ness – as they do to the Shakespearean imagination:

> I'd climb the hill on the Domain
> Before dawn, when the leaves were cold as iron
>
> Underfoot, and talk with the trees – this one

> Thinking she was ugly in her narrow dress of bark,
>
> That one a woman who'd had many children –
> The tree nymphs – their great beauty made me tremble. (*CPoems* 555)

XVI

Mannered and literary as it might be, Eileen Duggan's 'Country' concludes with the kind of anti-urban sentiment which, a few decades later, Baxter's writing was endlessly reiterating and broadcasting (Duggan 63):

> Towns are as vain as a king that is doting,
> Babbling to himself of laurel on laurel.
> I who shirked peace know north and south of trouble.
> Ah for my birthright, the green grass and sorrel!

While Duggan sought to replace the disordered, progress-obsessed life of the city with that of the orderly, cyclical garden, towards the end of his life Baxter was reaching for a socio-political alternative (with nature in an attendant role). He was looking to such possibilities as the marae, hippie commune, halfway house/drop-in centre or the combination of retreat and recovery facility which he experienced at Futuna, in the Wellington suburb of Karori.

XVII

In a 1968 article entitled 'The Angels', a family holiday in the Mount Cook region became a platform for the study of both natural history and spiritual matters. With characteristic fluidity, Baxter begins the single, unfurling sentence below with an explication of the scene before him, then moves seamlessly towards the 'beyond':

> The wind blowing over the rocks of that high glacial valley; the sound of the creek talking to itself among the boulders; the movements of light and shadow on the heads of tussock grass; the small wild flowers growing on the bank of the creek – the impressions I received from the place were no doubt wholly sensory; but the joy was not sensory, it was too profound for

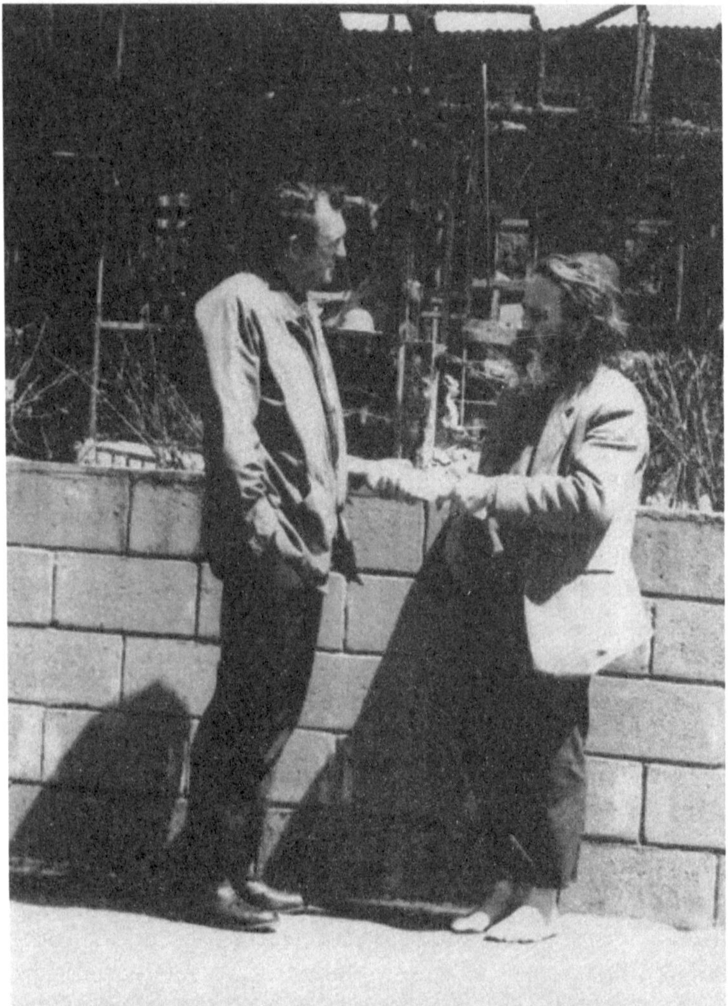

James K. Baxter handing a cheque to Fr Beban outside Futuna Retreat Centre, late 1971. When a fire destroyed an accommodation block, Baxter contributed money and the publishing rights to two prose-books to assist the rebuild.

> that; I could call it perhaps a remnant of the intellectual joy that Adam felt in paradise, a joy that comes from an inward contemplation of the forms of nature, yet obscurely reflects a light that comes to us from beyond nature. (2. 498)

In the same article, Baxter describes his experience of nature – with its cycles of birth and death – in terms almost identical to those used by Duggan and Bethell (harking back, in turn, to Gerard Manley Hopkins, Wordsworth and Keats):

> There was something grave and deep and massive about that joy, which has accompanied me from time to time throughout my life, like a music that fades away to nothing and then returns again just when you think it may have gone away for ever; it did not set life against death, but included both life and death in its strong current. (2. 498)

## XIII

Baxter describes this intuitive connection with Nature as 'one of the strongest human realities; and without it we would perhaps become less human' (2. 498). Besides the paradox that the individual might realise their humanity most acutely and profoundly in the absence of humanity, the statement begs another, related question: Do we go to nature to lose a sense of ourselves, or to assert and prove ourselves?

In Baxter's mind, up until shortly before his death, art played an important role in negotiating this existential territory. It offered a way of being *in*, as well as understanding, nature:

> Poems are statements of a theology of the Creation. You have the Creation; the Lord God made it and dwells in the Creation. He both made it, is beyond it, and is inside it. Look at the Hebrew Psalms – they're a theology of the Creation (3. 511).

## XIX

Like artist M. T. Woollaston (1910–1998), James K. Baxter increasingly saw New Zealand as a landscape of busted and altered things, in which scenic lake and mountainscape had to compete with cattle-trough, hedgerow, telegraph poles and entanglements of no. 8 wire. Painter and poet shared a vision of a functioning and malfunctioning, intensely humanised land, overlaid by a sense of tumultuous nature, of Hopkins-esque inscape, or rhythmical, symphonic effect.

> Through the green fabled
>
> Land of drenched willows, river-flats and farms,
> All of us acknowledge the matrix
>
> Of whatever grows in us. A broken springcart
> Falling to pieces in a farmer's garage,
>
> A church, a milkbar, any place or thing . . . (*CPoems* 424)

As a conservationist statement, the art of both Woollaston and Baxter is far from straightforward. Their work is predicated on a belief that the land comes into a new kind of meaning (and, at times, power) when humanity has placed its stamp upon it. A case in point, Baxter's *Pig Island Letters* offers a New Zealand that has been aggressively colonised, intensely and grittily overwritten with human history and present conditions – from 'an old house shaded with macrocarpas' to 'corrugated shack / with fried pauas in the pan, / Beside a bay somewhere . . .' (*CPoems* 277, 283). His 1967 prose meditation 'Kiwi Habits', which appeared in the *Otago University Review*, treads similar turf:

> Progress: an old railway line that ends in the bush. You climb out of a dusty truck (used once for carrying logs) and two hundred yards beyond the terminus you might as well never have seen a bridge or a railway sleeper. Bellbirds; dropping water; rotting leaves and branches; spider-webs glistening with rain – the bush is what it has been, living and dying beyond human help. Progress – the shunting of trucks, the

raising and lowering of signals – is not exactly a lie; it is merely totally irrelevant. (2. 398)

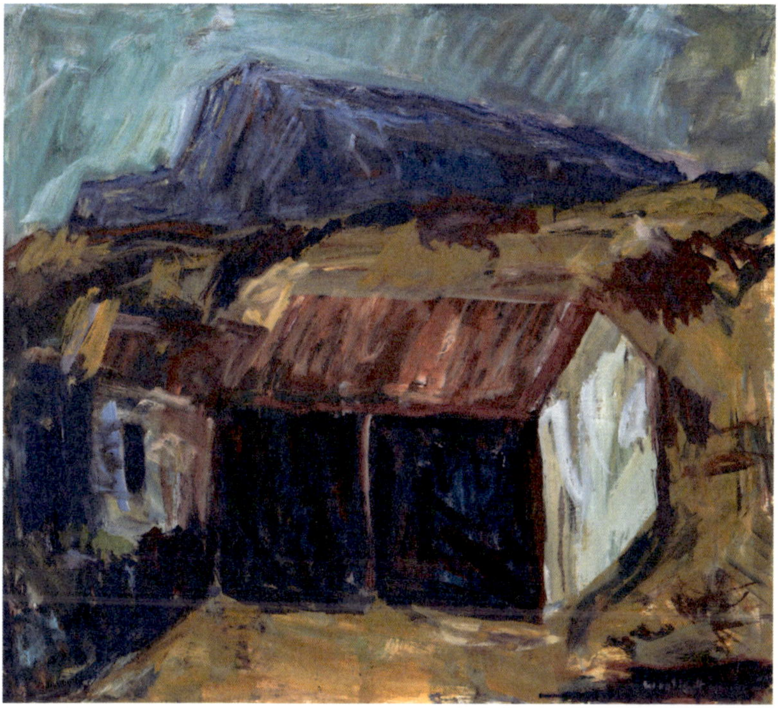

Toss Woollaston, Shed Upper Moutere With Ben Nevis, 1996, Oil on board, 983 × 1305 mm, Courtesy of Page Blackie Gallery and the Toss Woollaston Trust.

## XX

Peter Simpson has written extensively of both the vexed friendship and life-long artistic conversation between Baxter and painter Colin McCahon.[2] Not long before the poet's death, there had been a dramatic break, which McCahon came to regret painfully. (He memorialised his lost friend in many works painted at his Muriwai studio between late 1972 and 1974, including the celebrated 'Walk' series.) By the late 1960s, McCahon, like Baxter, had been looking for a new creative, social and spiritual impetus, exploring alternative social models and, far more directly than Baxter, engaging with environmental issues. His works were central to the 1971 exhibition of conservationist art, 'Earth/Earth' at Barry Lett Galleries, Auckland, and he wrote disarmingly, in the accompanying catalogue, about the degradation of marine and coastal environments.

Some years earlier, McCahon had been directly involved in the nascent 'Keep New Zealand Green' movement and produced a number of works on that theme. His Greenness, you could say, was fully formed and unequivocal, whereas Baxter's was evolving and just one part of a broader agenda which, for the time being, prioritised social over environmental activism.

Both were seeking to resolve existential as well as creative problems. Colin McCahon found a partial solution in withdrawing from social relations as much as possible and retreating to an isolated studio above Muriwai Beach, just outside Auckland. Rather more problematically, Baxter headed for Hiruhārama/Jerusalem with his shifting crew of young and outcast followers, the objective being to start a new society. Both McCahon and Baxter sought to make statements that went far wider than the usual high-art constituency; both questioned the notion of art for art's sake. 'Once the painter was making signs and symbols for people to live by,' McCahon stated in 1972, 'now he makes things to hang on walls at exhibitions' (26). To a comparable end,

2 See, for example, *A Candle in a Dark Room* and *Bloomsbury South*.

Baxter maintained that while he didn't advocate everyone putting on sackcloth and ashes, he thought 'it is reasonable and necessary that poetry should contain moral truth, and every poet should be a prophet according to his lights' (1. 356).

## XXI

As a public figure, Baxter took on the physical appearance of the archetypal Green Man – long-bearded and barefooted, an earth-bound if not entirely grounded individual. Very much in the tradition of the Green Knight (minus horse and footwear), by the late 1960s he had become the folkloric interloper, the outsider who effects a seasonal shift in a community. But the travails of the poet weren't entirely centred on social relations. Barefoot up the River Road was also a statement of relationship to landscape. So was sitting cross-legged at intersections or on roadsides and grassy verges:

> I learn my religion through my feet. The rock fangs of the road, set in tarseal, are designed for the rubber of car tyres to grip on, not for a man's bare feet to walk on . . . Te Atua speaks to me through my feet. He does not need words . . . Cold is another dialect of the same language . . . (3. 467)

Baxter should be thought of as a poet of the River Road rather than the river itself. It is his own singular journey he keeps returning to – on the human-made road – ghosted or echoed by the river-past of Māori mythology and human history. Such is the focus of the prose, as of the poetry. Landscape, for the most part, is reduced to the role of an accessory, the river-skirting mountains framing the terrestrial passage of the pilgrim-soul like the wings of an altarpiece. And the adjacent river minding, for the most part, its own business.

## XXII

In Baxter's mind, the fifty kilometres of winding road and surrounding hill-country between Hiruhārama and the nearest town, Whanganui, functioned primarily as a barrier – a wall separating the commune from outside realities. The settlement's isolation, as far as his social experiment was concerned, was its great virtue. The natural world, with all its idealistic, symbolic potentials, served an essentially pragmatic function: it became Baxter's bulwark, a fence or a screen to hide the social experiment from prying eyes or less-than-committed drop-ins.

## XXIII

It wasn't until the year of Baxter's death that the influential do-it-yourself-Green-guide, *New Zealand Whole Earth Catalogue*, was published (with further editions in 1975 and 1977). Said volume would, by various accounts, have come in handy up at the Top House in Hiruhārama. Baxter was far better at providing spiritual sustenance for his Tribe than he was at running the practical matters of food-gathering and horticulture. Returning to Hiruhārama after a ten-day absence, Baxter notes that weeds and thistles had taken over. 'God teaches me by means of the garden,' he writes. 'Now I am happy again, a newborn child resting freely at its point of origin, wrapped in God's overcoat, as Francis knew – wind, sun, stars, fire, earth, water, and the love for which even love is too weak a name' (3. 83). In 'Letters to a priest (second series)', Baxter's remarks on the therapeutic nature of his fellow commune-dwellers' gardening endeavours would have delighted Bethell or Duggan: 'Let them refresh themselves often . . . above all, digging gardens, so as to restore that awareness of the cycle of the seasons which our civilisation has fractured in us' (3. 151).

## XXIV

The greenest Baxter imaginable: the Price Milburn edition of *Jerusalem Daybook* (1971) features a florescent apple-green cover, with type and image printed green-on-green. The image could be a detail from a wood engraving by the rural English artist Thomas Bewick, with colour-treatment courtesy of the Psychedelic Poster Shop on Mount Eden Road (where Baxter was employed sporadically during the final months of his life). From a design point of view, the cover is at odds with the contents of the book, in which nature is never quite so homogenous, well-tended and *neat*.

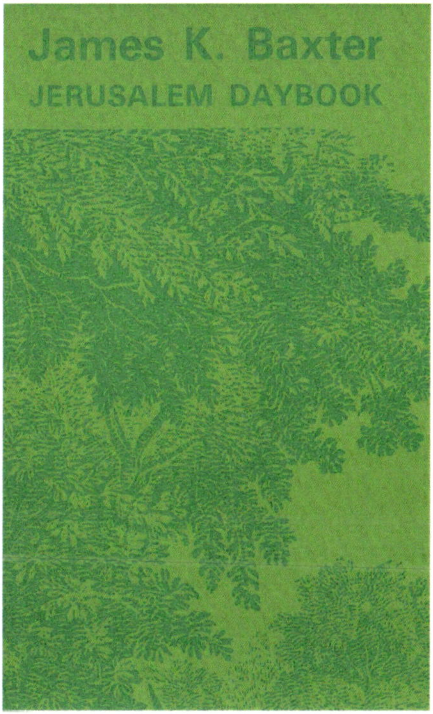


As in *Autumn Testament*, which appeared the previous year, Baxter's *Daybook* allows the Authentic Poet Baxter and the Prose Baxter to keep close company. In contrast to the poetry, Baxter's late prose is not so much an exploration or refinement of his thinking as it is a playing-out or broadcast. Whereas he wrote poetry to discover or find a new way of entering into a scenario/encounter, the prose tends to march a few steps behind experience, its mind already made up.

Often shaped by a sermonising inclination, the prose

is characterised by repetition, a tendency to underline, reiterate, paraphrase or call in an appropriate anecdote/ parable (from a seemingly endless supply). If Baxter's prose was a means of *conveying* meaning, in his poetry meaning was forged, tested and shaped. In *Autumn Testament* and *Jerusalem Daybook*, we witness the ebb and flow and tussle of these two modes.

Also notable is the fact that landscape – whether human-formed or in its natural state – is far less apparent in the late prose than it is in the poetry. Baxter's articles and sermons reflect – and risk being overwhelmed by – his preoccupation with the trials and travails of his fellow commune-dwellers: 'I have to be the sponge that sucks up the disordered / Humours of the tribe' (*CPoems* 574).

While the physical setting of Hiruhārama offered much potential for engaging with nature – Mount Ruapehu is clearly visible from the cherry orchard above the settlement – Baxter's attention as a prose writer focussed on social and spiritual realities, to the exclusion of much else. A compelling and essential element in the late poetry, however, the Whanganui River and environs grounded Baxter's verse in the quotidian while adding rich layers of metaphor and symbol.

## XXV

With the foundation of the Values Party in May 1972 – four months before James K. Baxter's death – the political arm of the Green movement was officially launched in New Zealand. Touting environmentally sustainable development and a rejection of the market mentality that had overtaken the policies of both main parties, the Values Party espoused the concept of 'zero growth', of a quiet, non-materialist, non-advancement-fixated societal model. (According to the Green Party website, the Values Party was 'the world's first national Green party'.)[3] The broadening of the Green Party into a mass movement can be dated from this time. Had he

3 'The History of the Green Party'. https://home.greens.org.nz/

lived long enough, it might have provided a political context in which Baxter could have flourished.

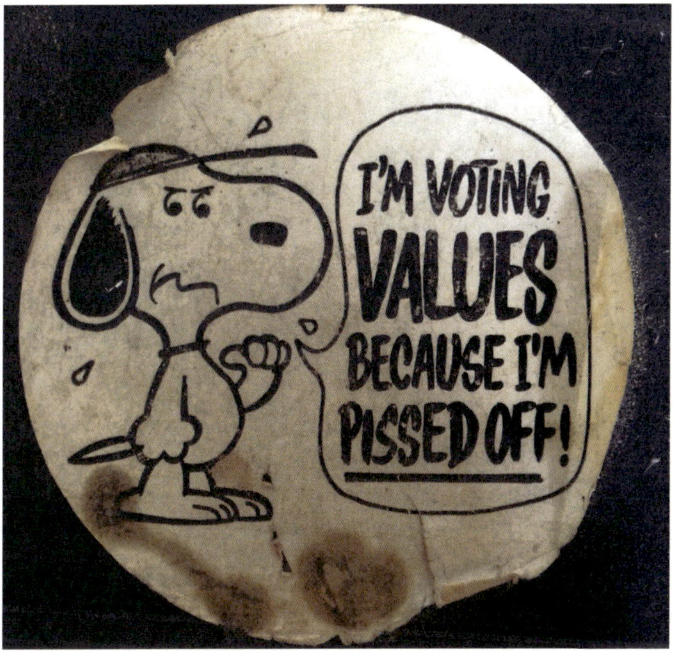


'Values Party' sticker, mid-1970s, courtesy of Robin Kearns

XXVI

> This same evening that I write I witnessed,
> Resting on a garden bench and looking westward,
> Sublime splendours . . . (Bethell 19)

As both a 'nature poet' and environmental ideologue, James K. Baxter exists in the space between Mary Ursula Bethell's 'Glory' (1929) – quoted above – and the following extract from the 1975 Values Party manifesto. The first quotation might be thought of as a point of origin, the second as a possible destination.

history-green-party#toc-origins Accessed 12 July 2017.

There is nothing wrong with man altering his environment. But it must be done carefully, so the alterations do not cause the breakdown of the natural systems on which every living thing depends . . . The urban environment must be kept on a human scale, because one of the prime causes of social problems is the alienation of people in the places where most of us live – the cities and towns.[4]

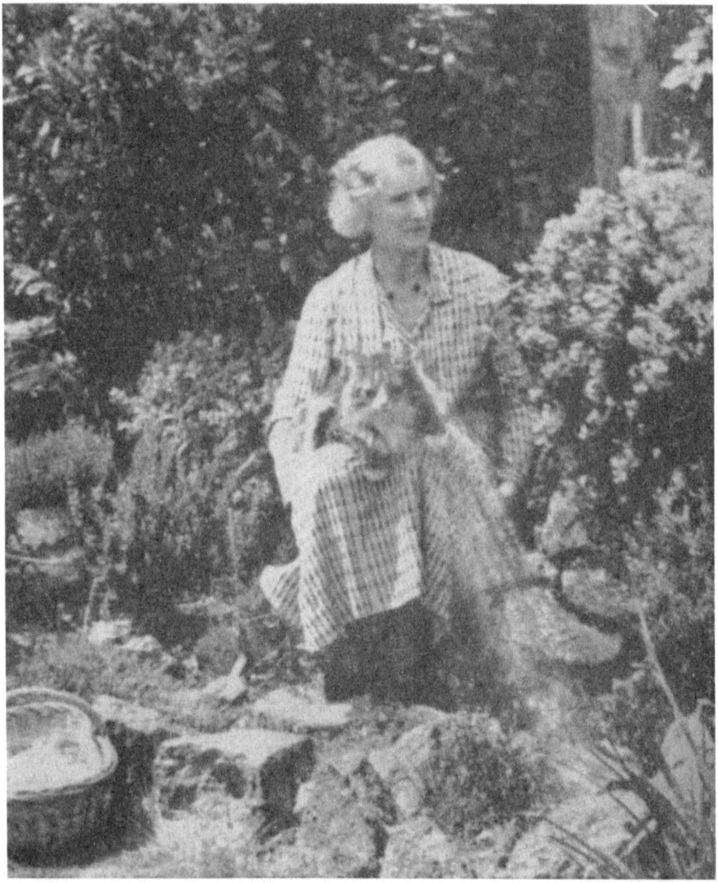

Ursula Bethell in the garden at Rise Cottage, with Michael the cat, c. 1930. Macmillan Brown Library, University of Canterbury.

4 'Beyond Tomorrow: New Zealand Values Party'. https://www.globalgrcens.org/green-party-platforms-programs-and-manifestos/nz_values_1975. Accessed 14 July 2017.

## XXVII

By the 1970s, alternative 'natural' toilets had achieved an almost iconic status within Green circles. Composting technology featured in the *Whole Earth Catalogue* and a variation thereof, 'the humus toilet', was championed by the notable Austrian artist Friedensreich Hundertwasser, who arrived in New Zealand in May 1973 – seven months after Baxter's death – and set up his Northland home, with a well-tuned humus toilet providing compost for his rooftop garden.

For Baxter, the outdoor lavatory was not only a naturally composting eco-experiment and a means to an end, but also a social and theological workshop. He sang the praises of the 'earth closet' in *Jerusalem Sonnets*: 'Man, my outdoor lavatory / Has taken me three days to build . . .' (*CPoems* 457). His late prose also frequents this lowliest of spiritual platforms, from whence he holds forth about the interconnectedness of different aspects of human and non-human life. A case could be argued, apropos of the Jerusalem years, for an Earth-coloured Baxter rather than a Green Baxter. The late poetry accommodates many soil and dung colours, the browns of clay-banks and muddy rivers – a far cry from the greens or blues that dominated *New Zealand in Colour 1*. As he writes in 'He Waiata mo Tana':

> Grey and muddy the waters of Babylon
> Flowing out of the broken hills,
> The river serpent swollen with proud silt . . . (*CPoems* 492)

The verse is populated not only by dogs, chickens and eels but also frogs, spiders and insects. Ursula Bethell's long view – with its sublime implications – has here been replaced by grunge; the mountain of detached observation has been displaced by the mole-hill of intimate communion. If early Baxter is high pastoral, then perhaps his final state of poetic being could be thought of as anti-pastoral. Eileen Duggan's 'green calm' was never going to engulf him, especially not now.

## XXVIII

Early in his career, Baxter fell comfortably into the role of the poet as landscape-seer, in such defining poems as 'Blow wind of fruitfulness' and 'The Mountains'. Through the varying phases of his poetry, he renegotiated the relationship between figure and land, absorbing along the way Māori and Greek mythologies, elements of Christianity and later Buddhism, while also keeping an ear to the mood of the times. The animism and anthropomorphism of his late poetry manifest as both an artistic device/conceit and an article of faith:

*Tangi*

They have taken the piupiu from the body of the land
Baring those wild timid limbs and thighs

Not in love, but in order
To see her as a thing. The crooked tree

On the cliff face is an old woman mourning
At the tangi of her daughter. Nevertheless

Day and night the waves move
On the broken dunes, caressing and reshaping

What will outlast the asphalt and the towns. (*CPoems* 449)

Written in 1969, 'Tangi' is close in intent to the art of his friend, Michael Illingworth, who was a committed environmentalist and contributor to the aforementioned 1971 'Earth/Earth' exhibition. Just as Illingworth merged human breast with headland in *Matauri Landscape*, Baxter's poetry became increasingly an expression of intimacy with nature – by turns erotic, maternal, elegiac, transcendent:

A man's body is a meeting house,

Ribs, arms, for the tribe to gather under,
And the heart must be their spring of water. (*CPoems* 568)

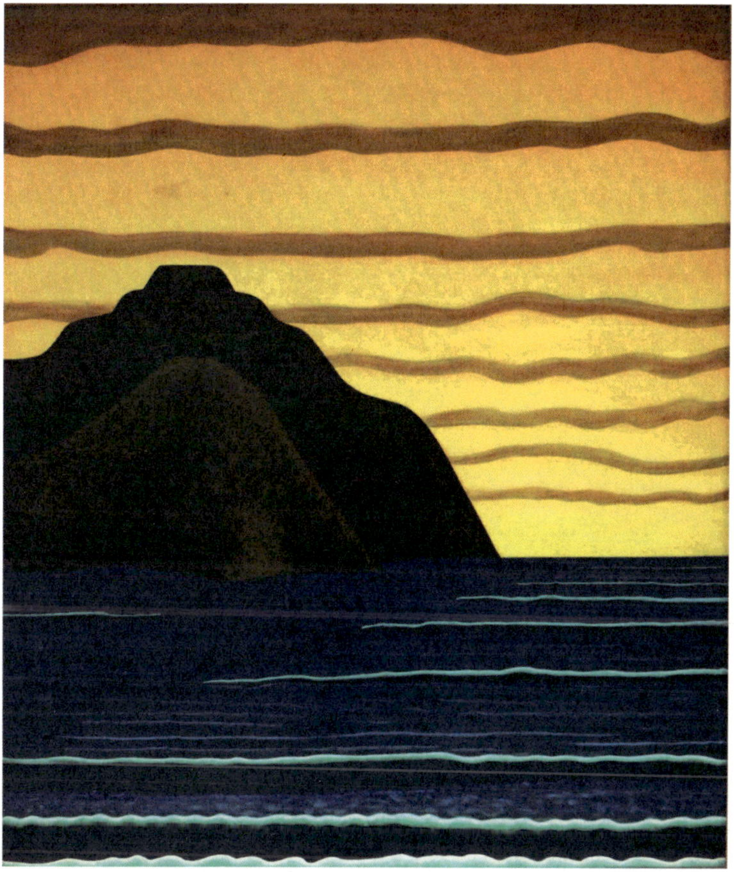

Michael Illingworth, ‘Matauri Bay’. Courtesy of the estate of Michael Illingworth.

## XXIX

Ecology and environmentalism were unfamiliar and under-utilised terms in Baxter's day. The word 'ecology' only appears once in the entire *Complete Prose*; 'environment' is more frequent, but it refers to working/teaching environments or suchlike, rather than to its prevailing usage in the present day. Words like as 'biosphere' and 'Anthropocene' were a long way off in the future. Yet there is a sense that Baxter's writing was linked to subsequent developments in ecological thinking. While his writing reflected its historical moment, it hinted at the kind of 'authentic human ecology' which Pope Francis has lately written of (*Laudato Si* s. 5). In *The Six Faces of Love*, Baxter stated:

> Well – we all live in a house God made for us – this earth with its rivers and trees and mountains and oceans. And we cut down the trees for no good reason, and fill the rivers with sludge, and destroy through greed the fishing beds of the ocean and carve up the mountains to make roads for tourists who will give us money. We ruin the ecology of the world because of our frantic pursuit of the dollar note, which is in a sense the god of our civilisation. (3. 253)

To that, the words of Pope Francis could be added: 'Everything is connected. Concern for the environment thus needs to be joined to a sincere love for our fellow human beings and an unwavering commitment to resolving the problems of society' (s. 91). Such a sentiment comes very close to the holistic message at the heart of the *Jerusalem Sonnets* and *Autumn Testament*, and which is abundantly present in much of Baxter's *Complete Prose*: an all-encompassing vision of humanity in deep relation to the universe.

In this schema, the Green Man – recently arrived on our doorstep and demanding of our attention – could be thought of as a personification of the planet Earth, calling us to a new kind of consciousness, demanding that we reconsider the divide between human and non-human nature.

'God has joined us so closely to the world around us,'

writes Pope Francis, 'that we can feel the desertification of the soil almost as a physical ailment, and the extinction of a species as a painful disfigurement' (s. 89). As a Deist and a believer in the transubstantiation, Baxter would have understood the direction of Francis's thinking: the world, as well as the word, made flesh: 'This is my body.'

On many levels, then as now, the writing of James K. Baxter is a call to new ways of thinking and living, and an acknowledgement of the need to reestablish deeper connections with each other and with the planet. It is only when this is achieved that, as he wrote in *Jerusalem Daybook*, the 'sacred universe' is restored, 'the river spirit is back in the river'. (3. 323)

## *Works Cited*

Baxter, James K. *Jerusalem Daybook*. Wellington: Price Milburn, 1971.

Bergoglio, Jorge Mario [Pope Francis]. *Laudato Si: On Care for Our Common Home*. Available at: http://w2.vatican.va/content/francesco/en/encyclicals/documents/papa-francesco_20150524_enciclica-laudato-si.html Accessed 14 July 2017.

Bethell, Ursula. *Collected Poems*. Ed. Vincent O'Sullivan. Wellington: Victoria University Press, 1997.

Bornholdt, Jenny, Gregory O'Brien and Mark Williams, eds. *An Anthology of New Zealand Poetry in English*. Auckland: Oxford University Press, 1997.

Duggan, Eileen. *Selected Poems*. Ed. Peter Whiteford. Wellington: Victoria University Press, 1994.

Schmied, Wieland. *Hundertwasser 1928–2000: Personality, Life, Work*. Vienna: Taschen, 2014.

MacFarlane, Robert. *Landmarks*. London: Penguin, 2015.

McCahon, Colin. *Colin McCahon: A Survey Exhibition*. Auckland: Auckland City Art Gallery, 1972.

Monk, Meredith. *On Behalf of Nature*. Munich: ECM, 2016.

Oliver, W. H. *James K. Baxter: A Portrait*. Wellington: Port Nicholson Press, 1983.

Simpson, Peter. *Bloomsbury South: The Arts in Christchurch 1933–1953* Auckland: Auckland University Press, 2016.

Simpson, Peter. *Candles in a Dark Room: James K. Baxter and Colin McCahon, July 1995–October 1996*. Auckland: The Gallery, 1966.

Stead, C. K. *In the Glass Case: Essays on New Zealand Literature*. Auckland: Auckland University Press, 1981.

# *'The Rich and the Poor': An Unpublished Essay by James K. Baxter*

Peter Whiteford

John Weir's 'Foreword' to this volume of essays describes the long genesis of the *Complete Prose*, its complicated bibliographical sources, and the industrious unearthing of texts that has culminated in the preparation of these four volumes. He will no doubt view with a wry smile, but with little surprise, the inclusion of the piece which follows, published here for the first time. For one of the inevitable consequences of the publication of *James K. Baxter: Complete Prose* – comprehensive though it may be – has been (and will continue to be) the emergence of additional lost or forgotten material that immediately gives the lie to the title of the compendium.

The genesis and provenance of this rediscovered essay, and its serendipitous re-emergence last year, have been revealed in an article by the custodian of the original autograph, Richard Hill. I am very grateful to him for the invitation and the opportunity to edit the essay for inclusion in this volume, for our conversations about the work, and for providing me with access both to the original manuscripts and to high quality, enlarged photographic copies.[1] Richard Hill's account of the genesis of the essay provides

1 I am also very grateful to Paul Millar and to the Baxter Trust for permission to publish the edited text here. Note that Hill's article includes a facsimile reproduction of the three pages.

a fascinating insight into some aspects of left-wing political activism in Wellington in the early 1970s, and illustrates at the same time just how peripheral Baxter's place in that was. There is no need to repeat the account that Hill is able to provide from his privileged first-hand knowledge. Rather, my purpose here is to provide an annotated edition of the essay itself, together with some comment relating it to Baxter's other prose.

The essay has been preserved on three foolscap sheets which show some foxing and discolouration. In Baxter's own hand, it is written on one side of each page only, in blue ink, with what looks to have been a biro or ballpoint pen. The sheets are numbered (top, centre), each of the six sections is numbered, and the essay is signed at the end. Both title and signature are underlined.

The hand is generally clear and legible (more so than is the case with some of Baxter's manuscript books) and has the appearance of having been carefully, even in places somewhat laboriously, written out. There are a number of authorial corrections to the text, most done at the time of writing and in the same ink, but one is done at a later time in black ink. On the second page, six words have been underlined in red. It is impossible to know who was responsible for the underlining. Richard Hill speculates that this may have occurred because 'they were difficult to read' (57), although he is unable to account for who made the underlinings, or when, as they seem to have occurred when the manuscripts were not in his keeping. If Hill is right, and this does seem the likeliest explanation, it would suggest that there had been some effort to prepare it for publication before the magazine for which it had been intended ceased to print.

Even had the circumstances of its composition not been available as evidence for the date of that composition, it would not have been difficult to suggest a date in 1971 or 1972, for the essay is very similar to some of the writing from that period, both in content and in style. The deep concern for disadvantaged individuals is manifest in Baxter's efforts to secure the services of Hector MacNeill in defence of the young Māori, R – , who had been charged with car conversion. Even more prominent, although here treated in general fashion, is the abiding concern for those who experience poverty. That concern has little to do with economic theory, or with Marxism, despite MacNeill's position among the left-wing movement. On the contrary, Baxter's interest is religious rather than economic, and here, as so frequently in these later years, his discussion of social issues reverts to a religious solution (in traditional religious language, the solution consists in the exercise of 'corporal works of mercy') or is made manifest through deliberate religious symbols and images.[1] Here, he draws throughout on the parable of Dives and Lazarus – a choice that allows him, on this occasion, to include criticism not just of the state and its bureaucracy but also of the Church, which he believes has lost its interest in serving the poor. In like manner, in 'A Handbook for the Christian Militant' he describes the Church as being 'married' to Dives, 'our capitalist Pharaoh' (3. 490).

Baxter's brief essay also makes clear that the antipathy he feels towards what might loosely be described as the forces of state is as prominent as it ever was. On this occasion, it is the police in particular who bear the brunt of his satire, in a manner that echoes his criticism of the 'Catholic pakeha sergeant' in the contemporary 'House of Lazarus' (3. 454); but as the striking image of the 'legal sheep dip' makes clear, Baxter's criticism extends to the whole of the legal system.

Equally prominent is his continued disdain for bureaucracy ('the boys in grey'), coupled with a contempt for the managerial class that he sees as guilty of the oppression of ordinary working people, and especially of those whose ability to maintain employment relies on the goodwill or even

1 The distinction between the political and the religious here should perhaps not be pushed too far. The famous saying of Helder Camara is appropriate: 'When I give bread to the poor, they call me a saint; when I ask why the poor have no bread, they call me a Communist.'

the whim of those managers. What is particularly noticeable in this essay is Baxter's recurrent description of this servile relationship in terms of being forced to lick someone's arse – an image which also recurs in the 'House of Lazarus' and elsewhere. Baxter's fixation with this image – it occurs three times in an essay of just over 1300 words – is of considerable interest.

Stylistically, too, this essay can readily be compared to the writings from the Jerusalem period: the prose is simple and without flourish; there is a natural blending of English and Māori; and rhetorical effects are more often produced by repetition than by grand gesture. For all its simplicity, though, there is a vigour and forcefulness in the prose, and the satire still has considerable bite. But as the final section perhaps indicates, that social satire is now more overtly presented within a religious framework, and is lightened by dry humour.

## The Rich and the Poor

### 1

I write these notes on the 25th day of a 30-day fast undertaken, among other reasons, to meditate in an appropriate manner on the parable of Dives and Lazarus. In Latin, 'dives' simply means rich; and this country is the country of Dives because an Asian family could contrive a living by use of the food and material any one of us throws out the door. Yet the poor man Lazarus is present with us. I meet him every day in the streets of Wellington. He bears the marks of heavy handling by the officials of Dives – the cops, the bureaucrats, the managers of factories who require men to lick their arses before they can get or hold a job. It is Lazarus whom I love, because he loves me and so obviously carries the peace of God about with him. But it is my job to love my neighbour Dives as well. If necessary I will chop down the door of his burning house with an axe. Christ said the rich men who have no mercy on the poor will land in Hell. If my words are sharp and vigorous, you may be able to ~~dect~~ detect behind them the rhythmical blows of an axe wielded on behalf of my neighbour Dives, even if not with his full approval and consent.

2

Today I lie on the floor of an office, with my head on a coat, and sleep. In a dream I am commenting to the New Zealand poet Allen Curnow that one of his poems has a line with such and such a meaning. Still in the dream, I can't remember the line. I see Allen Curnow's face very clearly. I wake and cannot remember who I am or where I am. This is an effect of having been for more than three weeks without food. One feels that one might die. A large minority of people in the world are feeling the same. It is a state with which Dives is rarely personally familiar. It is a frequent state in the kingdom of Lazarus.

3

Alongside the steps that go up to St Mary's church in Boulcott St somebody has created iron railings, painted green, with sharp points like javelins. This depresses me. The area of concrete thus fenced off has been used by the metho boys for many purposes. It is in fact the bedroom and lavatory of Lazarus, and on occasion his couch of unofficial marriage. But Dives, who has his own bed and lavatory inside the presbytery, has chosen to deprive Lazarus of the communal facilities provided for him by the Lord God. This is a sign of great spiritual enfeeblement and poorness of eyesight in the Church where Dives ~~is~~ too ~~much respected.~~ often governs.

[p. 2] If one of the meths drinkers, climbing clumsily over the railings, should fall and pierce his stomach or testicles, Dives will be to blame for it. He has an inherent tendency to regard as his own inalienable property the earth that the Lord God provided for the use of all. This tendency is peculiarly hideous when it is displayed in immediate proximity to the house of God.

I go in to Mass, and hear Christ telling the Pharisees, whom we so closely resemble, about the judgement of God and the wrath of the poor. He tells them also that not one stone of their magnificent Temple will be left standing

All that Dives needs is a hose and a water tap and a broom and a sunshiny day to clean up the bedroom and lavatory of the poor. He could take out a cup of tea in the morning to Lazarus, who may be suffering from the dry retches. If he stays and sits beside him, brother with brother, the peace of Lazarus will begin to pour into his soul.

4

It is not the agony of Lazarus that rends the world apart. That agony is real enough. But it is in the main a physical agony terminated by death by starvation, or a mental nausea generated when he is forced to lick the arse of Dives to keep himself and his family alive. The agony of Dives is a spiritual agony of blindness, deafness and asphyxiation, on account of his allowing attachment to material possessions to strangle love for neighbour, God, and eventually family as well. The flame of this agony is dense, piercing and terrible. It consumes the marrow of the bones.

When Dives wakes up from a bad dream about the Hell for which he is preparing himself, a million people have to die for it. 'They want my property,' he thinks. 'They want to kill me.' And indeed the wrath of the poor will one day swallow up his world of power and money. Yet he could exorcise his demon simply enough, by distributing what he did not himself need ~~and t~~ among his fellows who are needy. He cannot do this because he regards his surplus property as security. And he hates Lazarus because he fears him, as his terrible twin, as the image of his own starved and amputated soul.

The agony of Dives is shared by his wife and daughter. His wife licks envelopes for the Bishop or looks for love at the kind of party where no love can be found. His son curses him or inherits his business without thanks. His daughter emerges like a waif from the rich house with three garages and swallows pills night and day or gets pregnant to one of the sons of Lazarus. Madness is one of the ailments of his family. [p. 3] It is the madness of a dog driven crazy by being devoured by a thousand fleas. The cure for it is the acquisition of a spirit of poverty.

But I find the peace of Dives more terrible than his agony. It is the false peace that comes to a man who dreams that because his belly is full his house can be in no danger. It is the peace of the graveyard. The name for it is comfort.

5

In the police courts I observe the legal sheep dip in operation. One by one the sons and daughters of Lazarus pass through this ritual bath, receiving fines, imprisonment, probation and moral admonition. The oppression of the poor by the rich is endless. It began when time began. It will end when time ends.

My friend R – , aged 16, a Maori, receives probation for car conversion. Dives does not share his iron chariot with Lazarus. He locks it and leaves it at the roadside. Led by an ~~if~~ infallible instinct, Lazarus finds the unshared car, opens it, and shares it with his friends, abandoning it on Mount Victoria where the cops, the agents of Dives, can discover it and return it to him.

R – will very likely be put in a job where he ~~lick~~ has to ~~lick the~~ lick the boss's arse. When he eventually explodes, he will go to jail for breach of probation.

I tell ones like R – , 'Don't imitate the rich. You're like a millionaire aching to get his second million. Be content with kai and clothes and shelter and the company of your friends. Needs can be satisfied. Wants can never be satisfied.'

Yet, if they do this, they will still be oppressed by Dives. They will be picked up by the boys in blue or the boys in grey for being poor, for not having a job, for having long hair, maybe for being Maori. The charges will be laid under the I. and D. clauses of the Police Offences Act. I haunt the police stations like a bad smell, telling the police that it is wrong for them to oppress the poor. This process also is an endless one.

6

May Lazarus receive his brother Dives into paradise! That is what I want to see. But Dives will have to give him at least a few stale cracker biscuits to make it possible.

James K. Baxter

## Notes

line 3: 30-day] the figure 3 is unusually large, and appears to be written over another figure possibly the figure 2. Hill cites W. H. Oliver's belief that the fast was a 25-day one (56); Baxter also refers to having undertaken a 25-day fast in 'The House of Lazarus' (3. 461).

4: parable of Dives and Lazarus] see Luke 16. 14–31.

13: Christ said . . . Hell] not a direct quotation but essentially a summary of the parable of Dives and Lazarus.

18: of an office] Baxter had originally written 'on an office'.

27: St Mary's church in Boulcott St] formally St Mary of the Angels, an imposing Gothic Revival church run by the Society of Mary.

34: too often governs] this change was made at a later stage of composition, having been added by Baxter in a different pen.

40: Mass . . . Pharisees] numerous passages within the Gospels record Christ's condemnation of the Pharisees in these terms. See, for example, Matt. 5. 20; Luke 11. 37–54; Luke 16. 13–15.

42: not one stone . . .] see Matt. 24. 2; Mark 13. 2.

50: starvation] underlined in red; see Hill 57.

52: deafness] underlined in red; see Hill 57.

54: strangle] underlined in red; see Hill 57.

59: demon] underlined in red; see Hill 57.

60: among, fellows] underlined in red; see Hill 57.

62: terrible twin] compare the passage in *Conversation with an Ancestor*, in which Baxter writes of his 'schizophrenic twin' (2. 135).

79: my friend R] has not been identified.

84: where he . . . boss's arse] Baxter has made a few contemporaneous corrections in the line.

90: boys in blue . . . boys in grey] 'boys in blue ' is a common shorthand for the police force; 'boys in grey' no doubt refers to the public service bureaucrats (see line 9) against whom Baxter so often railed.

91: I. and D. Clauses] Part II of the 1927 Police Offences Act deals with Indecency and Vagrancy and includes a section dealing with 'Idle and Disorderly Persons' (preceding sections that deal in turn with 'Rogues and Vagabonds' and 'Incorrigible Vagabonds').

92: like a bad smell] Baxter similarly described himself as a 'bad smell' in two other texts from around this time: *Jerusalem Daybook* (3. 303) and 'A Scorpion Circled by Fire' (3. 413).

96: May Lazarus . . . into paradise] the language is reminiscent of the 'In paradisum' antiphon of the Catholic Requiem Mass, said or sung as the body is being taken from the church. The antiphon includes the prayer 'May the angels lead you into paradise . . . May the choir of angels receive you and with Lazarus, once a poor man, may you have eternal rest.'

## *Work Cited*

Hill, Richard S. 'Literature, Politics and Activism: "The Rich and the Poor" (1971) – A Rediscovered Essay by James K Baxter.' *Journal of New Zealand Studies* NS23 (2016), 54–63.

# *Biographical Notes*

**John Davidson** retired as professor of classics at Victoria University of Wellington in 2010. He has published extensively on ancient Greek literature and mythology, especially tragedy and the intertextual relationship between Sophocles and Euripides and the Homeric corpus. Since the 1970s he has also been writing on the reception of ancient Greek and Latin literature in New Zealand poetry, with special reference to James K. Baxter. With Geoffrey Miles and Paul Millar, he is co-author of *The Snake-Haired Muse: James K. Baxter and Classical Myth* (VUP, 2011).

**Doreen D'Cruz** has been a senior lecturer in the School of English and Media Studies at Massey University, Palmerston North, from March 1987 until April 2017, and is currently an Honorary Research Fellow there. She is the author of *Loving Subjects: Narratives of Female Desire* (Lang, 2002) and co-author with John C. Ross of *The Lonely and the Alone: The Poetics of Isolation in New Zealand Fiction* (Rodopi, 2011). Her recent articles have been on New Zealand authors Maurice Gee, Patricia Grace and Fiona Kidman.

**Lawrence Jones** is emeritus professor of English at the University of Otago, where he taught from 1964, and in 1966–67 had the office across the corridor from James K. Baxter's Burns Fellowship office. He has written many books, chapters, articles and papers on New Zealand writers and their works and on New Zealand literary history, including *Picking Up the Traces: The Making of a New Zealand Literary Culture, 1932–1945* (VUP, 2005); 'The Novel' in *The Oxford History of New Zealand* (1991); and *Barbed Wire and Mirrors: Essays on New Zealand Prose* (Otago UP, 1995). From 1990 to 2000 he was editor/co-editor of *JNZL: Journal of New Zealand Literature*, and helped to organise the 1994 'James K. Baxter: Poet and Prophet' conference, papers from which appeared as *JNZL* 13.

Previously the owner/manager of Wellington's iconic 'Costume Cave', **Sharon Matthews** completed her PhD at the University of Otago in 2016. Her thesis, 'The Monstrous Mother and the "natural man": Mythic Figures and Recurring Metaphors in the Plays of James K. Baxter', was recognised by the Division of Humanities as being of exceptional quality. She has published on Baxter's drama in *Journal of New Zealand Literature* (2013) and in *Athens to Aotearoa*, edited by Jeff Tatum and Simon Perris (forthcoming VUP, 2017).

**Geoffrey Miles** is a senior lecturer in English at Victoria University of Wellington, where his research focuses on classical receptions in English literature. He is co-author (with John Davidson and Paul Millar) of *The Snake-Haired Muse: James K. Baxter and Classical Myth* (VUP, 2011), and has published several articles on Baxter and mythology.

**Paul Millar** is deputy pro-vice chancellor of the University of Canterbury College of Arts and head of the School of Humanities and Creative Arts. He is also professor of English, with extensive publications in New Zealand literature, particularly the poetry of James K. Baxter. His literary biography of novelist and cultural commentator Bill Pearson was a finalist in the 2011 New Zealand Book Awards. Millar has long been involved in digital humanities projects and research. In 2001 he co-founded Victoria University of Wellington's New Zealand Electronic Text Collection (NZTEC). Following the 2010/2011 Canterbury earthquakes he led the development of the CEISMIC Canterbury Earthquakes Digital Archive (*www.ceismic.org.nz*), a cultural heritage database that collects stories, images and media about the earthquakes' impacts for the purposes of commemoration, teaching and research.

**Kirstine Moffat** is a senior lecturer in English at the University of Waikato. Her research focuses on New Zealand settlement writing and performance culture. She has been preoccupied with the Puritan legacy in New Zealand since embarking on her doctorate and has valued this opportunity to grapple with James K. Baxter's complex thinking about faith and culture.

**Paul Morris** is professor of religious studies at Victoria University of Wellington, where he holds the UNESCO Chair in Interreligious Understanding and Relations in New Zealand and the Pacific. His research focuses on religion, politics and culture in New Zealand, the Pacific and the Jewish world. He has recently completed a monograph on radical theologies, and his current research is on religion and development in the Pacific; religion, identity and happiness; and comparative religious diversities. His current teaching in religious studies includes: What is Religion?; Confronting Death; and Arguing about Religion. He was awarded the 2007 Gold Medal for Peace through Dialogue by the International Council of Christians and Jews (Heppenheim, Germany) and in 2013 was Dorset Fellow at the Oxford Centre for Hebrew and Jewish Studies.

Born in Matamata in 1961, **Gregory O'Brien** has lived in Wellington since 1989, writing and painting full time. He was Stout Memorial Fellow at Victoria University of Wellington, 2015–16, during which time he worked on a book exploring the relationship between the imagination and the environment. Recent publications include *See What I Can See: New Zealand Photography for the Young and Curious*, and a collection of poems, *Whale Years* (both AUP, 2015). He also recently edited a collection of writings by ceramicist Barry Brickell, and, with Nick Bevan, co-edited a study of Wellington's Futuna Chapel, *Futuna: Life of a Building* (VUP, 2016).

**Hugh Roberts** teaches in the English department at the University of California, Irvine. He has written widely on New Zealand literature and Romantic period literature. He is the author of *Shelley and the Chaos of History: A New Politics of Poetry* (Penn State University Press, 1997).

**John Weir** was born in Nelson in 1935. In January 1961, while training to become a Catholic priest, he became an intimate friend of James K. Baxter. At Canterbury University his Master's thesis and doctoral dissertation explored Baxter's prose and poetry and provided him with the literary resources that enabled him to edit nine collections of Baxter's work, including his *Collected Poems* (Oxford University Press, 1980) and *Complete Prose* (VUP, 2015). More recently Weir has been preparing for publication both Baxter's letters and an edition of his verse which includes more than three thousand poems.

**Peter Whiteford** is professor of English at Victoria University of Wellington, where he has been a member of the English programme for over twenty-five years. His teaching and research cover a number of different areas: medieval literature, New Zealand literature and the poetry of Gerard Manley Hopkins. With respect to New Zealand literature, he published the *Selected Poems* of Eileen Duggan, selected letters of Ursula Bethell and John Mulgan, an uncensored edition of Mulgan's *Report on Experience* and an edition of Mulgan's previously unpublished *Journey to Oxford*, together with numerous essays and articles. He is the general editor of *Kōtare: New Zealand Notes and Queries*.

**Janet Wilson** is professor of English and postcolonial studies at the University of Northampton, UK. A New Zealander, she formerly taught at the University of Otago, Dunedin. She has published widely on the postcolonial/diaspora writing and visual culture of the white settler societies of Australia and New Zealand, with a focus on writers like Fleur Adcock, Dan Davin and Katherine Mansfield. Other research interests include literature and fundamentalism, subaltern cosmopolitanism, liminality and diaspora, the global fictions of Mohsin Hamid, and refugee and slum narratives. She is currently patron of the London-based New Zealand Studies Network, vice-chair of the Katherine Mansfield Society and co-editor of *The Journal of Postcolonial Writing*.

**Nicholas Wright** is a lecturer in the English department at the University of Canterbury where he teaches New Zealand and American literature. He is currently working on a book of critical essays – *The Enchanting Remains* – on contemporary poetry written in Aotearoa.

# Index